My Days of Strength

Anne Walter Fearn

My Days of Strength

An American Woman Doctor's Forty Years in China

By
Anne Walter Fearn, M.D.

"I think of things past; my days of youth and strength;
Slowly pacing back and forth, I sigh long sighs"

Tu Fu—Chinese poet, A.D. 712–770
Translated by Florence Ayscough

ILLUSTRATED

HARPER & BROTHERS PUBLISHERS

New York and London

To

IRENE

My Sister and My Friend

CONTENTS

Contents

viii

ILLUSTRATIONS

Illustrations

x

FOREWORD

WHEN DR. ANNE WALTER FEARN MOVED FROM SOOCHOW to Shanghai we residents of that colourful and odorous city had no inkling of what was going to happen to us and to our traditions. Her arrival was unobtrusive and, in any event, we seldom paid any attention to outport women who moved in on us. They came and they went and made no more of an impression on our big sophisticated city than the week-end visit of a Massachusetts farmer makes on New York. They never bothered us for they usually knew their places and kept out of the way of us Old China Hands.

But it wasn't very long before Dr. Fearn was not only underfoot but in everyone's hair and no one seemed to mind. She didn't like the way things were being done in Shanghai, but she didn't say much about it. She just changed things around for us. Being a friend of everyone she couldn't understand why the little American community should be divided into a lot of impervious compartments. She noted that business men not only didn't mix with missionaries but didn't mix very well with each other. It surprised her that American women played bridge with wives of husbands who worked for the same company and rarely with any others. This had been going on for years before she came, the same little cliques cementing old prejudices or forming new ones.

Being naïve and unsophisticated, Dr. Fearn thought this didn't make sense and she proceeded to mix us up and see what would happen. She started with the saints and the sinners, as represented by the missionaries and the business men. It was an enlightening experience for both of them. The missionary learned that the sinful Shanghai business man might drink a cocktail or two without falling into a drunken frenzy and beating his wife. The business men found that the missionaries were not the Bible-pounding fanatics they had thought them to be and that you could have interesting conversations with them without their trying to fill your pockets full of tracts. Pretty soon they were speaking to each other on the street and joining the same organizations.

Having made the Americans acquainted with each other, Dr. Fearn then turned to other sections of the community. She had met and liked the British, French, Germans, Italians, Russians, and Scandinavians, to mention but a few of the many nationalities in Shanghai, and she didn't see why they shouldn't like each other. So she started in mixing them up, in the same way she had mixed her fellow Americans. When you went to her house for tea or cocktails or dinner you were never sure whom you were going to meet, but it was a moral certainty that you would meet a lot of people you had never heard of before and that you would hear something besides English spoken. It would never have surprised me a bit if I had found the Grand Lama of Tibet at one of her parties. In fact he may have been at one to which I was not invited. There was no Social Register in Shanghai and Dr. Fearn just made one of her own inviting everyone she liked. Before many months passed she had mixed the various foreigners of Shanghai so thoroughly that we couldn't be unmixed for, much to our surprise, we had blended.

In the meantime the foreigners and the Chinese remained aloof from each other. The foreigners took Kipling too seriously and the Chinese took the foreigners too seriously. Dr. Fearn's formula for friendship worked here just as it had in the narrower fields. Often the prettiest girl at her party—sometimes several of the prettiest girls—were Chinese and West met East and liked it. Sometimes the foreign women didn't like it so well, but when they found that a Chinese girl was often able to redouble a grand slam bid and make it, Kipling's reputation

Foreword

slumped and the relations between Occident and Orient were placed on a new and entirely different footing.

After Dr. Fearn had mixed us up and got us acquainted with each other, she was always thinking of something for us to do. There was always some cause which needed supporting or funds to be raised for something or other. The proportion of men in Shanghai who will cheerfully serve on committees is certainly no greater than in any other part of the world and most of us were rather expert at avoiding work of that kind. But we soon found that when Dr. Fearn had made up her mind to get something done, we might just as well tear up our alibis and get to work. It wasn't because she browbeat us or was unpleasantly insistent. But when she started to do anything she was so enthusiastic about it and worked so hard herself that she shamed everyone into trying to help her. And she was always just as eager to help everyone else.

Nor was it lack of anything to do that drove Dr. Fearn to these activities, for she was one of the very few foreign women in Shanghai who had an occupation of her own. She owned and operated a highly successful hospital and personally brought an amazing number of babies into the world. It finally got to be a kind of social distinction to be born with the aid of her tiny but capable hands. There are dozens of young men and women living in various parts of the world who enjoy that honour and are known collectively as "Fearn babies," a classification they are proud to acknowledge. All of them seem to feel that they have an obligation to live up to.

It is a pleasure and an honour to introduce Dr. Fearn. It would be presumptuous to introduce her in the Far East for she is the best-known and best-loved woman between Suez and the China Coast. Everyone who knows her loves her, as, I am sure, will the reader who meets her in the pages of this book.

CARL CROW

ACKNOWLEDGMENT

I wish to thank Miss Frances Russell for her assistance in preparing the book for publication; Major Arthur Bassett and Dr. H. S. Wainwright for much useful information. I also wish to acknowledge my indebtedness to Dr. F. L. Hawks Pott's *A Short History of Shanghai*.

A. W. F.

My Days of Strength

Chapter I

Walter House and My Youth

A SMALL GIRL WITH CROPPED, CURLY HAIR WAS PERCHED PRE-cariously on the edge of the veranda. Her hands were folded primly in the lap of her starched white dress and she was being very quiet because she was supposed to be safe inside the house with her three sisters and little brother. But the excitement in the air had been too strong to resist; like a magnet it had drawn her out of doors. Half hidden by a pillar she listened to the strange sounds; she heard the rush of many feet, the rising murmur of the confused crowd that filled the yard. She watched the townspeople mill around the man on the steps, imploring him to stay with them. She looked up into the man's face and thought of lions, so wonderful were his eyes, so full of power and strength.

I was that eleven-year-old child, and the man was my father, Colonel Harvey Washington Walter. That was my last sight of him, standing there with his three grown sons behind him, and telling his neighbors that as long as life lasted he and his sons would remain there with them.

I didn't know then why the women cried, why the men walked about with faces drawn and tense. Later I was to learn. That was the summer of 1878, the never-to-be-forgotten year, when the terror of the South—yellow fever—raged all around us.

New Orleans, a constant victim of its ravages, was in the grip of an epidemic and slowly the disease had made its way northward. Holly Springs, with the highest altitude in Missis-sippi and heretofore immune, grew apprehensive as first

Grenada, then Water Valley and finally Oxford, the university town thirty miles to the south, were stricken. My father, the ruling spirit of Holly Springs, had been away somewhere at court. He returned to find that in his absence his fellow citizens had established a shotgun quarantine. Grieved by this seeming heartlessness, and strong in his faith in the immunity of our hills, he had induced them to raise the quarantine and welcome refugees from the neighboring towns. Soon sporadic cases appeared in our midst, and then the courthouse bell tolled ominously; the epidemic was upon us.

The morning after the meeting on our front lawn my mother, with the younger children, took "the last train that stopped." It was all very thrilling to a little girl who liked things to happen, whose mind was stirred by adventure then and always, and who didn't realize the seriousness of that trip or the tragedy left behind. My father and older brothers stayed on, as my father had promised, tending the sick and burying the dead. Our house was turned into a hospital. Every household was in mourning and in many cases whole families were blotted out. But it was not until the frost had fallen, the greatest danger past, and the end of the epidemic in sight that my father and brothers fell ill with the fever. Then, within one week, all four were dead.

My mother was left desolate. Of our homecoming I cannot speak.

We were in Huntsville when the first mail reached us in all those weeks of exile. Even before the news came my mother had an experience that made an indelible impression on me. I usually slept in the same room with Mother and I was awakened suddenly one night by her cry. My married sister, Minnie (Mrs. H. C. Myers), who had joined us there, was in the next room. She came at once and I was shifted to another room. It was not until many years later that I dared ask my mother about that night. She hesitated before replying and then said,

"It distresses me to speak of it, but since you have asked, I will tell you that I was awakened by a light that shone about your father, who stretched out his arms to me as he said, 'Dona, my wife, it has come upon me like a thief in the night.'"

Among the letters we received in that first batch of mail was one from my father to my mother. It began: "Dona, my wife, it has come upon me like a thief in the night."

During that long, sad autumn I have fleeting memories of my mother wandering drearily from room to room in the big house which had been so easily filled by the presence of the large-hearted man who was gone. It was years before we heard her laugh again.

It was incredible to us children that Christmas should not be as we had always known it. Hospitality had been the family watchword, and Christmas the time when the house overflowed with gaiety and friends and happiness. But we learned, with sorrow and surprise, that we were not even to speak of Santa Claus, nor expect any festivities. On Christmas Eve the five of us, Irene, Pearl, Lillian, Brother Harvey and I, Annie, were grouped on the floor around a glowing fire, ready for bed and unhappy that we were not allowed even to hang our stockings on the mantel. It was all so different from the other Christmas Eves that we had little to say and sat silent until the baby, Pearl, held up a soft and worn-out shoe and said timidly, "Can't I even hang up my shoe?"

We hung them—five in a row and Santa Claus did not forget us completely.

One incident of my very early childhood remains stamped on my memory. My father was host at a large luncheon to many distinguished men. Mint juleps had been served, and after the guests had gone into the dining room I, then a child of about five, slipped into the parlor and ate the sugar left in the glasses. How long this orgy lasted I do not know. I do remember being found on the upstairs balcony in great distress, hold-

3

ing my arms out toward Sally Knapp's house. Something was wrong with me. I wanted something—but what? I had always wanted Sally's house so it must be that. My next recollection was of being in bed. My mother was sitting beside me. She was crying. It puzzled me that she should cry when it was my stomach that was aching in such a surprising manner. I remember my mother's tearful words, "To think my little daughter is drunk!"

I had never heard that word before. I had no idea what it meant. It must mean sick. If so I was dreadfully drunk.

When I was twelve, having exhausted the educational advantages of our Presbyterian Sunday School which served also as day school, I was sent to the Charlotte Female Institute in North Carolina (now a part of the Woman's College of South Carolina). There I spent three years, getting only the little learning which I could not manage to escape, although, coming from a scholarly family, I probably retained more information than I thought. However, after three years I passed my examinations and came home. Music I really loved, and my training in voice and piano was of the best. I seriously considered the stage and grand opera. To be honest, I hardly think anyone else considered it for me. I was qualified for nothing but the life of a social butterfly; a bitter disappointment to my mother and, I must confess it, somewhat of a shock to myself.

Our home, the Walter Mansion as it was called, was the gathering place for the youth of the town. It was a great red brick colonial house with octagonal towers at each side. Huge Corinthian capped, fluted columns supported the roof whose eaves formed the covering of the wide veranda. But the real source of its popularity was not its spaciousness but my sister Irene, who had graduated with distinction from Maury Institute, and had developed into an exceedingly beautiful girl.

It was with reference to this house that Genevieve Wilson Bartlett wrote the following poem:

4

Walter House and My Youth

To WALTER HOUSE

With Appreciation of Her Children

It stands a pile of glowing brick
Built of the soil that gave it birth
By pliant hands of happy slaves.
A hundred years and still it braves
The future, Walter House.
Around the park swift shadows race
All sights translate inherent grace
And loveliness reveals its strength
Where tapered columns rise.
Deep ripples wave the lily pond
The dark deodars pierce the skies.
Crepe myrtle flaunts its scarlet plumes.
In green magnolias' white-cupped blooms
Enchanting incense lies.
The mocking bird proclaims that day
Is done. Its note brooks no delay.
Alfred comes with julep tray.
Here now it stands still sheltering
A virile race that calls it home
A race that wills to do, to roam;
A place of peace to all who come;
Inspiring Walter House.
Here now it stands embodying
Through fertile years and years of drouth
The gracious living of the South.

On my return from Charlotte I immediately fell in love with
a boy named Levi Manning, the son of our Congressman. He
was later to become one of the West's most influential men,
and Governor of Arizona. But at this time I was fifteen and
he sixteen. One moonlight night we sat under an old oak,
dreaming of the future and making plans that never were to

5

materialize. The town clock struck eleven and my mother called from the veranda, "It is time to come in, Annie."

Hand in hand we walked to the house. At the door he placed his fingers under my chin and tipped my face that he might look into my eyes. Then quickly, lightly, his lips touched mine. My first kiss! He rushed down the steps, troubled. Would I ever forgive him? I closed the door, trembling. Was it a sin? Would he ever kiss me again?

With the passing of the summer, plans were made for my coming out. I was staying at that time with my eldest sister whose husband, Henry C. Myers, the handsomest man I have ever known, was Secretary of State. This longed-for event was to take place under very auspicious circumstances. The invitations were issued by "Uncle" Robert Lowry, Governor of Mississippi and an old friend of my father, and the party was to be held in the stately ballroom of the Governor's Mansion at Jackson. There was little money for the purchase of the necessary frocks, but in the upstairs hall was a large cedar chest, filled to the brim with gorgeous satins, brocades, silks and velvets, which in former days had been worn by my mother and my sister, Mrs. Myers. These were transformed into dresses for me and thus clad I went forth to conquer.

My coming-out dress had a skirt of gold brocaded satin with paniers of white satin and a tight-fitting pointed bodice with a Medici collar. I thought it was beautiful. I wore a patch and my hair was done high on my head in puffs, and lightly powdered. It was not the style, but I carried it off, and from the beginning my quaint gowns were the envy of the other debutantes.

By day I was a hoyden, stealing jelly with my friend, the Governor's daughter, raiding the pantry shelves, and then, to conceal our guilt, smashing the glasses with their official emblem. But when evening came I donned my debutante airs and set about collecting hearts.

It was a gay winter but hard times were upon us. Year after

year came devastating floods. The Mississippi overflowed its banks and became a river one hundred miles wide. Either the already planted crops would be swept away or the water would remain too long to permit replanting. Even when in desperation the land was planted, it would be a late crop and the cotton would come into boll after the beginning of the autumn rains. Though faced with ruin we were helpless as we had always been.

After my father's death, great changes had taken place in the family fortunes. During his lifetime, with a rich Delta plantation and a good law practice, he was counted one of the wealthiest men in the state. But his income was barely sufficient to meet the demands of an unlimited hospitality and a large and expensive family. As was the custom of the time, he had charge accounts at all the stores in town that sometimes ran for months. Periodically he would go around and ask how much he owed at each store, paying each bill without question.

My mother, the daughter of a prosperous planter and the wife of a successful lawyer, knew nothing of finance and less than nothing of economy. In our home lavish expenditure alternated with grueling economy, a practice which has been unfortunately characteristic of my own adult life.

My grandfather Brown gave each of his children several servants and a large plantation as a part of their dowry when they married. This small, dainty girl with the very blue eyes and very black hair, had as her portion several thousand acres of black alluvial soil forty-five miles from Holly Springs in the heart of the Mississippi Delta, just across the river from Friar's Point. Its richness, increased by the frequently recurring floods, was capable of producing great wealth; but without money for taxes, wages and the ceaseless war against the floods, it brought us only annual deficits. Many years later its sale brought us a small profit but much freedom from worry.

But it was our only hope and haven for some time. My

7

brother-in-law had served as Secretary of State for eleven years (the first three by appointment), and was unable to run for a third term. He suggested that we all take up our residence for awhile on this plantation, so in the autumn of 1888 we moved from our Holly Springs house to live in what the Negroes called the White House. It was a spacious log cabin set high on a grassy knoll, overlooking fields that extended for hundreds of acres; fields which should have been covered with cotton and corn, but which, because of the threatened flood, were lying idle, unworked, bringing in nothing.

The next year the rain fell unceasingly and in torrents. Day after day we watched Brother Henry, with a look almost of desperation on his face, staring toward the sunset at the western sky, praying for just one red streak to indicate a change of weather. Nearly every day brought a fresh calamity. The best mules died; a near-epidemic threatened the cattle; and still it rained. In the evening the sun continued to go down in a sodden gray sky.

Several times each day word came. It was always the same: the river was rising. One evening just at dusk a messenger brought word that the levee had broken forty miles away. The Negroes, already organized into working parties, were sent to throw up private levees around the place. All night they worked, singing, and as the water in the bayous rose, the words of their song came to us. It was "Roll, Jordan, Roll," and we breathed a fervent prayer that the "Mississippi" Jordan would turn and roll the other way. Late that night we went to our rooms. All the doors were open and but for the far-off singing of the Negroes there was an unearthly stillness.

About four in the morning we heard old Uncle Charlie shuffling to Brother Henry's room. We heard him whisper, "Marse Henry, she's a-creepin' in."

Down to the banks of the bayou we rushed, and sure enough, she was "a-creepin' in." Down the center of the water in the bayou, a tiny red stream, thick with sediment from the river, was pushing its way in. While we waited and watched it widened and the water began to rise. At six we went to breakfast and when we came out of the dining room what had been land was a sea.

Chickens, cows, mules and pigs and fleas took refuge within our small levee, the pigs beneath our house. Our cabin on the mound and the cabins of the hands as well were built on piers. We never lost a building in flood time.

Always it was the back water coming in through the bayou which found its way to us first. But it was not long until the Mississippi was flowing past our door. Houses went down. Bellowing, struggling cattle went floating by, and an occasional bale of cotton, carrying human freight, passed us on its way to the sea. Sometimes whole families crowded on a single bale and once a small melodeon completed the outfit. One day a Negro floated by singing "I'm gwine to join ma' Savior." On another five small children were swept from one bale by low-hanging tree branches and before our eyes disappeared below the swirling yellow waters.

Those were sad and lonely days, corralled as we were upon our knoll. Occasionally we rowed in a dugout or canoe for miles and miles in the calmer waters, passing through second-story windows of deserted houses, over roofs of others. These little excursions were none too pleasant or safe. At any time a snake was likely to drop into the boat with us, for they had sought refuge in the upper branches of the trees.

Weeks passed, and at last the waters returned to the bayous and thence to the rivers, leaving behind indescribable desolation and despair. Dreadful things were found in the soil, and once or twice treasures were unearthed by the Negroes when they returned to the fields. It was a hopeless situation. The levees were breaking everywhere, as they had been doing for years, but there was no money for rebuilding or even for repair work.

My Days of Strength

The government helped somewhat, but without millions for reconstruction work it was a forlorn hope. And always there was the question: was it better to build levees or deepen the river bed?

The levees on the Mississippi side were higher than those on the Arkansas side. The only hope for protection the Arkansas planter had lay in the breaking of the Mississippi levees and to that end, in spite of shotgun patrols, desperate men sometimes crossed the river under cover of darkness. Often a dangling corpse, hanging high on a rudely constructed gallows, and left as a warning, told its own ghastly tale.

The winter which stands out most clearly in my memory was a white winter when for weeks the snow scarcely left the ground, a most unusual occurrence in that southern climate. Night after night we heard the howling of the wolves and not infrequently during those cold weeks, packs of them came runing across the fields. One never-to-be-forgotten night I watched them as they came. To my terror they tore straight through the open space to our log cabin, right past my bedroom window, great shaggy, hungry, food-hunting beasts.

Exactly when and how our luck turned I do not remember. Possibly there was more assistance from the government. At any rate, as troubles had come in battalions, so now relief came on the same large scale. About this time my sister Irene married Oscar Johnson who, though he afterward became a great financier, was by birth a man who knew and loved the soil. He, with Henry Myers, did wonderful things, and once again we knew security and comfort.

Chapter II

Shades of Dr. Mary Walker

J UST ABOUT THIS TIME I HAD A SEVERE ATTACK OF MALARIA, which altered the entire course of my life. I went to California in the summer of 1889 to recuperate and visit my brother Harvey, who was then in business in San Francisco. On the train I was attracted by a lovely looking woman and although I never spoke to her I overheard her brilliant conversation with others. I was told that she was a "woman physician." Incredible! Dr. Mary Walker in gentlemanly attire was our idea of a woman doctor and we, in our ignorance, considered her a sacrilege against womanhood.

I never learned the name of the woman who made such a deep impression on me, but I never forgot her. In San Francisco I plunged into the social life and soon I met the orthopedic surgeon Dr. Harry Sherman. To him I poured out the story of my chance encounter and my enthusiasm for this unknown woman doctor. He suggested that it might interest me to meet a few of the women doctors of San Francisco and not long afterward he introduced me to Dr. Elizabeth M. Yates. Through her I met others.

A new world was opened to me. None of these women was a coarse-grained freak; they were fine, gentle and sensitive. They lived full lives, fighting against great odds with energy and courage. There were few women in medicine at that time and they were none too popular anywhere. People jeered and scoffed, and obstacles impossible for this generation to imagine were put in their paths. Women in any profession were having a hard time in those days, but women physicians seemed particularly obnoxious to the average man and woman of the eighties and nineties. Study of the ills of the human flesh was a disgustingly unladylike occupation. The young woman student of medicine faced the reproaches of a "disgraced" family, social ostracism, and incalculable difficulties in the struggle to build up a practice.

All of this I knew quite well, but into my happy-go-luck life there suddenly came a purpose; and opposition served rather to spur me on than to deter me. I had begun to realize that the life of a social butterfly was only half a life; my new friends lived completely and nobly. My overflowing energy suddenly became a rope which pulled me (at times much against my frivolous heart) toward a definite goal. I wrote to my mother, telling her I had decided to study medicine. She replied by wire:

"No disgrace has yet fallen upon your father's name. Should you persist in carrying out your mad determination to study medicine I shall never again recognize you as my daughter."

I knew the shade of Dr. Mary Walker, in trousers and a long-tailed coat, was stalking through my mother's mind. That settled it; I just had to study medicine!

I smile now as I recall Dr. Sherman's remark when Dr. Virginia W. Smiley told him of my determination. "As a social butterfly Miss Walter would be a great success, as a physician never—there is nothing in her." He lived to rejoice with me over the opening of the Fearn Sanatorium, the ultimate result of my right-about-face from the social to the professional life.

My brother approved and encouraged my ambition but my mother's attitude was one of unmitigated reproach. It was no wonder, for if the women in this profession were looked on askance in other parts of the country they were distinctly taboo in the South. It was a question of propriety as to whether or not they should even be discussed in polite society. But I was in the freer air of the West, far from the staid old traditions; I had found the thing I wanted to do, and I had faith in my ability to swing Mother around to my way of thinking. This I set out to do during the next months, by means of tactful descriptions and suitable anecdotes about the various women physicians I was meeting. Eventually I won her over.

In the meantime I was without money and I could not remain indefinitely a burden on my brother. The summer was coming to an end and I did not know what to do when Dr. Yates and Dr. Smiley suggested that I go to San Diego for a winter with Dr. Lucia Lane, Dr. Smiley's friend. I could begin my studies in her office under her wise direction. It was an ideal solution to my problem and it gave me a better start than I could have found in any other way.

In San Diego I discovered that I did not know how to study. I didn't know anything! Many a night Gray's *Anatomy* was dashed to the floor, while I sobbed myself to sleep on a pillow wet with tears. Long bones, short bones, flat bones, articulations, muscular attachments—these were only on the edge of the morass of knowledge into which I stumbled and floundered.

An inherited obstinacy came to my rescue, and when the spring term of the Cooper Medical College in San Francisco opened I was one of the nine women who matriculated among hundreds of men. At Cooper women were not only admitted but welcomed.

On my first day one of the men students offered to guide me around. On the top floor we came to a door with a sign, "Dissecting Room." The letters stood out as big as cartwheels and whirled dizzily; my escort stepped aside politely to let me enter first. I wondered if I were going to disgrace myself forever by being sick. I was certain I was going to faint, but I walked through that door!

Money was scarce, as usual, and I did not know how I could complete the course. Again Dr. Smiley came to my rescue with the suggestion that I try for a scholarship in the Women's

13

Medical College of Pennsylvania. I wrote some of Father's friends, Governor Stone, Governor Robert Lowry, and one or two others, asking them for references. Their response was extremely cordial and as a result I was immediately awarded a scholarship which included only tuition and laboratory fees. Dr. Yates advanced the money for expenses not covered by the scholarship.

I reached Philadelphia in the autumn and was warmly received by the College Board and Faculty who were pleased to have the name of an old southern family on their roster. Signs of the changing times, indeed, for a southern girl to choose deliberately the lot of that scorned and struggling group of women doctors!

My first year at Women's Medical was a repetition of my previous work but I managed to find an outlet for my energy. Because of the work I had done at Cooper I was made curator of the museum and given the position of presector for the professor of anatomy. This latter job meant dissecting at various odd hours, but I had long ago acquired the matter-of-fact attitude of the medical student to such things. There was one time——

It was very early morning at that hour just before the dawn when the world is wrapped in a peculiar, eerie silence and I was all alone in the dissecting room, preparing a "stiff" for the next day's demonstration. I was sleepy and anxious to finish my job and hurry home to bed. Impatiently I tugged at the tendon of the arm outstretched on a board. The arm jerked, clasped itself around my waist, and stayed there. That was too much for my "hardened" nerves. I don't know how I disengaged myself from that gruesome embrace, but I remember that I was afraid to run for fear of rousing the shades of the desecrated occupants of the other tables. Somehow I put out the lights and found my way down the long, spooky flights of stairs into the street. I vowed that never again would I do such work alone in the small hours of the morning.

My special friend, Sarah Poindexter, and I did light house-keeping together. I have mentioned the unknown woman trav-eler as the particular agent responsible for my entry into the medical profession, but in reality it was Dr. Poindexter who determined my future by the influence she exercised over me in a critical hour of my life.

Many years before, my father had returned from court feeling feverish, with an annoying pimple on his forehead. It was diagnosed later as varioloid. I, a baby of three months, devel-oped confluent smallpox. Owing to my mother's care, my life was saved though my face was deeply pitted. Strangers passing me on the street would exclaim, "Oh, that poor child, she has had smallpox," a remark that invariably sent me sobbing to my mother's arms where I would cry, "Why didn't I die? why didn't I die?" My horror of this disease increased with the years. Although the scars gradually faded until they became almost imperceptible, the word, "smallpox" mentioned in my presence continued to make me faint.

One morning the professor of medicine announced that on the morrow he would begin a series of lectures on smallpox. All that day I went about my work as if stunned. All that night I lay sleepless, wrestling with my problem. Could I go on? I knew that if I lacked the backbone to conquer this case I was conquered for life. At eight o'clock my state of indecision was as complete as my state of physical exhaustion.

All night long Dr. Poindexter had lain awake there in the room with me, saying nothing but surrounding me with sym-pathy. She brought me my breakfast saying, "See Nan, I've brought you the scrambled eggs, bacon and coffee that you love. You must eat, little one." At eight forty-five she took my hand and we went out together to the college and to the lecture on smallpox.

My Days of Strength

Sarah Poindexter was a tall, thin, remarkably fine looking woman, a graduate of Cornell, a student of biology and a lover of mankind. She was the most unselfish of mortals. Nothing was hers but everything was ours or Nan's. Her life, while in China, did not lie in pleasant places. Her husband, Mr. Rufus Howard Bent, was stationed in the bandit-infested districts and after repeated, nerve-racking experiences they were forced to leave. Now she is in Philadelphia again, happy in her children and grandchildren. But it was her confidence in me at that time which got me over the smallpox hurdle.

How I studied. For the first time I was awake to my responsibilities in life. Those were three happy years for me. For my mother they were by turns anxious and exultant ones. Having reconciled herself to having a woman doctor in the family, her revolutionary daughter became a matter of pride. At last the day for the final examinations came. We had agreed that the result would be wired her. It was long after midnight before the lists were out and the notice of success or failure alphabetically delivered. My name, Walter, coming so near the end of the list meant centuries before I could rush to the telegraph office.

My mother, rising with the dawn after an almost sleepless night, sat dressed in a fresh, cool morning gown, in an old rocking chair on the veranda, and waited for the message. Hours later she saw the messenger boy sauntering down the street. Seeing her he increased his gait, waving the telegram and shouting, "Good news, good news!" He handed her the folded slip and seeing that she could not read it for her tears opened it, and though he (and all Holly Springs he had met on the way) knew it by heart, read her the words:

"Hurrah! I've won my degree!"

My life heretofore had not brought much joy to my mother

but for the joy which came to her that day I shall always be grateful.

Dr. Joseph Price, a Southerner and one of the world's greatest surgeons and obstetricians, had for some reason taken a fancy to me. He had unlimited faith in my future success and had given me every possible opportunity to see the best surgical and obstetrical work, including that at his own hospital and the Preston Retreat, at that time one of the largest maternity hospitals in the United States.

One way in which he provided me with experience was to allow me to accompany him as a nurse and later as an assistant when he went into private homes to operate on those who refused to come to the hospital, then a none too popular resort. Once when he was to operate on a Negro woman somewhere in the slums, he took me with him. It was my birthday, a fact which I casually mentioned. When all was ready he motioned me to the operator's side of the table. In real consternation I demurred.

"Your birthday present," he said, tersely.

My first abdominal section. I was carried away with excitement and when it was over I persuaded him to let me take the place of the district nurse and take charge of the patient; spend the night there. Much against his better judgment he consented.

I was left alone with the Negress in her corner tenement room, three stories up, over a carpenter's shop on one side and a shoemaker's shop on the other. It was about four in the morning when I happened to glance at the uncurtained window. There, pressed close to the pane, I saw a Negro, his face bestial, malignant. At once it disappeared. With the courage of desperation I managed to move and pinned my underskirt across the window. Suddenly, I heard steps on the stairs, stumbling as they came. They passed the carpenter's shop, passed the shoemaker's shop, stopped at my door. There was a fumbling at the knob, and all the while, I sat paralyzed with my back to the

17

door, waiting in terror. The door opened, quick steps came to my side—and Dr. Price's voice said:

"I couldn't sleep for fear of what might be happening here."

Had an angel from heaven stood before me I could not have felt greater joy—or astonishment. I burst into uncontrollable sobs. He stood by my side until I was quiet and then he put the ironing board (which had served as the operating table) across two chairs, and with his coat for a pillow I slept there while he took my place at the patient's side. In a few hours his carriage came and in it, to my intense relief, another nurse.

This kind and able man was destined to die on the operating table while undergoing an appendectomy, an operation he had done hundreds of times with particular success.

It was my experience under him which led indirectly to a fateful conversation one noon shortly before commencement, when we were all gathered in the college mess hall. Dr. Margaret Polk, President of the College Association and one of my warmest friends, mentioned that if she had had my unusual advantages in hospital work she wouldn't mind going to China. She was then preparing for work in the mission field as physician in charge of the Women's Hospital in Soochow.

"I'll go in your place for a year, M. P.," I said, "while you take another year's work in the hospitals."

The twenty or thirty fledgling doctors seated around the table thought that was a grand idea and chipped in with suggestions. By the time the meal was over a plan had been evolved down to the most minute detail.

"I'll pay your expenses to China," said M. P., growing enthusiastic, "and the Women's Board of Foreign Missions can pay your salary for a year."

"All right," I said, "but I won't go as a missionary. I'm not even a church member. I'm a physician."

"That can be settled, I think," said Margaret, then suddenly practical. "The Board will have to pay my expenses out there. You must pay your own way back."

That was agreeable to me for then I could take up my postponed internship and when that was over settle down somewhere in the South. It was all only a lovely dream but it was fun dreaming.

However, that very evening I received a note from Margaret Polk asking me to come to her room. When I arrived there she handed me a telegram from her brother. His wife had died.

Our plans were carried out with the additional clause that if she were not ready at the end of the year I would continue for another or even two more years. I was to work as a salaried employee, not as a missionary. Dr. Polk thought that by the end of three years her brother, with his family of four small children, would have adjusted himself to the new conditions. She was right. At the end of the third year he remarried and Dr. Polk was free to take up her long delayed work in China.

It was in June, 1893 that I received my degree. I was so bursting with a desire to use my full title that stopping over several hours in Norfolk, on my way home from Philadelphia, I signed the hotel register with a flourish—"Dr. Anne Walter."

The news spread like wildfire and in short order curious people were hanging about the lobby and street, craning their necks for a glimpse of the creature who had disgraced her sex by becoming a doctor. That experience taught me a lesson; not for years did I use my title in registering at a hotel.

I spent a brief holiday in the big, high-ceilinged home of my childhood, recapturing my past but ever aware of my future. My precious medical degree aroused little enthusiasm or trust among my fellow-townsmen. I was forced to sit idly by while across the street a friend nearly died from a dangerous delivery, attended by doctors far older than I, but far less skilled in obstetrics.

My decision to go to China was a shock to my mother, but

she conceded that it was a wonderful chance for me to see the world. Naturally I would return via Suez and Europe, thus encircling the globe, at that time a great event. When the hour of my departure came she pressed into my hand a ten-dollar gold piece, a coin never too plentiful in our household, insisting that with that special gold piece I should cable her the one word, "Safe," immediately on my arrival in Shanghai.

I sailed with Dr. Poindexter who was to work in Tsinanfu, and with Dr. and Mrs. J. B. Neal with whom she was to live. The whole trip was packed with pleasure and excitement, although I remember very few details, only the general sense of adventure and joy.

And then came Shanghai with its wonderful Bund, its splendid buildings, its carriages, its rickshaws, and race course. It so filled me with amazement that no word so prosaic as "safe" satisfied me. The word I sent across the seas was "Delight." That alone could express the feeling that possessed me then, as it does now and will as long as I live.

Chapter III

Sounds, Sights and Smells

In soochow there is a narrow, straight street beneath which lies the patron dragon of the city. He is a kindly dragon, a monster in appearance only, and wells are never dug along that route lest his back be scratched unpleasantly. The citizens were struck with awe when the nine-story pagoda was set on his head, and later when the Confucian Temple was built on his tail to keep it from wagging either in joy or in wrath. History does not tell by what geomancy he was lured from his home in the Taoist heavens to be set down so firmly beneath the Street of the Protecting Dragon, but the poor beast has been long in exile, for when Venice was conceived and built on a similar plan, Soochow was a bustling, prosperous city, a thousand years old.

When Confucius was traveling from court to court, in search of a virtuous ruler, Ho Lu was overlord of the petty kingdom of Wu. After attaining this eminence by beheading his predecessor, he decided to make use of his authority to build a city worthy of his new-found dignity. In the midst of a score of lakes, with a series of low hills in the west and the Great Lake, Ta Hu, to the south, he swept a rectangle clean of hovel and fishing village, and threw a wall around it. Fifteen miles of brick work, bastioned, was that wall set between two moats. Interlocking canals paralleling the walls were dug within the city with eight-foot streets between them. The Grand Canal sweeping down from Peking through the Yangtze valley to the sea became part of the Soochow water system, joining the moat along the western wall.

My Days of Strength

This ancient city was to be the setting for my life for the next fourteen years. Here, very young and inexperienced, I was to fling myself headlong, with the blind, enthusiastic courage of youth, into a job that would have taxed the resources of a diplomat, a Sinologue and a scholar. I was to drudge like an Israelite to make bricks without straw, sometimes weeping over my failures, sometimes rejoicing in accomplishment, but never wholly satisfied.

An American bishop who visited in my home once described Soochow as a "city of unmentionable sights and indescribable smells." Certainly beauty and filth jostle each other with unconcern in the narrow, shop-lined streets. The overhanging carved balconies are decorated with the family wash hung out on bamboo poles next to gaudy signs and the brilliant draperies of the dyers. Dainty women float in flower boats along canals where the rice is washed and the refuse dumped; the streets where gorgeously dressed dandies walk, bird afinger, are used by incredible numbers of small children for every natural purpose. For a pittance a day sixty thousand weavers bend over hand looms, weaving exquisite satins; and back of the teeming, putrid streets are fragrant gardens where the women of the rich, shut away from the world, live as divorced from reality as in a dream.

Just outside the city is Tiger Hill with the Leaning Pagoda, around whose ruins mynas and great gray hawks wheel and call. There is a rambling monastery, and capping the hill is the shrine and main temple. It is as serene and awesome as the strikes of the temple bell. From the tiled rock foundation to the chasmed stream whose waters flow from an unknown source, it is mysteriously holy, utterly withdrawn from the turmoil of the city.

Then, in sharp contrast, there is the Great City Temple, in the busiest street in Soo. In a squalid courtyard of perhaps two acres there is a gateway and an enormous temple, gems of

22

architectural beauty. Within the courtyard goods of every description are laid on the ground while the vendors protect themselves from the beating sun by matting stretched between bamboo poles. One may buy anything from a cat to a fiddle, have one's fortune told by a geomancer, or listen to a tale of ancient lore. There is the shouting of the hucksters, the wailing of children, shrill voices raised in bargaining. Within the temple itself there are scores of pictures of the sainted Confucius and his disciples offered for sale. One may kneel in worship before a statue of Buddha or in awe before a Taoist devil.

"Above there's heaven; below are Han and Soo" (Hangchow and Soochow), says the ancient Chinese proverb. Although this may be unfair to other cities, from my first delighted sight of Soochow forty-five years ago, I can understand the enthusiasm which prompted that description.

But to reach Soochow from Shanghai in the year 1893, one had to journey sixty miles by slow boat up the Soochow Creek Canal. Mrs. Josephine Campbell, the hospital matron and head of the private training school for nurses in Soochow conducted by the Women's Mission Board of the Methodist Episcopal Church, South, met me in Shanghai. On the Monday following my arrival we started out. For three days and nights the panorama of China spread itself before my eyes—my real introduction to the country, for Shanghai is something apart.

We passed water wheels, turned by patient blindfolded buffaloes; cormorant boats paddled slowly upstream, the birds sitting solemnly along each side with rings around their necks to keep them from swallowing the fish they had just caught; remarkably long bamboo rafts poled along with utter disregard of other traffic; farms clustered around huddled groups of village buildings. Once in a larger village we saw lively evidence of the weekly market day, that red-letter event in the monotonous life of the Chinese farmer. Frequently our boatman hopped off at some hamlet to buy eggs, fish, pork and rice. Our boat was propelled by a yuloh which is a kind of oar but unlike any I had ever seen. It is shaped rather like a fish-tail and fastened to the rear deck, extending out behind the boat. The boatmen sway rhythmically in unison with its motion, and croon strangely haunting minor airs whose tuneless-ness, to Western ears, is in fantastic harmony with the scene.

With the coming of evening that first day the head man or *laodah* came to us and squatting down, asked in a sepulchral whisper if they might tie up near a village, for the night was dark and before us lay the wilderness. This network of canals was in those days haunted by bandits and our boatmen were afraid to traverse it alone at night. When we gave our consent they tied up by sticking a long hook into the bank. All that night I lay sleepless, listening to the bullfrogs in the ponds near by, the tree toads in the overhanging branches, the occasional twitter of wakeful birds, and the soft, mysterious thud, thud of oars as boats passed us in the darkness. All such familiar sounds I might have heard any similar night on my own plantation home, but now they were touched with an almost fearful strangeness.

In the early morning we were awakened by the deep tones of the temple bells. At noon of the fourth day we came to the walls of Soochow.

Word of our approach had reached the hospital as soon as we had passed the gates. At the hospital landing stage the entire staff and all the foreigners in the community waited to welcome the new doctor. I suppose that in every place the world over where there is a small group of aliens one finds the same hospitality, the same eagerness to greet a newcomer, and the same natural curiosity about this person who has come to share their lot.

As soon as we could get away Mrs. Campbell took me to the Hospital Home which we were to occupy together in the work

I had so lightly undertaken. My responsibilities were already beginning to weigh on me like lead.

We had just stepped inside the doors when the Chinese preacher's wife rushed up to me with her sick baby. Tears streamed down her face as in a broken voice and quaint, careful English she told me that she had been praying for my coming.

"Now all will be well!" she ended happily.

Her faith in the new doctor was touching but at the moment it was also embarrassing. What the matter with that child was I could not make out, nor, worse luck, what to give it. The entire staff stood by expectantly while I examined the infant and when I finished (for want of further inspiration) someone solemnly handed me a prescription blank.

My mind was as blank as the prescription form. I looked as wise as I could manage, and then had a brain wave.

"Castor oil!" I clutched at the straw, a perfectly safe remedy which would tide the child over until I could collect my wits. I dared not write the common name; only the Latin would do, and how to spell Ol Ricini I could not think. Was it "si" or "ci"? I had not yet mastered the art of writing illegible prescriptions, but bravely I made a stab at illegibility and gave the scrawl to the anxious mother with what I hoped was professional calm and efficiency.

By the time the oil had taken effect the child was well and my reputation was saved, for the time at least.

About two o'clock that same night a call came for the new doctor to visit one of the girls in the school dormitory. As we stood by the side of the bed with only a single light to lessen the gloom I could faintly distinguish innumerable faces and silently flitting forms, hundreds of them it seemed to me. The entire school had risen to do honor to the occasion and catch a glimpse of the new doctor.

25

As the novelty wore off and they grew bolder I heard whisperings.

"What are they saying, Mrs. Campbell?" I asked.

"They say you are like Mrs. Burke."

"And am I?"

"Oh no," she answered, "Mrs. Burke is beautiful."

On Sunday afternoon, while Mrs. Campbell and I were walking on the breastworks of the city wall, our only place for exercise, I suddenly became conscious that the farmers were at work in their fields. Everywhere about me the ordinary weekday life was going on. I had come straight from the Quaker City of Philadelphia where every frivolous and mercenary activity was strictly taboo on Sunday.

"Why," I exclaimed, "see how everyone is working! Don't these people pay any attention to Sunday?"

"My dear," said Mrs. Campbell, "would we be here if the Chinese knew anything about Sunday?" and she laughed at my absolute ignorance of the people among whom for a brief season I had elected to cast my lot.

The brief season stretched out to forty-four years. Looking back after all that time I think it is the fragrance of the night and its sounds during that early period of my life in Soochow which linger most clearly in my memory.

A word, a sound, a fleeting perfume annihilates time and distance. Again I am sitting at my desk at one end of the large, pleasant living room of the Hospital Home. The air is heavy with the scent of sweet olive, of jasmine or tuberose, those heavily perfumed flowers of China. The school clock strikes nine; a bell sounds sending the boys to their dormitories. Ten o'clock, and the light appears on Dr. Parker's veranda across the street. I know that when he has taken the day's record for the Royal Asiatic Meteorological Bureau I shall be left all alone with the night sounds.

Eleven o'clock brings the shuffling, muffled sound of the

water buffaloes, as the milkman leads them past the gates on their way to the pasture from which at five o'clock they will return. For everything in China is reversed. Even the cows are stabled during the day and pastured at night. A topsy-turvy, fantastic world it seems at first; a world that makes one's childhood speculations over the big globe and the Chinamen who must walk upside down seem quite reasonable.

At hour intervals all through the night I hear the night watchman beating his drum, blowing his horn and rattling his stick as he calls "coming, coming, coming," to frighten the thieves away and to avoid the embarrassment of being frightened himself.

An occasional Chinese passes by the window as speedily as possible, whooping and yelling at the top of his lungs to scare off all evil spirits as he nears the houses of the foreign devils. Upon the grave mounds in the lot in front of my window where for centuries coffins have been deposited, all the *wonks* (stray dogs) of the city collect night after night, to bark through the long darkness or to sit yapping at the moon.

But the noises and the pervasive smell of China soon ceased to disturb me. I was able to sleep serenely through it all, no longer feeling myself a stranger in an alien and rather terrifying land.

CHAPTER IV

Loh Kwei Kyu
(Old Customs and Superstitions)

TIEN SZ TSUNG—"THE HEAVEN GIVEN PLACE," OR IN OUR MORE
prosaic language the Soochow Woman's Hospital—had
been organized and built by Dr. Mildred Phillips. She had
chosen a site next door to the Soochow Men's Hospital and near
by was the Davidson School for Girls. All the buildings were
close to the canal, spacious affairs, architectural hybrids of the
East and West. When Dr. Phillips married and left Soochow
the hospital was closed and unused for two or three years. There
were so few women doctors at that time that the problem of
finding one suitable for the post and willing to come all the way
to China was difficult. Margaret Polk's acceptance of the position had been hailed with joy, but I must say that they welcomed me as a substitute as if I had been the merciful dispensa-
tion of a kind providence.

My first job was to pick up the pieces of the organization Dr.
Phillips had started and put them together again, a not too
difficult task, especially with the friendly help of the staffs of
both hospitals. The hospital was well equipped; and as we
ordered drugs in large quantities from the leading wholesale
druggists in the United States and paid no duty (the hospitals
were under the Mission Board) there was no trouble on that
score.

But there *were* handicaps, principally the Chinese fear of the
"foreign devil." Often in the midst of a recital of woes a patient
suddenly would be overcome by the realization that she was

28

in the presence of a foreigner and before I could speak she would be gone. The soles of her feet and the hem of her garment would be the last I saw of her.

Frequently a patient whom I wanted to stay in the ward for additional treatment or observation would draw away in open terror and either depart immediately or huddle in a corner to discuss the question with the inevitable relatives who had come with her. I soon learned that argument was useless and left them alone to chatter about it as they liked. But when the next patient was urged to stay there would be an eruption from the corner and the first group would add their entreaties to mine, extolling my wisdom, my marvelous success, of which they knew nothing, and the delights of the hospital of which they knew still less, praising everything in such terms that often in convincing others, they convinced themselves and it ended by all of them staying.

In spite of their fear, however, there was great excitement throughout the city when it became known that a woman physician had arrived and that on a certain day the hospital and clinic again would be opened. It was a memorable experience. On the first day they arrived in hordes, most of them drawn out of curiosity. Some were brought on litters improvised from doors. Many came quite frankly to see the new "foreign devil's" mysterious healings and there were hundreds of beggars, afflicted with all sorts of diseases which were their stock in trade. Feeling helpless and woefully ignorant, I faced these strange patients with as much equanimity as I could muster. Mrs. Campbell sat at a table beside my desk with the big ledger before her in which she recorded the cases as she interpreted. The patients brought their bundles of bedding, which might be all their worldly goods, and whole families came with a single patient to scream her symptoms into my deafened ears.

Our little clinic was very modern and quite up to date for 1893. Its adjoining pharmacy was well equipped, and the druggist, trained by Dr. Phillips, did splendid work. The Chinese nurses, many of whom were graduates of mission schools, were heroines, bright and engaging, not afraid of work, stanchly loyal to their teachers and determined to succeed. Without them I could have done nothing.

If I have any criticism to make of the Chinese nurse, it is that she lacks initiative in times of emergency. An accident, an unexpected hemorrhage, sends her scurrying to cover.

But one who never lost her head, even under the most blood-curdling conditions, was Ling Tsu who came only to my shoulder and I was just five feet tall. It wasn't long after my arrival that I chose Ling Tsu for my personal nurse and she was with me continually, accompanying me everywhere until the very day I left Soochow. I chose her for two reasons, she was unusually bright and she was the only nurse who could speak English. Her father was an American educated Chinese doctor and her nephew later was President of Soochow University.

As the hospital gradually ceased to be a curiosity it became less of a task to sift those patients it might be possible to help from the many who, for one reason or another, were far beyond our assistance. As the hospital filled and the women discovered that the "foreign devil" doctor was not so devilish after all, it was the morning clinics that I found most interesting and it was a matter of pride when first one and then another woman begged, of her own accord, to be allowed to remain for treatment.

One morning a young epileptic girl came to me, saying she would be happy if she could only have a fit to show me how sick she had been before her cure. I told her that I would take her word and excuse her from the fit. I do not think that there was a square inch of her body that had not been treated for some imaginary trouble. She was so afraid of being sent away that she developed a new disease every time I visited the ward.

It was through these clinics that I learned many phases of Chinese life and customs and gained a knowledge of the people and their character that could not have come to me in any other way. I remember once a man staggered into the room, bowed under the burden of the woman he carried on his back. Groaning and grunting he deposited her on the chair in front of me. She was garish in her dress of green upper garment, brilliant red divided skirt, white stockings and shoes of a startling yellow. We learned that she lived one hundred miles from Soochow, across the Great Lake, and that she had been dressed for her grave before leaving home. It was just as well because I was forced to tell them that there was no possible hope for recovery.

Hearing my verdict the husband threw her back over his shoulders and went off, sorrowfully, to his boat. Before leaving he told us that he would go by the temple to invoke the mercy and the blessing of the gods that his wife might be spared to reach home alive; prayers failing he was prepared.

He had taken the precaution of bringing along a live chicken and if his wife should die on the journey home, in spite of all prayers, her spirit in its flight to realms unknown would be caught by the chicken. Then the chicken would be slaughtered by the graveside of the woman and the spirit released near the family burial plot. Otherwise the spirit might never find its way to its proper shelter.

Another time a patient remarked matter of factly that if we could not cure her she would be forced to hang herself. She had come to us as a last resort after the Chinese doctors had done their worst. It was the first—but not by any means the last—direct evidence I had of how lightly life is held by the Chinese.

Zing Sie Lu—Seeking the Death Road, they call it, and it is done most often by means of the rope or by opium. Not only suicide, to use our less poetic term, but the taking of another's life is regarded with comparative casualness. There was no legal punishment under the Manchu code for a father who had put an unfilial son to death.

My first experience with suicide also involved the mother-in-law problem which in China, among the poorer people principally, was anything but pleasant. The women of this family were clinic patients and I was called to their house just inside the city wall. The daughter-in-law of the house had "sought the death road" only a few days before by garroting herself over the doorway of her mother-in-law's room. She had succeeded in her twofold purpose: death for herself, disgrace for the mother who now lay dying, horribly and painfully, from eating raw opium.

The daughter-in-law, I learned, had been treated as a slave until unable to bear the brutal treatment any longer, she had taken her own life, deliberately hanging herself outside the old mother's door. It was spring and the continuous call of the bottle bird (so named because foreign tipplers declare its cry is "one more bottle, one more bottle") had haunted the old woman. Its *Lao ta-ta, veh hao,* which the Chinese say means "the old woman is bad," had driven her finally to a realization of her cruelty and to suicide.

The girl paid a high price for her revenge but innumerable daughters-in-law were willing to sacrifice their lives to escape from their slave-like existence.

The people themselves were anxious for relief from their illnesses, even at the hands of the foreign devils, but the influence of the priests was great. They, with their antiquated superstitions and fear of losing power, bitterly opposed our Western science, and by their tales of horror, prevented many sufferers from coming to us for help.

The natives of a distant village up the river heard of our hospital and one day a boatload of eighteen or twenty men and women journeyed to Soochow "to see the foreign doctors who

The dissecting class at the Women's Medical College of Pennsylvania in 1892.
I am sitting on the edge of the table at the extreme left; Sarah Poindexter is the tall girl in the middle.

In cap and gown, as I was graduated from
the Women's Medical College of Pennsylvania, 1893.

could cure all diseases." But before coming to the hospital they went to the temples to pray and ask advice. Here they were told by the priests that I would take out their eyes and mix them with copper to make silver, and that I would do many other horrible things to them. Many of the sick were frightened away but two very brave ones decided to come and see for themselves. After seeing they were persuaded to enter the wards. They stayed a few days and then returned to their home to bring another boatload to us for treatment, with no stopover at the temple.

This time they brought with them a man who entered Dr. Hart's hospital and six or eight women for mine. One morning one of the women came to me in great distress and asked me to look at her husband's "rotten throat" (an accurate description). She pleaded for just one word of encouragement. Dr. Hart had told her that the case was hopeless and if I agreed with his diagnosis she said, "the tears would begin to fall and never cease to flow" for the family loved him greatly.

She caught her daughter by the arm and baring it to the shoulder, showed me a hideous suppurating sore just above the elbow. Then in a tragic manner she demonstrated how this girl had bitten a piece from her own arm to make soup for her father to drink, and as she bit herself she had knelt and prayed to the Supreme Being that her sacrifice would save him.

This case of the girl biting out her own flesh to compel the gods to heed her prayer for her father's life is the only one of its kind that came to my personal notice, although such stories are often related in Chinese ethical works. To give one's living flesh as a sacrifice to save a parent is the highest example of filial piety. Some of the beautiful marble triple-arched *pailows*, erected along the banks of the inland waterways are to commemorate such deeds. Others, it must be confessed, merely extol the virtues of some rich landlord or landlady whom the villagers wished to flatter.

33

One still hears much, mostly from tourists, about the killing of girl babies. This belief probably arose from the Chinese custom of wrapping the bodies of still-born infants in straw mats and throwing them into the canal, or leaving them on the city wall where dogs occasionally destroyed them. Personally I have never known a case where a living child was thrown into a canal or exposed on the wall unless death was inevitable, and then only when gangrene had set in and the *chi mien* (awful odor) forced the family to dispose of the rotting body. As a matter of fact it has been my experience that girl babies are as well loved as the boy babies, though they may not be so important. As in every other country in the world, the father desires a son to carry on his name, but in China a son is even more desirable because of ancestor worship. Through the son of the house the family is assured of an unbroken line to burn incense to the ancestor-gods. I was made aware of this when a woman carrying a rather large child came into the clinic and sat down before me. It soon developed that the child could neither see, speak, hear, nor walk. On inquiry I learned that she had two more at home in a similar condition. When I asked why she didn't bring them all she answered, "Oh, the others are just girls and it doesn't matter about them, but this is a boy!"

Parents have complete control over their children and the father remains the head of the family with power of life or death even though his sons may be grown men, married and with children of their own. Theoretically girls are at a discount. Should they find no husbands they become economic liabilities. When they marry they transfer their services and their expenses to their husband's family. Actually a strong-minded woman has about as good a chance of ruling the household in China as in our country, and usually does.

The Chinese attitude on family affairs is startling to the newcomer from the West. Our cook, Sung Mai, for twelve whole days had been the proud possessor of a daughter. Early one morning the screams of the infant sent me flying across the compound to its rescue. Much to my surprise I found the grandmother wielding a dull razor and shaving its tender head. On the top she had left a patch of downy hair in the shape of a peach, emblem of prosperity, longevity and progeny.

"Why do you do this?" I asked. I knew that the Chinese custom does not require that a child's head be shaved until it is one month old.

"Well," she replied, brandishing the queerly shaped instrument which was more like a meat-axe than a razor, "two months I have waited here to plait the hair of Sung Mai should she die, for only a mother-in-law may perform this duty. She did not die. I have wasted enough time on her and her child. Tomorrow I leave, therefore it is necessary I do this today for only the grandmother is permitted to shave the baby's head the first time."

Although in China women are subject to the three laws— obedience in childhood to the father or elder brother, to the husband after marriage, and to the eldest son if widowed— human nature remains much the same. Only a week after my arrival in Soochow I was called on a case with a little story behind it that illustrated this.

It was midnight when the call came to go at once to see the wife of an ex-mandarin. Mrs. Campbell went with me as interpreter and after an hour's drive we reached a wretched straw hut which seemed a strange domicile for an ex-mandarin and his wife. There were fifteen or twenty men, women and children huddled together in the one room, but even in that cramped space I noticed that one elderly woman sat somewhat apart from the others, holding herself aloof from the whole proceedings but watching, with the eyes of a bird of prey, every move that I made at the sick woman's bed.

She was the man's Number One Wife. He had been a man

of wealth and after a few years of married life he took his wife's younger sister for his "small wife." Number One objected strenuously. He persisted; it was all too evident that the small wife was the favorite. Wife Number One ended by turning both husband and sister out of the house, vowing that she would make her sister "die like a beggar."

The sisters had not met for two years but Wife Number One had come that night in the impatient certainty that her vow would be fulfilled.

The husband told me that the Chinese physicians had given up all hope six days before but that if I would save his "small wife" he would send her to me in the morning. It was apparent that her only chance for life lay in an operation of a very grave nature. I told him we never guaranteed a cure but as death without operation was inevitable, he could do no less than give her the benefit of this one last chance. He agreed sadly and in the morning, just as I was sitting down to an early breakfast, she arrived at the hospital. The Number One Wife did not see her oath fulfilled on that occasion, for the woman lived.

After the operation was over we observed an eager, curious crowd surrounding the hospital. The news had been broadcast that something unusual was going on. At that time surgery was practically unknown and the slightest operation was miraculous to the Chinese. The priests objected to it and the people feared it because they believed that to be deprived of a member or any part of a member in this life meant everlasting existence without it in the spirit world.

I bumped into this almost impossible barrier of superstition one day when an old woman came into the wards with a gangrenous finger. In a fit of temper her son-in-law had snapped her finger backward and splintered the bone. The whole arm was swollen and black. I thought amputation might save her but she preferred certain death to having even the finger removed, for to her its loss meant a beggar's existence through eternity. This belief worked both ways. When a woman died in childbirth they always wished to have her delivered after death and thus be relieved of the eternal burden of an unborn child.

It is also very important to keep one's six ghosts and three spirits intact. During an unusual press of work a woman was called to assist the hospital amah. After her return home, unfortunately, she became ill. The following night two men came to the hospital, bringing a dress that the woman had worn and several sticks of incense. They asked permission to go into the room where the woman had slept to call back one of her six ghosts which she believed she had left behind. The woman's faith was so strong we feared a refusal might cause her death and so we allowed them to proceed with their treasure hunt.

One of the men went first into the room with the dress outspread and with sticks of burning incense, calling as he walked:

"*As-tisiau le! Ah-tisiau le.*" (Come sister! Come sister!)

And the second man following, answered:

"*Le tse, le tse.*" (Coming! Coming!)

Thus they captured the errant spirit and went home happy to put the clothes containing it upon the sick woman. We hoped it helped to make her well.

The superstitions of the Chinese were difficult to combat. At times they were amusing and caused no harm, at others death might have been prevented had not the patient fled from the "foreign devil's" medicine because of some superstitious fear.

One morning when I was extremely busy in the clinic, every time I raised my eyes from my desk I noticed a man conspicuously searching for something in the panes of glass, in the corners and under the furniture.

I called one of the nurses to me and asked why the man was searching so diligently.

"He is hunting a spider," she said.

I raised my eyebrows in wonder and she explained:

"He brought his baby to you yesterday for an examination. Today the baby is worse. He thinks that if he can find a spider, take it home and kill it by the side of the child he will be killing the evil spirit that entered the child while he was in your presence."

One day I was called to see a young boy who had a piece of lead from a bamboo toy in his larynx. Tracheotomy alone would save his life. This I explained to the assembled family. A discussion followed, and a wonderful chart representing the upper part of the human body was produced. It showed the esophagus terminating in the heart, in evidence, I suppose, that the heart and stomach in China as elsewhere are sometimes confused and thought to be one and the same thing. I got lost among the tangled ends of the trachea, which on the chart lost itself in what would be the gastric region of the European.

This ended my thirst for knowledge of Chinese anatomy. I pointed out the spot in the median line of the trachea where the operation must be done. They preferred the side. As I could not agree with them or persuade them to agree with me, there was no operation and the child died because of disagreement between family and doctor, one of a thousand similar cases in China.

A man once brought his baby to me. The baby was very precious but even so it had a typical case of scurvy. Several times a week the father returned for medicine and fresh fruit, always happy and always giving a good account of the patient. At last he said that while nine-tenths of the baby's trouble was well, the other tenth was as bad as it had been. I never knew what the other tenth was, but it killed the baby.

There were countless such incidents resulting from ignorance and superstition, but when the people finally made up their minds to put themselves entirely in our hands they usually obeyed orders as well as they knew how, and they were grateful and generous.

In one case only was my charge of five dollars a visit (Mexican dollars normally are worth only thirty cents American money) ever questioned. I was called to see a baby who was in a violent convulsion. I found the room crowded. Two men were busily running sticks up the child's nostrils to make it sneeze; while ten or twelve women stood by ready to yell and jump wildly around whenever it seemed necessary to frighten off a convulsion. I stopped the yelling and forbade them to hold seven lighted candles and a few lamps to the child's face when there were symptoms of an attack. The child recovered from this example of Chinese doctoring plus that of a foreign physician, and the family thought the recovery sufficient remuneration for the services of the latter.

A few months later, while I was away, the child died. Shortly afterward a "tribute board" inscribed with some high-flown compliments was presented to me, not because the child once had recovered under my treatment, but because they knew that I could have saved him if I had been there. The board cost many times the sum total of my bill.

I once received a wire asking me to come, "like an arrow shot from the bow," to see a youth who was dangerously ill. I was yulohed on a slow boat, our fastest transportation at the time, for two days and nights before I reached the large village where I found the only son of an official dying from malaria. Fortunately he had much in his favor; the gods were kind and he recovered.

Three years later came another urgent call from the same family, but on arrival I found the young man already in his coffin. I asked why they had not sent for me sooner, and reminded them that he was brought back almost from the dead three years before.

"Yes, Doctor," said the father, "but it is this way. We talked about it and much as we wanted you, we finally decided to let nature take its course. For suppose there are sixty chills in his system and you give him the white medicine when he has had only ten, what becomes of the remaining fifty?"

It was impossible to combat reasoning like that.

CHAPTER V

Ancient Chinese Cures

WHEN I ARRIVED IN SOOCHOW I WAS ONE OF A VERY SMALL handful of foreign women doctors in all that huge country. Dr. Mildred Phillips had married and gone home. Dr. Mary Fulton was in Canton and Dr. Mary Garner and Dr. Elizabeth Reifsnyder were in Shanghai. There may have been others in North China, but I am not sure.

The women doctors, and the men too, received only the most distasteful and hopeless cases because in those early days the foreign doctor was called only as a last resort. When the native physicians had done their best, or worst, a friend, or even a servant, would remember that strange stories had been told them of a foreign doctor; then—and only then—we would be called. The ignorance of the native physicians in their treatment of disease was remarkable. I was always stumbling over some queer treatment, and now and then, much to my surprise, discovering that these centuries-old ways were as effective as our modern methods; more often they were hideously primitive and immersed in superstition.

Early in my clinic work I was astonished to find that one hundred per cent of the Chinese whom I examined had already had smallpox. I asked why this particular disease was so prevalent, and was told that the people had not had the disease. They had been inoculated! On further research I learned that the Chinese method of inoculation was totally unlike our Western way of vaccination. The actual exudate from the ulcers of a smallpox patient was blown up the nostrils of the person who was to be vaccinated. This was called inoculation. It was most efficacious. It always "took," but it did not always kill. It gave the patient smallpox in a mild form instead of producing the reactions which one gets from vaccination as we know it.

It was almost impossible to control the spread of disease. If one Chinese had smallpox the entire city contracted it, for quarantine, then as now, was unheard of except for a red rag tied around the head. Smallpox is no respecter of persons; old and young, rich and poor, Chinese and foreigner, fell before it. I was immune but I dreaded it even more than cholera. In the spring a garment would be removed from a smallpox patient, carefully folded and tenderly tucked away until the autumn when winter garments again were brought out. Then the carefully protected germ would pop out and smallpox would be with us again. A man might hail a passing rickshaw in which the previous passenger had been a person with confluent smallpox, for no Chinese would think of letting a case of smallpox prevent him from going about his daily affairs; that is, not until he dropped down dead.

All during my stay in Soochow I came to expect the yearly epidemics and look for them as I did the blossoming of the peach in the spring and the turning of the tallow leaves in the autumn. Smallpox and cholera led, but pushing forward in the procession of diseases were diphtheria, malaria and scarlet fever. As far as malaria was concerned it was *M'fah* (fate) with the Chinese, and they did nothing but sit and point heavenward when the chills and fevers came upon them.

For centuries the Chinese have had a queer but effective cure for diphtheria. I have never encountered it myself but this, I've been told, is the method: a turtle is obtained from a native medicine shop and taken to the home of the victim. Its head is inserted in the patient's mouth where it sucks the diphtheritic membrane. This ancient method of tracheotomy was sometimes as successful as our more modern and hygienic way of inserting a tube in the trachea below the larynx. It wouldn't do for the squeamish or anyone with a turtle phobia.

As far as I could find out the most popular method of curing a convulsion was to frighten the child to death.

For cholera the Chinese had another odd cure of their own. They chewed copper coins! This is hard to believe unless you've actually seen it and the only way of proving the efficacy of this treatment is to have cholera and try it out for yourself. However, there is some element in the saliva of the cholera patient that makes it possible to masticate the coins. Perhaps European medical science, seeking a cholera cure, went back to ancient Chinese lore, for one of our remedies in the treatment of this disease is *tinct. cupri sulpha.*

My first experience with the copper coin cure occurred in Soochow toward the end of my sojourn there. I was just closing my office for the day when Dr. Margaret Polk rushed into my room.

"Look," she said unclenching her fist. And in the palm of her outstretched hand I saw something that looked like coffee grounds.

"This," she continued, "was a copper cash less than one hour ago." (A copper cash at that time was a coin of infinitesimal value.)

She went on to tell me that she had been with a cholera patient when the woman's servant had dashed in from the street, carrying a string of copper cash. Quickly, before Dr. Polk had a chance to snatch them away, she tore one off and popped it in the patient's mouth.

The patient had chewed the coin steadily for five or ten minutes before Dr. Polk could persuade her to spit it out. Then, much to Dr. Polk's amazement, she received in the palm of her hand not a coin but the tiny fragments. She hurried immediately to the wash basin, disinfected her hand and its contents,

43

and then hastened around to astonish one doctor after another with her find.

The cholera patient recovered. It may have been because of the copper coin; it may have been due to foreign hospital treatment. But in spite of Chinese and foreign cures, death came surely and often suddenly to almost everyone who was attacked by cholera.

One horrible summer Soochow was swept by cholera. It was like a mighty threshing machine working its way through the city with sinister efficiency. Hardly a home escaped. Victims fell by the hundreds every day, until at last the mortality reached a point far beyond computation. The dead were thrown into trenches; coffins could not be procured in sufficient number. People went about the streets with haggard, frightened faces, and no one knew who would be struck down next. Such a season of horror is not uncommon in China.

The Chinese continued to use the canals for all washing and dumping purposes, but in some way they had grasped the truth that the cause of the cholera lay in the water. Night after night they lined the canals with weird charms; they shouted and screamed and cried aloud to frighten away the cholera demons. There were endless numbers of processions, all directed toward the same worthy end. The streets each night were thronged with a hooting, chattering multitude.

One night, as my nurse and I were on our way to see a cholera patient, we found ourselves heading a procession, and for nearly an hour we added our forces of two sedan chairs and eight bearers to the general noise and confusion. Several days later we heard that the sudden increase of deaths which had occurred at that time was laid to the unfortunate presence of the foreigner.

It was during that same epidemic that my nurse and I inadvertently joined a funeral cortège. Our chairs unfortunately fell in behind the one which held the Chinese paper image of

44

the deceased. This raised us automatically to the post of chief mourners. Everybody laughed. It would be difficult to imagine the immense hilarity of that funeral procession. The paid mourners stopped mourning to laugh; the priests forgot to clang their gongs; the real mourners left off wailing, lifted the curtains in which they were enshrouded, and laughed aloud; while we dropped the curtains of our sedan chairs and did likewise. Sudden outbursts of merriment in our wake announced that the joke was shared by the rest of the populace.

When we reached home the head chair bearer said,

"*Oh, yeh!* (It is so.) That family will have to eat much bitterness because of you, Doctor."

But I hope the six ghosts and three spirits of that cholera victim are not still wandering aimlessly about the earth, homeless because of the baleful influence of our presence at the funeral.

It was during another of our many cholera epidemics that a woman living across the city from the hospital set out in her sedan chair to bring her dying baby to us for treatment. When the chair was put down at the door of the hospital, the mother was taken out dead. She had died en route from *cholera sicca,* this strange form of dry cholera which creeps up on the unsuspecting victim. In this form there are no stools and no vomiting, but the same poisons are there and the body liquids are emptied into the body cavities instead of being expelled.

The dying baby survived, and is now a hale and hearty man who has weathered cholera epidemics for over forty years.

Although I treated everything from toothache to cancer, most of my experiences were with obstetrical cases, and I had more opportunity than I really wished to study the crude, cruel methods of the midwives.

I had been in Soochow but a day or two when late at night, according to the best traditions of people everywhere, I was

45

called to the home of a wealthy Chinese. I was met at the door by the father, waving a tiny arm.

"We got this much," he said.

I was horrified. The midwives had gone about their task with more strength than science. It was apparent that the arm had been twisted from the shoulder by brutal force. Still somewhat dazed by my shocking introduction to Chinese midwifery, from sheer habit I proceeded to clean the mother up although I had little hope of saving her. This was the first of many, many emergencies where I was forced to do the thing I could do rather than the thing I should do.

The child, naturally, was delivered dead; the mother not only lived, but showed not the slightest septic manifestations. This only goes to prove the truth of my contention that the average Chinese patient is so impregnated with germs that a few million more or less make no impression. Even if by some miracle a Western woman had managed to withstand the ordeal of the midwives, she never in the world could have survived such an influx of germs.

Another time I was called to assist in a particularly difficult case of retarded labor. When I arrived I found all doors of the house unlocked and open. All the trunks, chests and everything unlockable was unlocked; everything openable was open. The midwife had done this to enable the patient to loosen up and expel the child freely.

I used the forceps, just the same.

On another occasion I found a labor patient covered with dry lizards, scorpions, beetles, and other swift moving insects and animals fastened on her garment with their heads pointed downward. Another instance of mental suggestion, but again I used the instruments.

Many of the Chinese remedies were simple and could not hurt—much. A hot drink of some kind was prescribed for almost every ailment, and the sick were placed in darkened

46

rooms. Most rooms were windowless, anyway. The hot drink and the dark helped considerably in smallpox cases, or at least they did no harm. The hot drink induced sweating and caused the poisons to be eliminated, and the dark room prevented too much exposure to light and air which have much to do with the irritation and deep pitting of that disease. But as for cancer! The common cure a half-century ago was to apply a red plaster on the outside of the afflicted spot.

The following description of a cancer by a Chinese doctor of forty-four years ago is fairly indicative of their knowledge of medical science at that time.

Description of disease of M. Pan Ying: In the left wrist the inch pulse is deep and low, and the middle and deep pulses are deep and fine, and also slow. In the right wrist the inch pulse is full and large, but with little strength; the middle and foot pulses are deep and quick. The coating of the tongue is white. The Yang (front) side of the right leg involves the Yin (back) side and is slightly red and swollen. The base of the swelling is large and scattered and slightly raised. The disease is half Yang (positive) and half Ying (negative). It is called yung-tee (cancer). Food is difficult of digestion. The place swollen but will not break because the stomach is weak. There is a thirst but no desire to drink.

It is of the utmost importance that the patient take some medicine that will bring the disease to the surface and strength the stomach. If the abscess is allowed to remain another half a month and does not swell or break open, the poison goes down into the bone and forms pus, while the appearance of the skin on the surface remains unchanged. A needle must be used, and if on insertion of one inch or two inches, no pain is caused, the needle may be thrust in deeper. This disease is attached to the bone and there is pus, but it does not appear on the surface. There must be an application on the outside, and some medicine must be taken to strength the vital breath and bring life to the blood.

This doctor was fairly advanced. He apparently grasped certain rudimentary facts, though he failed to use much sense in

47

applying them, and of course his theory of the pulse is absurd.

Their prescriptions were even more laughable. Here is one for snake bite:

A portion of the jaw of a wild hog
A portion of the jaw of a tame hog
A portion of the jaw of a goat
A portion of a goose bone
A portion of a peacock bone
A portion of the tail of a fish
A portion of the head of a venomous snake.

And another which seems to be a specific for the bites and stings of insects as well as snakes:

Powdered snake	two parts
Wasps and their nests	one part
Centipedes	six parts
Scorpions	four parts
Toads	twenty parts

Grind thoroughly, mix with honey and make into small pills to be taken four times a day.

Today your Chinese servant does not hesitate to borrow an aspirin from your medicine cabinet if he feels a headache coming on, but when I was a young doctor in Soochow a headache was often a fearful and wondrous thing. There are headaches of varying degrees of severity, but there was one headache in particular that I shall never forget.

A messenger came to the hospital late one night to say that I must make haste. Mme. ———, wife of an influential war lord, had a "great headache." I hastened and was deposited breathless in the courtyard of an immense house, closely shuttered and barred in medieval fashion. I was led to a large ceremonial hall where the entire household sat in family conclave. I was a bit bewildered. The husband stepped forth.

"You are not afraid?" he asked.

Some of my patients at the Mary Black Children's Ward.

The street entrance to "The Heaven Given Place," Soochow.

Gradually I collected around me a number of derelicts . . .

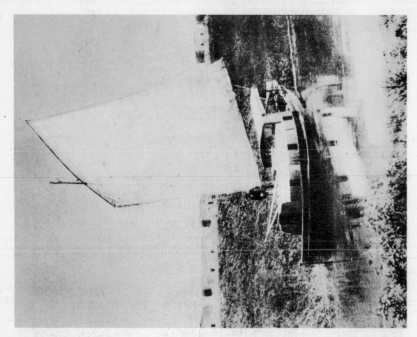

I was yulohed on a slow boat,

The first thing I did was to fall in love . . .

"Afraid of a headache? Certainly not," I replied.

"But you are very tiny," he said, "and so is she," pointing to Ling Tsu, the nurse who accompanied me everywhere.

Finally I convinced him that I was not afraid, but by this time the family's voices shrilling in consultation were beginning to give me a headache. Much ado about nothing in my opinion.

I was led through court after court, room after room, and at last the procession of family and servants, led by the husband, Ling Tsu and myself, stopped before a heavy door. The husband again asked if I were nervous.

I assured him, with a stamp of my foot for emphasis, that I was not. At that I was pushed inside quickly and the door closed and locked between me and the others. My first thought was that I had been abducted.

For a moment, in the semidarkness of the room, I thought I was alone. Then I heard a woman crying, and almost immediately I saw her sitting by the bed. She rose and came toward me and I could see then that she was stark, raving mad!

"You killed my child," she screamed, "you killed my child!"

By this time she was standing over me, hands raised, about to spring. I grabbed her by the wrists with a strength I didn't know I possessed. I was frightened but I steadied my voice as well as I could.

"I did not kill your child," I said. "I heal, not kill." I pushed her backward to the bed and held her there, repeating those words over and over again.

In a few minutes the family, not hearing screams or cries, first peeked, then tiptoed into the room. I prescribed for her headache—a headache I'll always remember—and slipped out quietly.

From this experience I learned that when a Chinese speaks of a "great headache," he does not necessarily mean something that a headache powder will cure but rather that the person is suffering from *chi*. Such noted Sinologues as Dr. Morehead,

49

Dr. Medhurst and Arthur Smith agree that this same *chi* is the Chinese equivalent of the Biblical term "possessed of the devil." In another word—insanity.

This also is *M'fah*, and no cure is provided.

Although all headaches do not terminate in insanity, a great many of the *chi* headaches I encountered did. Many who came to us for treatment claimed that their trouble began either with a "great anger" or a "great headache." The paroxysm may have occurred twenty years before but they had never forgotten it, though its relation to their present trouble was probably imaginary, unless the result happened to be insanity.

It was not at all uncommon while passing along the street to hear the sudden cry, "Save life! Save life!" and to come upon a man or woman or even a child who had fallen down in a fit, while the person who had been the cause of the "great anger" called for help, lest everlasting punishment fall upon his unlucky head.

I never knew whether the following incident was caused by such a fit of anger or was merely an exhibition of parental authority. One afternoon, sitting at my desk, I heard a fearful noise just outside the gate. A child's screams, piercing and shrill, sounded above the general hubbub. Rushing to the rescue I found a woman beating the child's head against the brick wall.

Snatching the child from her I prepared to deliver myself of the "great anger" which boiled up in me. Just at that moment my Chinese teacher passed by and seeing me in the midst of so much excitement, stopped.

"What's the trouble, Doctor?"

"She was banging her child's head against this brick wall!"

A stare of surprise was his only comment.

"Don't you understand?" I cried. "She was beating her child's head against this brick wall, and she's got to stop it!"

"But it is her child," he protested with genuine bewilderment. "She can bang its head against the wall if she wants to."

My anger collapsed like a pricked bubble in the face of this calm acceptance of traditional authority.

"Well, not against my wall," I answered lamely.

When I first went out to China the insane were chained to trees in the courtyard in summer and locked in a cell-like room in the winter. Today there are only two hospitals for the mentally afflicted in all of China, one in Canton, the other in Shanghai, and the insane are still chained like dogs or given the run of some tiny cubicle.

But Chinese medical methods have given way largely to Western medical science in the last half century. A woman who lived just across the way from the hospital was pronounced incurable by the Chinese doctors. Rather than call a foreign physician she sought "the death road" by means of a rope. That today such fear of Western science is extremely rare, if it has not altogether disappeared, is owing largely to the establishment of several excellent medical schools where the Chinese students have all the advantages of scientific methods.

It is a far cry from that day over fifty years ago when Dr. Elizabeth Reifsnyder performed the first abdominal operation on a Chinese woman in China, removing a tumor weighing over sixty pounds. The idea of an operation was so unusual that a Chinese artist drew a picture of it, entirely from his own imagination. His conception of what went on in an operating room was reprinted in all the Chinese publications. A copy of his drawing adorned our office wall. I remember it well. It showed the patient lying on a table, her knees drawn up in an agonizing position. Also on the table, standing over her in high-heeled shoes, was the foreign woman devil doctor, battle-axe in upraised hands.

CHAPTER VI

The Heaven Given Place

THE CHINESE CALLED IT "THE HEAVEN GIVEN PLACE," BUT AT times it was anything but that. Not even in a nightmare had I ever dreamed of such confusion in connection with a hospital. All my experience with hospitals had been in San Francisco and Philadelphia where I had found them to be quiet and well-ordered places. I was totally unprepared for the daily disorder of a Chinese hospital. It is true that the doctors in charge were foreigners, but the nurses, the patients *and* the visitors were Chinese, and it was all new to them.

I started in a whirlwind of energy to open the hospital, establish some sort of system, clean up the building, the compound, the servants, the patients and the houses of the patients. I even had a few nebulous notions about cleaning up the city. My endeavors along these lines created considerable amusement among the Chinese who immediately gave me the nickname, *Tai Foong* (Great Wind or Small Typhoon). They continued to call me this, behind my back, of course, for as long as I lived in Soochow. Naturally I overheard them, although to my face they were respectfully polite and addressed me by my formal Chinese name of *Waung me-tu*, which merely meant Dr. Walter. It is the custom of the Chinese to bestow nicknames on everyone; usually they denote some physical infirmity as "Mr. Lame-leg," "Mr. Blind-in-one-eye." They are seldom complimentary, and few foreigners escape.

I was quickly dissuaded from any ideas I might have had of sanitating the city. It would have meant demolishing Soochow and beginning again from scratch. I decided to concentrate my clean-up campaign on the hospital; that, I found, was task enough. I instituted rigorous rules of cleanliness. All the servants on coming indoors were made to change their shoes; the walls were whitewashed once in two weeks, oftener if we had a pus case, and the straw fillings of the mattresses were burned for fuel after each patient. I remember that we were always in great need of washable blankets since I never allowed two patients to use the same bedding until it had been washed. Spit has never been a horrid word to the Chinese; it was natural for them to expectorate wherever they happened to clear their throats, in the halls, at the table, beside the bed. This I tried to stop. It was fairly simple to maintain a semblance of cleanliness but not so easy to enforce order.

It was impossible to keep regular visiting hours, for time has never been important to the Chinese. Relatives, friends, servants cluttered the corridors from morning until night. A patient would arrive with her entire household, and the amahs would set up housekeeping outside the room, brewing tea and boiling rice, their tongues clacking over the latest morsel of gossip.

At one time there were twenty-three patients in the wards, and each patient had her own amah and at least one relative to assist and console her. I soon bowed to the inevitable; and among other compromises all private rooms were equipped with at least two beds, one for the patient, the other for the amah. Another disturbing influence was Mo Nyang-nyang, the hospital Bible woman (native teacher of Christianity), who spent the entire day working among the patients. When the other Bible woman could no longer bear the discrimination they decided to come into the wards every morning for an hour or two after prayers. Ostensibly they were a flower committee, bringing fresh flowers to each patient, which was very nice for the patients but disconcerting to the doctor.

At first it was difficult to regulate the diets, but after the hospital gained a firmer foothold and the people lost their fear we were able to enforce a rule: we refused admittance to patients unless they promised to accept our diets and stick to them. If they didn't they were packed off home in short order. Despite the constant observation of assistant doctors and nurses, the family and friends surreptitiously slipped them delicacies such as chopped chicken, ducks' tongues, boiled eggs and *hai sung* (sea slugs resembling tomato worms, gelatinous, and of a rich brown color).

Another factor contributing to our disorganization was the special kitchen we were forced to maintain for our Mohammedan patients, who brought along special food and their own cooks to prepare it.

In our desire for cleanliness, and in our anxiety to provide only the best of foods for the hospital patients and for the students at the Davidson School for Girls, which we supervised, we inadvertently were responsible for bringing two dread diseases into the compound, tuberculosis and beriberi.

Tuberculosis is not new to the Chinese. They've had it for so many years they've built up an immunity to it. The soil for tuberculosis has always been in their system and when they are brought into a changed environment the latent disease manifests itself. This was true in the case of tuberculosis among the school girls. The cleanliness and change of diet proved to be too much for them, coming as they did from homes where ancient customs were observed. They quickly developed the disease and we were at a loss as to the reason. In their homes they'd always eaten the cheaper unpolished rice. At the school we gave them what we thought was the better (it was more expensive) polished rice. All unknowingly we took away the very vitamins they needed because, aside from their *san woen van* (three bowls of rice), they ate little else save a flavoring of cabbage, pork, chicken or fish. First one girl and then another was sent home to die.

We were at a loss, too, when one patient after another in our nice, clean hospital developed a multiple neuritis affecting both the motor and sensory nerves, followed by a pain in the knee and then by a continued dropsical condition. It was the strange Oriental disease beriberi, and years later we learned the cause and the simple remedy. It, too, was caused by the radical change from unpolished rice to polished rice with no other foods to complete the diet. They suffered until they went back to their diet of unpolished rice or were given the costly tincture of rice polishings.

Everywhere about us there was filth and prejudice; and we battled both. The houses of the clinic patients, poor people mostly, were either floorless, windowless, great brick barracks with no provision for heating, or they were nothing but straw mats hung on bamboo poles, with a pile of straw in the corner for the sick. Sickness, suffering and death were in almost every house. Once I was called to a house within a stone's throw of the hospital where there were three coffins. Those were the times when in despair I wondered if they were ever going to learn to trust us, until it was too late.

Prejudice permeated the very air we breathed. The notices of our hospital work, plastered on walls and buildings throughout the city, were torn down within three days after they were posted. The people were much more willing to go to their charity dispensaries and to their native physicians who had taken vows to give their time, life and means to the healing of diseases. Our greatest rival was a native dispensary adjoining a pleasure garden just outside the largest city gate. This pleasure garden, noted for its beauty and rare amusements, was patronized by the Governor of the Province and all the high officials. Here they gathered to celebrate their birthdays and other festive occasions and the rich would order one of the many theatrical troupes to perform for the entertainment of their guests. The entrance fee was nine cents (Mexican) and there was always a small income which grew to quite a sum on

My Days of Strength

gala days. All the money was turned into the treasury which supported the dispensary. The gardens and the dispensary, established for years, were owned by one of the richest men of the province. The dispensary, which was in the name of the gentleman's philanthropic-minded wife, was also sanctioned by the Emperor who had ordered erected before it a slab bearing his approval. This was only one of the many benevolent institutions, and of course all those who gained a livelihood practicing medicine in them bitterly opposed us and our scientific methods.

But in spite of opposition there was much for us to do. The winter of my arrival there was a fearful increase of pneumonia. One night seventy-five children died and one afternoon Mrs. Campbell gave out fifty-seven packages of medicine to people who met her on the street, begging for help. In February, 1894, we established a dispensary at Sung Nga-Zien in connection with the Industrial School for Girls there, and Mrs. Campbell and I added to our labors by working in it one day each week.

My nickname was well earned for I moved like a small typhoon from one thing to another. I couldn't be still; there were so many things undone. Oh, how I wished I knew the language! It was exasperating to sit calmly by and listen to an animated conversation about a strange and marvelous disease which you would be expected to cure and yet have to wait until the very last to understand what you were impatient to know. The Chinese were so slow and I was all eagerness. It was an excellent school for cultivating patience, but I was never patient. I at once started the study of Chinese.

This was an amusing time for others. Many Chinese words sound strangely similar to the Western ear. One word may have several meanings, a matter only of the varying inflections. My early efforts to master the language, although a source of amusement to others, caused me much embarrassment. I made the frequent mistake of confusing *tskoo* (fruit) with *kootsz*

56

(pants) and many times I asked the boy to bring pants when of course I meant fruit.

But I was not alone in the careful selection of the wrong word. One of the oldest missionaries in China, a real Sinologue, stepped into her rickshaw one day and said quietly and sweetly to the puller, "Go to hell."

The coolie stared at her in amazement and made no effort to move. She realized that something was wrong and, almost at once, her mistake. She spoke again, this time giving him the right word. *"nyok dien,"* she said and he trotted off to market. Her first command had been *dien nyok,* the Chinese word for hell.

One morning as I was talking in Chinese to Li Sien Sang, one of the teachers at the mission, he laughed all the time. At last I said:

"Sien Sang, you may laugh if you like, but I intend to use Chinese until I learn to speak it well."

"Waung-me-tu," he said, bowing and then continuing in English, "sometimes we laugh because we marvel that some speak this language so wonderfully well, and sometimes we laugh because we marvel that they speak it so very badly."

He didn't say to which class I belonged and I didn't ask.

But my efforts to speak Chinese were no funnier than the Chinese attempts at English. I had my first pidgin English experience when a rich *ta-ta* (old woman) came to me for a slight operation. She was frightened nearly to death when she found it was over and she had felt no pain. The accompanying relatives likewise were frightened but after awhile, when they began to feel more assured of her safety, her nephew said to me:

"I speakee easy you. One piecee father have got. He seventy-one years have got; ten years no have eyes can see. I bringee he here, havee you he see."

We had trouble with the Chinese patients who went on the

assumption that if a little was good, a whole lot was better. Often a patient would drink down an entire bottle of his medicine, a week's supply, instead of the prescribed half-teaspoon.

The great majority of the cases brought to the hospital for operation were in such a condition from long-standing filth that it was almost useless to attempt a cure. Antisepsis was an unknown word and for a long time we found it was foolish to take cases of a very grave nature; even with the perfect care of the nurses, cleanliness was impossible. Another trying feature of surgical work was that the patients in nearly every instance left the hospital before they were well. Their condition after the operation was so vastly more comfortable than before that they could see no reason why they should not return to their work at once. Often operations were done against my better judgment.

And the diseases! So often they were pathetically hopeless. Day after day the women came to us with the same sad story. They told of the dreary monotony of their lives; they pointed in silence to their tiny, tortured feet; they spoke with shame and helpless misery of the diseases that rendered them unfit for wifehood or motherhood, they related sorrows so deep that all the world seemed but a throbbing echo of their appeals for help.

One young girl from one of the wealthiest and most aristocratic families, when admonished for opium smoking, replied:

"What more can you expect of us? We have vague ideas of a better life but we have no escape from the life that is death to us mentally and physically. We have women's diseases and there are no physicians for us; when we suffer we must take opium until we become its slave. We would read and find out for ourselves what the world is like, but we have no education; we would study but we have no teachers. There is no help for us except through the foreigner. Without this help there is nothing for us but opium."

The Heaven Given Place

Syphilology was not so widely disseminated in those days as it is now, not even among practicing physicians. In many cases we did not recognize syphilis when we met it and in others we did not know exactly how to treat it. Syphilis is as old as China; it is one of the oldest known diseases of the East. However, I had very few syphilitic patients as such, although many suffering from it came to us for derivative diseases. Syphilis was responsible for much of the eye trouble and blindness that I encountered and for many of the difficult deliveries of childbirth. Probably because the hospital cases were more or less selected and the vast majority of women continued to use midwives I had few syphilitic obstetrical cases. We seldom admitted syphilitic patients to the hospital. For one thing there was the difficulty of carrying out a prescribed treatment and for another many of them were too far gone for any help. Also, there was the constant danger of their infecting other patients.

Once a girl came to me with an opening in the roof of her mouth that went directly into the floor of the nose. Preparations for the operation were under way when I delved deeper into the case history and discovered that the girl was a syphilitic and that an operation would do little good. I gave her some medicine and hoped that it would help a little.

There has been leprosy in China for over two thousand years. Lepers came to the clinic but we tried to keep them out of the hospital. I soon learned to tell my leper patients by the purple nodular spots on their bodies and by a certain peculiar expression. The leprosy I met in my clinic work was very different from the old Biblical form I had read about and I learned that it was not infectious by contact unless the germ entered the blood stream through a cut or an abrasion. Some of the best families in Soochow had leper cooks, a practice I would not recommend.

Only in the advanced stages do the toes and fingers drop off

59

and those cases we did not take for there was nothing we could do for them. We used chaulmoogra oil in the treatment of our clinic cases. When a leper appeared the nurses drew on rubber gloves saturated in the oil, and proceeded to rub it thoroughly all over the leper's body and well into the pores. The treatment did little lasting good, but it retarded the progress of the disease slightly.

Once, and once only, did I come in contact with a leprous mother in childbirth. She was in the early stages of the disease and there were few apparent symptoms. The delivery was perfectly normal and so was the child who was whisked away before there was any possible chance of infection.

The hospital was by no means rich and there was never any extra money for such luxuries as clerical help. I had all of this as well as the case work to do myself and I usually got around to it about midnight after the last patient had departed and it was even too late to be called out.

It was my first Chinese New Year and it was early in the year 1894. I was checking accounts and probing into the clinic record ledger when I heard the reports of rockets far and near on the night air. It was a weird sound and it seemed to bring closer to me the ignorance and superstition of the people I had come across the seas to help heal. The old year in China was drawing to a close and the rocket was the escort of some kitchen god on his journey to the skies. This has all been changed with the inauguration of the New Life Movement, but at that time, any night in the last week of the old year, the family would burn the paper god which had reposed in a recess of the wall above the kitchen fire and watched the proceedings of the household for the past three-hundred and sixty-five days.

This is the usual rite, and New Life Movement notwithstanding I'm sure it still goes on: before the god's ascension New Year's cakes (small white balls made of rice and flour, boiled) and a small bowl of vegetables are placed before him. Molasses is smeared on his lips so that when he attempts to give his detailed account of the family transactions to the gods in the other world he will be unable to speak. Then the head of the family takes him down from the shelf and holding him in both hands above his head, carries him to the door and places him in a sedan chair. The chair, made of paper about six inches square, rests on evergreen boughs and is surrounded by cakes, fruits and other delicacies made of paper. Ghost money is scattered around it; the match is then touched and as the flames begin to lick the paper image the firecrackers are set off and the god ascends in smoke to bear record of the family's earthly condition.

It really seemed as though the rockets, speeding the kitchen gods heavenward, cleared the atmosphere for "The Heaven Given Place." The coming of the new year brought a change in the attitude of the people. They suddenly right-about-faced and grew confident. There were the usual percentages of success and failure but patients flocked to us and the fame of the hospital spread. Among my patients was the daughter of a *tao tai* in Nganwui Province and from time to time the father sent a messenger two hundred miles to see and report the condition of his daughter.

The people permitted us to take many heretofore prohibited liberties. One little girl with tuberculosis of the hip joint consented to wear an extension apparatus, the first in Soochow. It was made at the hospital under my direction.

We were on our way at last. The first year there were twice as many patients as any other year in the history of the hospital and the second year there were three thousand more than the first. But I was not satisfied.

Hundreds and hundreds of children needed hospital care. Thousands of tortured feet were pleading for deliverance. Hundreds of thousands were doomed to lives of uselessness for the lack of a little medical aid. Day after day they came to us and we gave them cursory clinic care; then reluctantly sent them on their way. We had no place for them.

It finally reached the point where I couldn't stand it another minute. I decided that if it were at all possbile I'd have a children's ward, and that it had to be possible. An incident, small in itself, decided me.

There was a little girl, no more than a baby, in one of the overcrowded wards who at first was terrified beyond measure at the sight of a foreigner or even at the sound of a foreign footstep. She would cover herself completely with a great blue handkerchief when she heard me coming. Thus protected she submitted to my presence. By degrees we arrived at a game of "peeps" and finally the blue handkerchief disappeared. Every morning she would toddle into the empty chapel and climb up on the front seat, where she would stay through the day. There was no other place for her.

My request for a children's ward was endorsed by Bishop Galloway. He presented the project at the annual conference of the Women's Foreign Missionary Society of the Methodist Episcopal Church, South, who approved it. The only thing needed was the money, and The Bright Jewels of the North Carolina Conference raised the money to build it in memory of their "Aunt" Mary Black. In a surprisingly short time the Mary Black Memorial Hall, with the first sunroom for tubercular patients in all China, was built and at a cost of less than five thousand Mexican dollars. The building was completed in the spring of 1895 but it could not be occupied until the following autumn when the beds and other furnishings arrived.

While the children's ward was being planned and built and while he were waiting for the equipment to arrive I went on to other things. I had been in China only a short time when I realized that without native help we would be lost. But these agents, I knew, must be fitted for the work. There must be medical schools to train them. Our Chinese physicians, both men and women, must be given every advantage. They must be able to cope with every disease; they must meet on an equal footing and consult with physicians of all nations. They must be so well-trained that we need never be ashamed for them, nor fear the results of their work. To this end, my next step was the establishment of a co-educational medical school in connection with the Soochow Hospital, a hitherto undreamed-of possibility in China. I was flying in the face of all tradition but it was one of my most interesting experiences. Our efforts would be ridiculed, I knew, but it was the first step, and a very important first step.

Between the men's hospital and the women's there was a large hall. Down the length of this hall we hung a curtain, dark blue and opaque. The lecturer, coming in from either side, walked to the door of the opposite side and after ringing a bell to summon the students took his place facing the curtain. The boys entered from the right, the girls from the left, taking their places on their respective sides of the curtain. They never saw one another, never spoke; so far (it was amazingly far for the China of those days) was the school co-educational.

Astonishing things happened. I once asked one of the boys how many degrees he would consider a dangerous drop in temperature.

"About one hundred," he replied.

Later I asked the same boy to count the pulse of the one sitting next to him. After a time he reported that it was "somewhere around five hundred."

The medical school opened on November 13, 1895, with twenty-two pupils—sixteen boys and six girls. Dr. Fearn (my future husband) and Mrs. Park were in charge of the English department while Dr. Park and I had the medical. In spite of the difficulties we turned out some exceedingly good doctors, both men and women.

It was our urgent insistence on the necessity for dissection and our aggressive attitude which in part, at least, familiarized the Chinese with the idea. Opposition to this desecration of the dead was the last and apparently the insurmountable barrier placed in the way of Chinese who wanted a medical education and could not go abroad to obtain it. All the strongest Chinese traditions were against it, and local sentiment still makes difficulties in some sections. However, they have been able to dissect freely for many years now, at least since 1914, in the medical school connected with St. John's University in Shanghai. Most of their material is the unclaimed bodies of those dying in St. Luke's hospital. The Peking Union Medical College had a tremendous struggle in getting permission to use unclaimed bodies for dissection, with the Peking police putting every conceivable obstacle in their way. The National government within the last few years has made it possible for them to use the bodies of executed criminals. It was not so easy for us in 1895 and 1896 and it was a great occasion when on the afternoon of June 20, 1896, we held our first graduation exercises. My faithful nurse, Ling Tsu, and Miss Zak Foh-me, another ardent worker in the women's hospital, received their diplomas along with three students from the men's hospital. The graduation exercises were held in the sunroom of the Mary Black Memorial and officials of the highest rank mingled with the crowd who came to witness this, the first thing of its kind to take place in China. The Japanese Consul spoke in English. Mr. Tsai, the former magistrate of the Mixed Court in Shanghai, spoke in Mandarin. The valedictorian's address was on the efficacy of new things in general and the roentgen rays in particular.

It was a history-making event.

There has been great change since then. The attitude of the people has veered from distrust and hate to respect and friendship, from fear to absolute confidence in the foreign doctor. The homes of the richest and most influential citizens everywhere are open to the European doctors; they are welcomed as friends, relied upon as physicians, and sought as teachers.

CHAPTER VII

My Waifs and Strays

G RADUALLY I COLLECTED AROUND ME A NUMBER OF DERELICTS, offscourings of Soochow and the surrounding countryside, victims of unspeakable sanitary conditions and the vicissitudes of Chinese life.

First came Pau Doo, Big Precious, indirectly a gift from the salt smugglers. She was a large, husky girl still in her teens and she had worked as a field hand. During one of the raids on the smugglers' boats by government officials she was struck in the arm by a stray bullet. After gangrene set in she was brought to the hospital and my predecessor, Dr. Phillips, found it necessary to remove the arm at the shoulder. Soon afterward she became a mother.

Poor Pau Doo, useless as a farmhand and encumbered with a baby girl, decided to present herself to the hospital. There she proved useful as a water carrier and a waterer of the flowers, and in so doing grew fat. Her baby, Sieu Ling, also presented to the hospital, we named "Good Morning" because it was the only English her small mind ever encompassed.

The next to arrive was Cheng Li. The "Hospital Mop" we called her because wherever she went she left a shining trail on the floors that always, no matter how often polished, were covered with a film of dust blown down from the Gobi Desert, two thousand miles away. Professor Joseph Baily, the noted horticulturist of Nanking, brought her to us. He said he had rescued the child, no more than a baby, from a grave mound where she had only the goats for companions. Her mother had deposited her there, knowing that death was inevitable.

"What do you expect of us—the impossible?" I asked, as I

gazed upon that forlorn and gangrenous little object. Her feet were hanging by shreds, the tip of her nose was gone, and there were purple spots on her cheeks.

"At least you can let her die in your hospital and not on a grave mound with the goats. I'll pay for her coffin," said her cheerful friend and left us to care for his find.

We clipped off her feet as she sat there and dressed her to the best of our ability. We put her to bed and waited confidently for her to die. But Cheng Li did not die and it was not long before we learned to expect the unexpected from her.

All night long, that first night, she wept and wailed for her hard bed on the floor of her mother's loft and for her red quilt. Our bedsprings made her seasick and cleanliness made life seem unreal. She almost preferred the grave mound and the goats. But in time she came to love us.

One day when I went into the ward where she was a patient for some minor ill I discovered her buried deep under the coverlet which she clutched wildly over her head. She was sobbing, shuddering, almost in a convulsion of fear. She had heard her mother's voice.

"My mother, my mother!" she wailed. "Do not let her see me!"

Gone was her longing for the hard bed in the loft and the vermin-ridden red quilt, the grave mound and the goats. Cheng Li was ours.

We always intended to operate on the stumps of her feet, but somehow never did. In later years we discovered that Dr. Polk's shoes exactly fitted her. She wore the shoes, of which she was immensely proud, with heels to the front, which gave her the appearance of going when actually she was coming. She became the pet of the hospital as well as its scapegoat. And as she grew well and happy she became quite attractive with her abbreviated nose, retroussé by courtesy, and her funny little ways. Eventually she married and became the mother of a small family, but in spite of this conventional ending she continued to wear her shoes heels forward.

Then there was San Pau, Third Precious. In all the world nothing had exceeded the speed of San Pau's tongue unless it was the speed of her feet. Yet in some unaccountable way when San Pau came in from the country one day to see the sights, one of those fast flying feet was crushed under a fifty-pound bag of flour which fell from a third-story window on the Mo Lang Ka, to the utter destruction of the foot and leg to the knee. But when we had finished with her we found that she had not finished with us, and San Pau was added to our list of liabilities.

We sent her to the Girl's School where she absorbed learning as a sponge absorbs water. With flying crutch and one foot she sped schoolward, while with flying tongue she broadcast the news of the day to any who would listen. We gave her a wooden leg which she cherished as an *objet d'art*, but the crutch was her chief support.

During the Boxer Uprising, when Europeans and all Chinese associated with them were in hourly danger, San Pau was sent to her home in a near-by country village. No sooner had she arrived than she went into business; so many cash (hundredth of a Chinese cent) for a fleeting glimpse of the stump, more for prolonged looks, and a few extra cash for a sight of the wooden leg. She often returned to visit us and she sent us many patients. From a liability she became an asset.

So also were the three children I bought for a Mexican dollar apiece from their half-blind mother, who was thrown in for good measure.

I had operated on the mother for cataract when she was totally blind. All went well until the day came for removing the bandages. Just before this was to be done a woman came to see the patient, bringing her news that her husband had died suddenly during the night. We gave the visitor strict orders

67

that this was not to be mentioned. I think she obeyed but there are no secrets in China and the story found its way to the ward and to the patient. When I came into the operating room where she was waiting for me, I found that the bandages were wet.

It has all been for nothing, I thought, silently cursing the busybodies who could not wait to tell the bad news. But I removed the bandages, cleaned the eyes, and then asked the woman to open them and tell me if she saw anything.

For a moment she gazed at me blindly; then the blessed light came into her eyes and she cried,

"I see the face of an angel!"

No one had ever before accused me of looking like an angel, but if there was ever a bit of heaven on earth it was the operating room that day. Perhaps because of my happiness I exuded a halo.

Soon after she left us she returned, leading her three children, all of whom she offered me at a dollar a head. Three dollars she had to have. She was half-blind; she had no money, no food, no work. It was a fair exchange she thought, for would not these three liabilities become wage-earning assets in due time?

At last my derelicts mounted to such numbers that I determined to open a school for the maimed, the halt, and the blind. We fitted up a room in the gatekeeper's lodge and began with fifteen pupils. Each was given some manual training in keeping with his or her disability. It was the happiest school I have ever seen.

When people ask whether the Chinese are loyal, I think of my waifs and strays in Soochow. They gave me a thousand evidences of their loyalty and affection, but the one that I remember most clearly concerns the visit of a committee of doctors, the advance guard of the Northern Presbyterian Mission, who were investigating hospital conditions in China, preparatory to opening work at Peng-pu.

To my great disappointment the day set for their visit was during the Chinese New Year's holiday. It was a foregone conclusion the place would be practically deserted, that being the great home-holiday of the Chinese when everyone, unless he is dying or imprisoned, returns to the family hearth. However, there was nothing to be done about it, and after the guests had breakfasted I led them, with profuse apologies and explanations, to see the empty wards.

I was taken completely off my feet when the door opened on a busy scene. Every bed was occupied and every staff nurse on duty, standing at attention by the side of a presumably suffering patient. Hospital work was in very active progress.

Going to the first bed I gazed into the eyes of Cheng Li, eager, questioning.

"Is Cheng Li sick?" I asked of the attending Chinese doctor.

"Not exactly sick," he replied in Chinese. "Just heartsick because of the loss of face of our beloved doctor in having to show the foreign celebrities only empty wards."

Without pausing to inquire the symptoms of San Pau's or of Pau Doo's troubles I marched my astonished visitors between the two rows of beds and back into the living room. There were roars of appreciative laughter when I explained the situation. My hospital had made a hit, thanks to my staff and my loyal derelicts.

In our work we neither ask nor expect gratitude, but I have been repaid many times over by the open-hearted affection of my Chinese patients. One hears so little of this particular trait of the Chinese character, and yet those of us who have worked among them can give many proofs of their loyalty.

Reputations in China, as well as in other places, are often a matter of luck. I'm quite sure that I owe my success in Soochow to the fact that my first two "big cases" outside our hospital had happy endings and won me the friendship of the two most important officials of the Province. If it had not been for the enthusiasm these men expressed for my work the townspeople would not have been such willing followers, nor would they have welcomed me with cries of *"Sien Nyung"* (the Wizard) as I was carried through the streets in my sedan chair.

In those days, now nearly half a century ago, the Chinese stomach was virgin territory in so far as foreign medicines were concerned and reacted quickly to a drop of this, a grain of that. And although my first two important patients were in agonizing distress when they sent for me, remedies were simple and they were quickly cured.

The first case came up when I had been in Soochow only a very few days. I was called to the home of Tao Tai Jen, the Governor of Soochow. His wife was extremely ill and for days had been unable to retain so much as a drop of water. She was beyond hope of Chinese medical aid long before they had taken the unheard-of step and sent for me. I examined her and found that she was ill with the pernicious vomiting of pregnancy. I was young, inexperienced and brusque. I didn't bother to ask questions. I gave orders.

"I must send to Shanghai for a drug," I told the husband.

"Spare no expense," he replied and called servants to hasten on the errand. Traveling day and night they were back in an incredibly short time with the case of champagne I had ordered. I went at once to the Yamen (official residence) with this precious contribution. I poured out a few drops, which was all the patient needed.

The Governor watched me, smiled and said, "My storeroom is filled with *that* drug."

Fortunately the nausea was under control almost at once, the wife recovered, and lo, I was a successful physician. When the wife was completely well the Governor came in person to

70

offer his thanks and a magnificent "tribute board," the first of the many that eventually covered our clinic walls.

It was not long after this incident that I was called by the Treasurer of the Province, who had heard of the astonishing cure of the Governor's wife. On my arrival at his palace, I was met by an entourage of servants and escorted to an immense reception hall. In a few moments the High Official himself appeared. Although painfully ill, he had risen from his bed and donned his ceremonial gown to receive the strange foreign doctor. He stared at me for a moment, then turned and consulted with members of the household before addressing me.

"But you're a woman and so young," he said. However, he permitted me to examine him. He was suffering with a violent attack of acute indigestion. At first I feared appendicitis and suggested an immediate operation.

When the Treasurer heard this he was frantic with a fear that was terrifying not only to me but to all of his attendants. To my intense relief, on further examination I diagnosed a stomach ache.

Again, fortunately for my future, the Western medicine I prescribed was effective and the recovery was rapid.

Later I learned the cause of his fury when I mentioned the word "operation," and why he was so pleased when a cure was accomplished without resort to extreme methods. This man, so powerful politically, so ruthless in his handling of his vast armies of tax collectors and soldiers, feared the knife. Like so many strong men he was a baby when it came to his personal ailments.

An amusing tale is told about how this same High Treasurer's sight was saved by an itinerant French doctor. The official was afflicted with cataracts, and although he was almost blind he refused to have them removed because, as I have said, he feared the knife. Our medical group had given up all hope of ever inducing him to have them cut, when the wandering

71

French doctor appeared on the scene from no one knew where.

He was taken to see the Treasurer and forthwith disarmed the old man with his arguments, finally convincing him that he could remove the cataracts by "treatment," and would not need to use the knife.

The official consented and was doped slightly, preparatory to the "treatment." When he was well under the anesthetic the doctor cut the cornea and removed the cataracts. After the bandages had been removed the High Treasurer, who now could see perfectly, was shown the crystal lens that had been taken from his eyes by this mysterious treatment.

The doctor collected a huge reward and went on his way. Needless to say no one ever dared tell the old mandarin of the hoax.

The two officials remained my friends for as long as I lived in Soochow, and longer. Their friendship made it possible for me to enter official circles and created "face" for me and the Soochow Woman's Hospital as well. The Governor, who was really responsible for my successful start, was later to protect my professional reputation, my hospital and my life.

So much for Chinese loyalty to foreign friends.

Among themselves they are capable of a friendship and love that puts us to shame. The union of husband and wife is given the utmost sacredness by the solemn ceremonies with which it is celebrated. Friendship between Chinese has a depth and permanence all too seldom met with in the West, and unsurpassed examples of the love of parents for their children and of children for their parents may be found everywhere in China.

As everyone knows, the cult of family is an integral part of Chinese life; but it is more than a cult. A genuine affection for parents and relatives is the rule, although I suppose there are numerous exceptions. From the magnificent palaces of the officials to the lowliest hovel one finds in every home an altar dedicated to the worship of ancestors. This reverence for the past inevitably entails the "rule of the dead hand" but it also inculcates orderliness of mind, quietude and respect for authority. Ancestor worship is breaking down under the new regime, and it is probably well that the bonds to the past are being loosened. But in all likelihood the Chinese will never entirely lose their strong family feeling nor their reverence for tradition.

Chinese folklore teems with stories of love—love of husband for wife, of father for son, of friend for friend. Legends have been handed down for generations which tell of loves as great as that of Abélard for Héloïse, or Dante for Beatrice, legends that date back to the ancient beginnings of China. And where in the world of poetry are found love stories more beautiful than those exquisitely translated by Amy Lowell and Florence Ayscough in the *Fir Flower Tablets*?

Once I came in touch with the end of a love story as poignant and tragic and poetic as that of Romeo and Juliet.

An old and decrepit ex-official had returned to his home in Soochow to await the end of his days. He was a wealthy man with a house full of treasures, but the most priceless of his possessions was a concubine, so beautiful that she was spoken of only with bated breath. We heard rumors of this delightful creature; that she was as beautiful as dawn, lovely as a dew-drenched flower, rare as an orchid. They said that the old man kept her constantly by his bed, where he could touch her flower-petal skin or feast his eyes on her perfection.

Many were the visitors who came daily to pay their respects to the dying man, and among them was a young official, a relative. Because of the relationship and because of the frequency of his visits the "rare one" was not always sent from the room on his arrival. The young man was handsome, strong and gentle. They saw each other; perhaps they exchanged a few words in the presence of her master. Inevitably they fell in love. At last, perhaps from fear or shame or perturbation in

73

the presence of her lover, she voluntarily absented herself from the room whenever he came.

We shall never know just how it came about, but after weeks had passed someone, perhaps a jealous, would-be lover, suggested that the old man have himself carried to the window where he might see "an edifying sight." And what he saw below in the garden was his "rare one" and his young relative in one another's arms.

The old man asked to be carried back to bed and when the "rare one" returned, ignorant of his knowledge and with no warning of what was to come, she was told that she must "seek the death road" by one of two ways, the rope or opium. She chose the latter. A potion was administered at once and she was carried from the old man's room into another part of the house —to die.

But somehow word reached the lover, who came "with the swiftness of the wind." He sent for me and we worked together to bring that poor, exquisite child back to life. Gone was the young man's long gown, gone was his imperturbable dignity. Back and forth, back and forth, endlessly he dragged her limp body trying to make the tiny feet respond. We tried artificial respiration, and the lover himself tried electricity. There were times when it seemed almost as though by the sheer force of his will he might bring her back. But the dose had been too fatally sure and we were too late. She died in his arms.

His grief was terrible to witness. I left him with his dead, and not many hours passed before I was told that he too had sought and found the death road.

Do the Chinese love as we do? In a country where life is appallingly cheap, I have witnessed the violent grief of friends and relatives too often to doubt it. Their gratitude and loyalty are equally strong. During the frequent social or anti-foreign upheavals, many disasters were averted because grateful patients brought news to the hospital of impending trouble, though they came to us in the certain knowledge that the act might mean their death, should it ever become known.

Too little is known of this side of the Chinese character and yet to me, who have lived intimately among them for many years, it is one of their most outstanding traits.

Do the Chinese love? Do the stars shine?

CHAPTER VIII

Japanese Interlude

WITH THE BEGINNING OF THE SUMMER OF 1895, MY ENERGY began to flag so seriously that I found it difficult to get through the necessary work; it was decided that it was time for me to take a rest. Sarah Poindexter came from her home and language study in Tsinanfu, and we started for our vacation in Japan.

It was before Japan had become too Anglo-Japanese; and for a season we fell under the spell of its enchantment. Even then the cloven hoof was beginning to show in the many ceremonies and forms which, because of their newness, were done up with an extra amount of red tape and executed with a native tardiness. We waited a week for the necessary visas, obtained after arrival instead of before as they were necessary only for travel in the interior. But each day of that week was a joy, full of beauty and interest and vastly entertaining incongruities.

In front of a photographer's shop we stopped short, transfixed with amusement, to read the notice, "Babies skillfully executed here." Having no desire to witness such a sight regardless of the skill employed, we hurried aboard a *tallamer* (tram) where we found ourselves confronted by a placard, "Passengers are respectfully requested not to stick their elbows and knees out of the window."

This was at the very beginning of the transitional stage, when it was no uncommon sight to see an apparition in a top hat and coat sitting cross-legged and comfortable on the seat facing the window, his nether extremities bravely arrayed

76

in long underwear instead of trousers, and his foreign shoes on the floor beside him. But only a mental gymnast could conceive of a position which would enable even these gentry to stick their elbows and knees out of the window at the same time.

But that was years ago! Today there is no more perfectly groomed gentleman in the world than a well-to-do Japanese in European attire—except when he goes traveling by train. He still insists on partially disrobing, exchanging stiff collars, shirt, and trousers for the comfortable kimono, and shoes for the airy *geta*.

We visited one of the larger and better Japanese girls' schools, and were honored by an introduction to one of the pupils. Behold the young lady, shy, blushing and pigeon-toed, suddenly slipping her hands down to her knees and, with an audible, indrawing breath, making a deep, bobbing curtsy in which her body forms a perfect triangle, and then with soft, undulating grace, sinking into giggling oblivion between her fan and the wall! Sarah and I regarded her with respectful amazement, feeling ourselves grow larger and clumsier, and very far from oblivion, polite or otherwise.

We spent our days among the curio shops, sitting on our heels on the counter, drinking tea from thimble-sized cups while we bargained with the dealers. Occasionally stools were placed for us in the street by the side of the two-foot-high counters, though generally we were asked to remove our shoes and rest our honorable limbs cross-legged on the counter.

Learning how to shop in Japan at that time (and to a certain extent even now) might well have constituted the entire curriculum of a business school, for the knowledge thus acquired was in itself a commercial education. The curio-dealer invariably put an enormous price on his wares. We offered him half. He declined, with polite sorrow, to sell. After much discussion the desired article went back in stock and we bowed ourselves off the counter. An hour or so after reaching home the dealer always appeared with a package neatly wrapped in a blue cotton square in which was the object under consideration plus many others. Bargaining began again. As we raised our price gradually, he lowered his about a third of the original price, and the bargain was struck, the merchant moaning all the time that he had lost on the sale. In direct contradiction to his groans he would reappear the next day with a fresh lot of fascinating wares and an undiminished enthusiasm for a new bargain.

But having bought, we were marked; waylaid in the street by dealers with their packs; haunted by men who salaamed to the ground as they begged the honor of a visit to their *godowns* (storerooms), where everything was "cheap, so very cheap, please, lady can buy"; and followed by a procession of ignored but still hopeful merchants.

Our passports arrived and we started for Nikko, the shrine of the real organizer and ruler of Japan, Ieyasu, and of his grandson, Iemitsu. They were the first and third shoguns of the Tokugawa line. Ieyasu, it is said, selected this place for his tomb because of its amazing beauty. It lies high up on the mountain side among forty-seven waterfalls, overlooking ravines of tremendous depth, and above it is Nantai San, the sacred mountain.

It was dusk when we reached Nikko and as we passed up the street we glanced into the shops on either side. Bargain sales were in progress in some, and in others men and women sat cross-legged on mats while they drank their tea, the men thoroughly at ease, the women with babies strapped fast to their backs busily serving their lords and at the same time attending to the wants of armies of chubby children. Large yellow, red, blue and green lanterns were suspended from every available hook and carried in the hand of every passer-by, their soft, tinted lights adding a peculiar charm to the busy scene.

Every hotel was full, for it was the month of pilgrimage to Nantai San, but the one English-speaking hotel proprietor told us of an old temple he had rented for the summer, which was at our disposal if we cared to try it. "My Monastery," he called it. He led us up a long line of stone steps in the mountain side, past old stone gods, out of the light into the darkness, for the city was hidden by the shelving rocks, then at last into the temple which was luxuriously furnished—with matting. We took off our shoes and sat on the matting while we viewed our quarters by the light of a single lantern hung in space on the wall. Soon *futons* (padded quilts) were sent up from the hotel. We were to sleep after the most orthodox Japanese fashion, minus sheets and covered with a *futon* as heavy as that on which we lay.

It was my first experience in a Japanese house, where the walls disappeared at a handclap and reappeared at a word; where we used our feet for seats, and slept under the brazen image of Buddha and golden inscriptions to the Sun God; where we awoke to the sound of the priest monotonously chanting his prayers in an adjoining room and singing the delights of Nirvana. The air was full of the chirp of innumerable *semi*, calling always "me, me, me, m-e-e-e, me-ep." The raven chimed in with its caw, caw, caw, and the sound of the rushing water of the falls formed a deep, steady undercurrent.

In all the world, I think, there are no more beautiful temples than those at Nikko. For twenty miles in three directions stretch old avenues of cryptomeria trees, their branches meeting to form an arch.

During the month of August the sacred mountain, Nantai San, was, and it still is, open to pilgrims. Of all classes and ages, they came from all parts of Japan. Each one had a straw mat thrown over his shoulders and a staff in his hand, and was

My Days of Strength

clad in a single white garment, a wide straw hat, and straw shoes. They "provide neither gold, nor silver, nor brass, nor script for their journey; neither two coats."

At dusk each pilgrim launches a fantastic paper boat upon an uncertain voyage across Lake Chuzenji. In every boat is a lighted candle. By the time it is dark the lake is like a gleaming mirror flecked with dancing will-o'-the-wisps; the banks a seething mass of human beings, struggling and fighting for a place near the water's edge. About two o'clock in the morning they plunge into the lake and out again, and singing, start on their pilgrimage up the mountain to worship the rising sun. These ceremonies continue throughout the month.

A description of Nikko as it was then would not be complete without mention of the Suzuki Hotel. It lay in the hollow between two mountains, facing a splendid waterfall. Over the entrance arch were the words, "Suzuki Hotel. Great Study Than Before." We interpreted the somewhat ambiguous notice to mean that a greater study had been made for the comfort of the guests than ever before. The fare was good Anglo-Japanese. A tablecloth was used and, best of all, the proprietor showed a friendly willingness to change this cloth at the suggestion of his guests.

The menu I carried away with me and have saved all these years as entertainingly characteristic of the place. It is a good example of the naïve intermingling of East and West, which both Japanese and European, from different points of view, thoroughly enjoyed.

No. 1—Cold Sam (Ham)
No. 2—Cold chicken
No. 3—Chicken Sotee
No. 4—Hapshi Beef (Beef Hash)
No. 5—Beets
No. 6—Stewed Corn
No. 7—Potatoes

80

No. 8—Hambuku bi stick (Hamburger Steak)
No. 9—Compote de Peach
No. 10—Glasse and the Tea Cakes
No. 11—Fruit and the Castor Pudding
No. 12—Tea and Cafe

After one of these repasts we wandered to a spot high up on the royal hillside where we looked down upon the forbidden grounds—the home of the royal and sacred family where none but the elect may enter. Two young daughters of the Emperor were the sole occupants at the time and they, we were told, went out for their exercise at four in the morning before the street had been desecrated by the feet of common mortals. They were accompanied not only by a guard and female attendants, but by four or five physicians, each one a specialist.

Just beyond the palace grounds is a beautiful and musical little stream, crossed by a finely lacquered red bridge which stands as a monument to the worship given to a human being. It was built for a shogun, a ruler of a former dynasty, who used it once or twice; except on very special occasions it has not been used since.

Every American visiting Japan is told of the unique honor extended General Grant in offering to open this bridge for his use and of the rare courtesy which caused him to decline the honor, thus making for himself in the hearts of the Japanese a place among their saints and shoguns.

Everywhere, in all sorts of unexpected places, there are little shrines, or images of Buddha sitting in beatific passivity on a lotus blossom. These images are usually covered with stones left by devotees who believe that healing, as well as virtue, is to be obtained by rubbing any diseased spot with a stone and leaving it on the image of the one in whom, as the great healer, they have infinite faith.

My favorite walk was to the Gamman ga fuchi, a most suitable abiding place of the gods. One hundred and twenty stone images of Buddha adorn the path for three hundred yards along the bank of the Dai Yagawa. Each god has been deprived of his head by time, assisted perhaps by small boys. It is queer to see these gods, some holding their heads on their knees, many with reversed heads, some brazening it out under borrowed heads, and not a few with no heads at all. The river rushes madly along in front of the row of idols over a bed so rocky that great masses of spray and foam are constantly dashed into the air and it is sometimes hard to say in which direction the current runs.

From Nikko we went to Irenoyu, an out-of-the-way and very charming spot some six thousand feet above sea level. En route we stopped over night at a Japanese inn, where we slept on the floor under a dark-green mosquito net suspended from the four corners of the room. The night was warm so we had the walls removed and found that the edge of our room formed the bank of a goldfish pond where frogs croaked the night through. In the morning it caught the first gleams of the rising sun through the wisteria vine trellised above it.

For breakfast we ate Japanese food in the orthodox Japanese style, sitting cross-legged on *tatamis* on the floor. We clapped our hands; a section of the wall vanished and a maid appeared bearing our breakfast on a lacquered tray. Immediately after breakfast we continued on our way to Irenoyu, each of us seated in a *kaga*, a round, flat basket strung on a pole and carried across the shoulders of two men. We were carried over all the level places but used our own muscles for climbing. Sometimes we were borne on a man's back across a stream or over some narrow mountain pass where two men could not go.

At Karuizawa, our next stopping place after Irenoyu, we read the following notice in the hotel office: "Welcome information. Fresh milk make here every day. Extorted from the pure cow by the veterinary," and in the street near by we found a

82

sign which declared Ah Wang to be a "Wholesaler, Retailor, and Shirtailor."

The night after our arrival we joined some people who were planning to make an ascent of Asamayama, the active volcano. Late that night we assembled and tossed for pack-horse or sidesaddles. I considered myself in luck when a sidesaddle fell to my lot until I found the necessary accompaniment to the only sidesaddle was a raw-boned sorrel of evil disposition and worse reputation.

It was midnight when we reached the foot of the mountain after a ten-mile ride in the moonlight across the plain. Here we had a light lunch and after waiting for a few minutes for the pack horses carrying our baggage, started on without them, hoping that the luggage coolies would overtake us. An hour later we began the ascent on foot, up steep and slippery slopes where we slid back on the smooth pebbles far faster, it seemed to me, than we ascended.

After two hours of hard work we reached the lava beds where our feet sank into the deep sand; then came the final pull up the zigzag path to the top. Soon we came into a cloud belt and felt the cool mist in our faces. The moon was almost hidden by clouds and all we could see of our goal above us was a long, straight black line lying across the lighted sky. Miles above, it seemed to our tired bodies. Again and again we fell flat on the rocks; and again and again we gathered our strength and pushed upward. The wind was piercingly cold; we had no wraps and dared not rest long for we were soaked with perspiration.

And then, as we reached the first crater, the moon which had dropped behind the mountain top came suddenly into view from below; it shone out with such splendor, such a full, dazzling light that we were half-blinded. In a dull, senseless kind of way, the light irritated us as we went stumbling on over the level path that lay straight across the mountain.

My Days of Strength

We began the last ascent bravely, for we were near the end. It was fearfully cold and great waves of sulphur-laden smoke blew down upon us. As we climbed, we heard the low rumbling of the boiling lava; and coming gradually nearer, we were almost suffocated by the smoke. At a quarter past four in the morning we reached the rim of the crater.

It was like a small island in illimitable space, with the billowy masses of clouds all about and beneath us. We seemed to be resting on clouds with the sky thick with stars above us. In front was the crater, constantly belching forth great volumes of smoke; on one side the red, egg-shaped sunball rising from its cloud bed, and on the other the round orange moon sinking into space behind the mountains.

Looking down into the crater we saw a great rocky cauldron, two and a half miles in circumference. In the bottom was a bed of molten lava shot with occasional gleaming streaks, like forked lightning, where the surface cracked to show the boiling red lava below. Gradually growing bolder we went into the crater a short distance down its ghastly sides, but we turned back very soon. It was too much like descending into the mouth of hell.

In about ten minutes someone cried, "Look! Look!" Rising from the mouth of the crater was a column of smoke like a huge ostrich plume, at least a mile wide, towering over our heads and reaching into the sky. As if angry at the liberty we had taken with her awful presence, Asamayama seemed preparing to avenge herself upon us. There was a dull rumbling; a slight almost imperceptible trembling of the mountain; and the great, grayish mass of smoke and ashes slowly became motionless, erect, a mighty pillar hovering above us as if undecided what to do.

Hastily we fled down the mountain side, shuddering as we passed places we had carelessly and ignorantly traversed the

84

night before. Fast as we were, we could not escape the storm of ashes which began falling on us.

The night following, from dark to dawn, Asamayama sent forth great tongues of fire which sprang from a solid, pillar-like base of flame. This fiery mountain, which spits forth poisonous vapors, red hot lava and huge boulders, was created by the gods, a fact well known to the charcoal burners, who during the night hold converse with foxes and ghosts. Perhaps because of this divine origin visitors are never welcome. Three times I have made the ascent and each time I have suffered from her outburst of temper.

Shortly after this first ascent, I was recalled to Nikko to attend a confinement case. The patient was Mrs. Joseph Bailey (Dr. Effie Dean Worley), whose husband established and developed the agricultural center in Nanking where intensive farming was carried on for the benefit of Chinese farmers.

I stayed on there for a month and my life was a pleasant conglomeration of work and entertainment in beautiful surroundings, among charming people. All my professional work —and there was a good deal of it, both medical and surgical— was among Europeans, chiefly the representatives of the different legations in Tokyo who were spending their holidays in the mountain resort.

Before leaving I received an invitation from the Diplomatic Corps in Tokyo to take up my residence there as legation physician at the end of my contract with the Southern Methodist Mission. It was an appealing idea, but my agreement with Dr. Polk to remain at Soochow until she was free to take up the work there was outside my contract for one year with the Mission Board. The latter was to be renewed at the end of each year if my services were satisfactory, with the idea that I would continue there until Dr. Polk arrived. So altogether I was pretty well tied up for three years, and I did not like to make another contract for a still longer period in the Orient. I still held the ambition of my earlier days—to open an office in one of the larger southern cities; to return to my own land and my own people.

I took time to buy several boxes of toys for my children's ward. I had discovered that the children could bear almost any amount of pain for an unlimited length of time when hung up before them were playthings that might soon become their own. The Japanese toys were so cheap I could afford to buy them in large quantities, but their very cheapness made them easily breakable and I longed for good American toys.

CHAPTER IX

My Marriage and Some Other Dramas

I RETURNED FROM MY SUMMER HOLIDAY IN JAPAN REFRESHED and ready for my hospital work in Soochow, and looking forward to a busy year.

The first thing I did was to fall in love!

When Sarah and I, with the other missionaries who had joined us in Kobe, arrived in Shanghai we were met at the dock by the tall, handsome young man who had been left alone in charge of the hospital. This young man was John Burrus Fearn who had come out from America that spring, just a few weeks before my departure, to take charge of the Men's Hospital. He was replacing Dr. Edgerton H. Hart who had been substituting for Dr. Park during the latter's absence. He had been so lonely. He was glad to see us and welcome us home.

Less than one year later Dr. Fearn and I were married. This definitely settled my fate as far as my return to the United States was concerned for my husband expected to make China the field for his life work; as for me, I had grown to love the country so well that I welcomed the prospect of exile. But I am getting ahead of my story ——

We all returned to Soochow and the very next day I remember going to the Men's Hospital to see the husband of one of my patients. As I passed an open room its disorderliness caught my eye. It was nearly noon but the bed was unmade and the unattractive red hospital blankets were in a heap, dragging the floor. Never, I thought, had I seen such an untidy room.

"Whose room is this?" I asked. "And why isn't the bed made

at this time of the day?" I was ready to call the servants together for a scolding.

Dr. Fearn replied quietly that it was his room and that often the bed didn't get made at all. There was so much to be done for the sick.

I was surprised. "What, do you mean you live here in the hospital? Haven't you a house of your own?" We all had.

But it seemed there was no place for him. Suddenly I was filled with an overwhelming tenderness for this man who was so plucky and so uncomplaining, who had put in the whole hot summer working while we played, and who didn't even have a comfortable place to sleep. I scurried around and found a place for him with one of the missionary families and that was the beginning of a courtship which culminated in our marriage in Soochow on April 21, 1896.

It was odd that I had to go thousands of miles and across an ocean to meet a husband who was born in Jackson, Mississippi, and lived most of his life in Yazoo City, not far from my girlhood home of Holly Springs. As a matter of fact his sisters and I had been friends in those long ago debutante days when I was stealing jelly in the Governor's Mansion.

Looking back, it seems that my personal life at this time was more dramatic than ever before or since. Perhaps it is only the glamour that surrounds any young woman in love that makes the incidents of this period stand out with such startling vividness. Work and courtship, tragedy and comedy were interwoven in all their varying moods.

At least once in the life of any doctor there comes a period of depression and discouragement, when medicine seems a useless profession. Despite all available knowledge the patient dies. My first despair over my personal and professional failings came just before my marriage. The fault was not mine but just the same I had fallen short of my chief purpose—saving

88

life. I wanted to turn tail and flee into the wilds of Thibet, across the Pacific, anywhere.

It was winter, I remember. Indoor fires were burning brightly and outside it was cold and gray with that peculiarly penetrating dampness of China. I was giving thanks for a warm hospital and plenty of patients to keep me busy there when I received a message from an American-educated Chinese doctor, begging me to come at once to Naziang, a twenty-four hour trip by canal boat. The daughter of Mr. Chen, richest and most influential mandarin in that section, was ill.

I forgot my desire for warmth and comfort, and set out at once. Dr. Zau met me, and explained that when he had been called Mr. Chen's daughter already had been in labor for several days. A cursory examination had revealed that only instrumental interference could save the girl's life, the baby having been dead for some time. In those days Chinese men physicians never treated obstetrical cases and the use of forceps was taboo. Long before Dr. Zau had put in an appearance all the city's leading midwives had been in attendance, but their primitive ministrations had done more damage than good.

After one look at the patient I applied the forceps, although I realized from the beginning that the case was hopeless. The mother was cyanosed; her entire system had absorbed the poisons of the baby which was delivered in a semi-decomposed state. The midwives had not the slightest idea of cleanliness or asepsis and the woman had been badly torn from repeated unsanitary, unscientific digital manipulations in their ruthless examinations.

But somehow or other she lived through the operation and the rejoicing father prepared a great feast for the foreign doctor. Hardly had we begun when word came from the patient's room that she was having another hard chill. I was sick with discouragement, knowing what these chills meant and realizing the futility of the work done that morning. I told the father that death was certain. The feast was forgotten and all that night we worked over the girl. At two o'clock in the morning I informed them that I could do no more and that, if they wished, they might call in other assistance.

I crawled into the huge, canopied, curtained, four-posted Chinese bed. During the remaining hours of the dark a succession of native physicians, soothsayers and necromancers passed through my room to the patient's room beyond. Concealed by the draperies I listened to the stories told them of what had been done by the foreign doctor. Then I was forced to hear the criticisms of the Chinese doctors, not one of whom had ever seen a woman in actual labor.

All through those hours I lay and listened to the surging voices of the populace at the courtyard gates. The entire city was agog over this case, so prominent was the family, and hundreds waited for the answer to their question—"will she live, will she die?"

She died at dawn. I would have returned to Soochow at once but the father came to me in great distress; tears coursed down his wrinkled face. He told me of the imminent confinement of his son's wife, and he was afraid. I, too, was afraid, because danger of sepsis threatened the new patient. I consented to remain and ordered her placed in another part of the house, giving instructions that under no circumstances was a member of the family or a servant who had associated with the dead girl to go anywhere near my new patient.

Early in the morning of my third day there Mr. Chen appeared at my door to say that labor had begun. I went to the patient and during the day a strong, healthy son was born. Yielding to their pleas, I stayed on until all danger was past. As I was leaving the house with Mr. Chen we passed a newly made coffin in the courtyard. The father turned to me:

"This rare and precious wood," he said, "has been in my

90

possession many years. It was intended for my own use but now I have given it to my best loved daughter."

That was all I needed to send me weeping back to Soochow. My profession seemed senseless and I took little joy in my hospital and its patients or in the plans for my coming marriage. I was obsessed with the memory of that desolated family, and even now I can picture that splendid old man, wandering from room to room, dazed by his sorrow.

I dried my tears a few weeks later when a magnificent houseboat arrived in Soochow from Naziang, bringing Mr. Chen with gifts for the doctor who had failed to save a life. Among the gifts were bolts of the finest silk, pieces of silver, handsome embroideries and a large, exquisitely fashioned cup with my name inscribed on the bottom and four Chinese characters engraved on the sides. That gentleman translated them for me as meaning, "The Touch of Her Hand Brings Life."

Later I learned the literal translation was, "The Return of Spring Brings Life," but I've cherished the cup no less for the old man's translation which brought me up from the depths. For over forty years that cup was always on my desk where, when I was discouraged, I could reach out and touch it.

The members of the Chen family and I have been friends since that time. So greatly affected were they by the unnecessary tragedy of the daughter's death and so impressed by the easy delivery of the son's wife that they became willing and influential converts to Western science in all its branches. Sons and grandsons were sent to American and European universities and returned to introduce new foreign ideas to the old China. One son is now a high magistrate in Shanghai, another is a scientific authority in the University of Peking.

Dr. Fearn and I decided on April 21 as a good date for our wedding. We did not consult the soothsayers according to Chinese custom but Dr. Polk's long delayed arrival, set for the late spring, would release me from my contract. Dr. Park, for whom

My Days of Strength

Dr. Fearn had been substituting, was due back about the same time and in all probability Dr. Fearn would be sent to an outport.

But before the wedding took place I had my first experience with mob fury; and only by sheer good fortune did I live to tell the tale.

One spring night, two or three weeks before my marriage, a messenger arrived at the hospital around midnight. He had been sent to fetch me to an ailing and, at the time, unknown patient. Little Ling Tsu, the nurse who always accompanied me, and I were carried posthaste to the house designated. We found the customary assemblage of family, relatives, friends and servants, all in the patient's room, surrounding the patient.

I asked the nature of her illness and was told that she had "a rotten throat." One glance satisfied me that the throat really was "rotten." It had been eaten entirely away. It was futile to attempt any treatment but the distracted husband was so persuasive that against my better judgment I gave in and promised to do what I could if the patient were taken at once to the hospital.

They promised that she would be with me by break of day, so after doing what was possible for her immediate comfort I returned to the hospital. Dawn saw the patient, plus many interested spectators, at my door.

We began treatment at once. I waved good-by to the doctors and nurses who were starting out early for an all day picnic which the entire mission was to enjoy among the azaleas. I was left all alone, the only doctor, the only foreigner in the compound.

I had retired to my room, hoping for at least an hour's sleep, when one of the Chinese nurses came to tell me that great crowds were gathering in the courtyard below and that curious sight-seers were thronging the hospital wards. I ordered doors closed and gave instructions that no one, not even the dying, be allowed to enter.

In the meantime weird tales spread that a member of one of the city's richest families had been "bewitched" by the foreign woman doctor. Excitement grew proportionately with the increasing crowd. The coolies closed and locked the doors of the chapel which gave entrance to the hospital, but the crowd rushed them, smashing the doors and breaking the locks.

At ten o'clock in the morning the patient died; instantly rumors circulated that the doctor had killed her by applying medicine to her throat. I could feel the hostility of the crowd oozing up from the courtyard and when I walked through the wards I was met with ugly looks and threatening gestures.

I went to the patient's room and asked the family to remove the body at once. They gazed at me in stupefaction.

"What," they cried, "take the body away from the place of death so soon? Impossible!"

"Yes," I said, with firmness. "You have upset the hospital routine. There are other patients to be considered."

They insisted that the body be left as it was for at least three days. I had a mental picture of the hospital in ruins with myself a corpse if I complied with their request. I said "No." Then, wearily, I acted on my nurse's wise suggestion and went to my room. I dared not face the anger of that ingravescent crowd, for by now it seemed to me the entire population of the city had surrounded the hospital, and my presence excited them to further fury.

Suddenly I sensed a change. My nurse came to inform me that the mob had grown quieter. I sent her to find out why. Not until several hours later did we learn that while the clamor was at its peak a hundred or so men had circulated among the people, refuting the evil tales against me with stories of my magical and miraculous healings. The healings were mostly imaginary but they served their purpose. I discovered much later that the men had been sent to protect me by the Tao Tai Jen, the husband of that early patient whom

I had cured with a few drops from the whole case of champagne; and that he had been ready to come to my aid in person if necessary.

It was a hectic day. Finally with the roar of voices all around me, I fell asleep, exhausted. I was awakened by an awful stillness, and called my nurse, Ling Tsu. "Where are all the people?" I asked.

She didn't know; all that she had been able to gather was this: a message had come from some important official who had ordered a mat-shed built in the empty compound across the street, the body placed in this before midnight and the clothes burned there and not on hospital property.

His commands were followed to the letter, and from my windows I watched the glow of many fires and heard the wailing of the relatives who performed in traditional Chinese fashion. Then again I fell asleep and slept until the dawn. Awakening to an even greater stillness, I looked out. The compound was again empty; the mat-shed and coffin were gone. All this time I had been the only foreigner in the compound for the merry picnic party had reached the city after the gates were closed for the night and could not enter until dawn. When they finally returned only scattered heaps of ashes remained to give proof to my story of that horrible day.

Then came the day of my wedding, the one day I can't remember much about. I only know that it was a day of confusion. I delivered four babies to inconsiderate Chinese mothers who might have had them one day earlier—or later—before I could rush into my wedding gown and down into the parlor of my house. There missionaries, doctors and other foreign friends from as far away as Shanghai had already gathered to witness the ceremony—a very pretty one I've been told. And it must have been, with the flowers and the green grass, the cherry and peach trees blossoming, and one stately magnolia in full bloom in the front yard.

My Marriage and Some Other Dramas

We went to Hangchow for our honeymoon and returned to take up our work in the adjoining hospitals as before, until the almost simultaneous arrivals of Dr. Park and Dr. Polk.

The beginning of our life together did not give promise of a useful happy marriage. For many years our attempts at adjustment seemed futile and many were the tempestuous disagreements from which we emerged with a courage born almost of despair. It could not have been otherwise, so different were the schools of life from which we had been graduated. My husband had grown up in the church. I had not. For every hour he had spent in Sunday School and church I had spent two in dancing and similar pleasures.

He was dominant and born to give orders just as definitely as I was born not to take them. I often told him that our life together would have been much happier had I been six thousand coolies. It took the Great War to make him realize that others had a right to their opinions even when those opinions were diametrically opposed to his. He became less critical of the "small sins" of his wife and friends.

I honestly endeavored to follow his wishes. One of his obsessions was that the day should begin with prayer and Bible reading, and that the Bible should be read through methodically once or twice a year. It was his desire to see me started on this course so we allotted ourselves five chapters daily and ten on Sunday, beginning with the first chapter of the Old Testament and not omitting a single begat.

This hour immediately after breakfast was to me the most important of the day. Wards had to be visited, the hospital inspected, operating room treatments given, and operations performed. While I read Isaiah, Jeremiah and other books of the Old Testament, all hospital work stopped. The nurses were annoyed, the Bible women (native teachers) lost control of the growing groups of clinic patients. The little child whose eyes fell out every time she sneezed or prayed, so slack were

95

the muscles and ligaments, cried for me to come quickly for I had "magic" in my fingers and she would not let the nurses apply the packs. Patients pleaded frantically to see the doctor while the doctor read the Bible, wondering if any good could come from the reading at such a price.

One particular morning a Caesarean operation was set for eight o'clock. We began the reading of the five chapters of Isaiah while the patient was being prepared. With every nerve in my body on the jump we began our reading, and the nurses began coming for me. They stood outside the study door at my husband's unseeing back, but facing me.

I smiled as I nodded to them. "In a minute," I said, and asked my husband, "How many more chapters, dearest?"

At his reply, "Three," my heart almost jumped from its moorings.

Again a nurse appeared, adjuring me with clasped hands to come. "The patient is ready, Doctor."

Again I said, "In a minute," and to my husband, "Dearest, I must go." His answer to the effect that the Bible reading was the most important duty of the day unloosed the rebellion in my heart, which even under ordinary circumstances was more like a repressed volcano than a normally functioning organ.

Springing up tempestuously I cried, "I can't bear it! I can't bear it! I wish I'd never seen the damned thing!" And flinging the Bible to the floor I rushed out, straight to the operating room where, after cleaning up, I got busy on one of the most vitally important of all abdominal operations. Fortunately the mother survived this combination of surgery and fury. The child had been dead several hours before the patient had been brought to us.

This little flare-up ended the Bible readings. The subject was never mentioned again but Dr. Fearn never forgave nor forgot, and I lost forever my taste, if I ever had any, for the Old Testament.

The water buffalo on which the Big Miss Fee often rode.
Though usually gentle with children, these buffalo
were responsible for many bad horn-rip cases.

When she was three, she learned to ride a donkey . . .

We called Ming Tse, "The Regular Boarder" . . .

She was fair of skin, blond of hair,
and dressed always in white from head to toe . . .

CHAPTER X

Dzang Dzok

SOON AFTER THIS, MY HUSBAND WAS TRANSFERRED TO DZANG Dzok, to open medical work there, and I accompanied him. It was the beginning of a period of confusion; of upheaval and tribulation for the Chinese; of travel, trial and great happiness for us. For during this time of chaos and change our child was to be born. It seemed a little strange but altogether delightful that I, who had delivered innumerable babies under every imaginable condition, should now be going to have one of my own.

Dzang Dzok was a city of wealth, aristocracy and great beauty, about a day's journey by boat from Soochow. There is a pretty little legend that the dragon who lies sprawled under the earth's surface became annoyed many, many years ago at the frequent disturbances of the soil above him. With an irritated heave of his great body he produced an eruption of earth which formed the high hill on which Dzang Dzok is situated. The corresponding depression soon became a great lake. It has always seemed to me one of the most beautiful places I have ever seen, and the city itself is untouched by Western culture. High upon the hilltop stands a *ding tze* or pavilion placed there for the use of the spirits which keep guard over the grave of a much loved scholar which lies at its foot.

Our experiences there were many-sided, for not only were we working hard to inaugurate hospital facilities, but our position as the only foreigners in the city made our home the center for great social activities and the meeting place for officials and the aristocracy. The people welcomed us at first with true

97

Chinese hospitality and the clinic was well attended. Then fewer and fewer came; and finally the clinic was stopped entirely.

All over China at this time hostility to foreigners was increasing. Anti-foreign riots occurred frequently, and we came in for our share of the antagonism. We heard ugly rumors about ourselves; we were necromancers and worked only evil to people. When we passed children in their parents' arms their faces were covered with handkerchiefs to ward off the evils of our eyes. Constant and increasing reports reached us that we and all the Chinese who worked for us were to be killed.

Our old cook came back from market one day with word that our house was to be destroyed that night, and ourselves and our servants murdered. My husband called the servants together and told them that he had provided a boat for them; that they must leave at once for Soochow where they would find safety. They filed out silently. Ten minutes later they filed in again to say that they had talked it over and had decided that as we had been their friends in their hours of need they would remain with us in our trouble. In our over-wrought condition, this evidence of affection and loyalty almost brought us to tears, for the danger was far from imaginary.

Fortunately government troops arrived from Soochow in the late afternoon. In time the trouble blew over, but this was another experience which I'd rather not relive.

There is another Dzang Dzok incident I never recall without a shudder and a smile. As I have said, we were the only foreigners in the city. Ours was the only cook nearer than Soochow who could prepare European food, and a jolly good cook he was, with a temper as vicious as his cooking was perfect. He and the laundryman hated each other and it was the cook's favorite stunt to put ashes in the tub with the freshly laundered linen.

He was told that one more offense meant instant dismissal

but he could not resist temptation. He was discharged and told to take the evening launch to Soochow. In the meantime we dispatched a message to a friend to send us a cook by the return launch which would arrive in Dzang Dzok the next morning.

All that day the cook went about his work, voice raised in song. My husband remarked, "It sounds ominous."

He left, after getting dinner. I was ill in bed but my husband, who on various camping expeditions had learned to make baking powder biscuits and scrambled eggs, rose to the occasion and in the morning turned out hot biscuits in such vast quantity and of such perfection that he had a fine orgy sampling his own culinary efforts. Fortunately I was too ill to eat. Before he had quite finished breakfast he appeared at my bedside, green of face and violently nauseated.

Simultaneously Mr. Edward Pilley, an old Soochow friend, appeared with the new cook. In a little while the amah, the laundryman and the Boy, who evidently had partaken of master's cooking, also became ill. Mr. Pilley announced that it was all foolishness, just imagination, and that he would eat breakfast. He did. He ate hot biscuits and joined the others.

Meanwhile, word had reached the Chinese minister and his twenty church members that all the Fearn family and servants were dying and they came to assist in making our passing as comfortable as possible. The minister tried to get a boat to take us to Soochow but the captain of each boat came, looked, and left, saying a curse would be upon his boat were we to die on it. After awhile the pastor and his flock left; going through the dining room they saw the beautiful biscuits and the cook, practical in his generosity, offered them some, pointing out that we probably would not live to eat another. That night every Chinese Christian in Dzang Dzok joined the ranks of the retching and the nauseated.

The peculiarities of the condition were the nausea, griping abdominal pains and a burning, quenchless thirst. In desperation the victims drank their fill of what was supposed to be a deadly poison, water, for we had reached the conclusion that it was water that had caused all the trouble.

By this time even our new cook was ill. It was up to me to do something about it. I dragged myself up and into our spotless kitchen. Picking up the baking powder tin I asked, "Isn't baking powder white? This seems to be pale orange." And pale orange it was. At first we thought it had been mixed with bichromate of potash since we knew that drug, used largely in photography, could be obtained in Dzang Dzok. As an antidote we drank vinegar as one would drink water, but with no relief.

Further investigation proved the poison to be bisulphide of arsenic.

And the net result of my husband's biscuit-making was that he, Mr. Pilley, and thirty-five Chinese in different parts of the city were ill. We had never realized until then how many were fed from our table.

Suspicion at once fell on the old cook who was brought back to Dzang Dzok and questioned. In the meantime everyone had some remedy. One friend brought a prescription calling for lamb's blood, snail-shells and other things. The green pea is supposed to be a specific in arsenic poisoning but none of these remedies seemed to be efficacious in this case.

"Why did you do it?" I asked the old cook. "We have never treated you with anything but the greatest kindness."

He replied that he loved us enough to lay down his life for us but that he could not bear to leave our house. Hoping we would think the new cook's efforts had made us ill, he had purchased from a barber the red arsenic used in that profession as a germicide. His intention was to make us "slightly ill." He had bought enough to kill a regiment but the salvation of the biscuit eaters was that the quantity of arsenic in one biscuit was enough to make it come up almost before it got down.

The old cook was imprisoned but my husband interceded for

him and after a month's sentence he was released, only to die a few weeks later of grief and shame.

About this time we journeyed to Changchow to decide on the advisability of opening medical work in that city of wealth and learning. As it was early summer and exceedingly warm when we left Dzang Dzok I dressed in light clothes, but a sudden cold spell made a wrap necessary. Our arrival was heralded abroad and runners came from the Yamen, the official residence, with an invitation to dinner that evening. This was about one month before the birth of my baby and, with anything but a sylph-like figure at best, I added to my bulkiness by wearing as a wrap an eiderdown bath-robe, the only warm outer garment we had with us on the boat.

As I stepped from the houseboat to the shore I overheard this remark:

"It is true that these foreign devil women have waists like wasps," said the voice. "See, her waist is as fine as a needle." So much for the psychology of preconceived impression.

While we were in Changchow I operated on the only son of the city's highest official, doing a tonsillectomy and removing the child's adenoids. This simple operation assumed major proportions in the eyes of the Chinese and won for us the lasting affection of the official.

Owing to the unforeseen reduction of our medical staff, our visit there was cut short and it was thought best to postpone the building of a hospital in Dzang Dzok, and to put aside plans to open one in Changchow.

My husband was soon to be stationed again in Soochow, but we were still residing in Dzang Dzok when I returned to Soochow for my confinement.

The birth of a baby in China is not news; thousands are born with each tick of the clock. By the time I was ready to give birth to Elizabeth I had delivered upward of three thousand babies since my medical school days, a number that was to grow to six thousand and seventeen recorded births before I was through practicing medicine. But when an obstetrician gives birth to her own child it ceases to be an incident and assumes proportions of grave magnitude.

I approached my confinement with the usual nervous trepidation of any normal expectant mother but I was not overly frightened. I was to have the medical services of two of the best obstetricians in China, my dear friends, Dr. Margaret Polk of the Soochow Woman's Hospital, and Dr. Sarah Poindexter, who had come down from her mission station in Tsinanfu to be with me. And then, I had little time for worries about accidents and what-might-happens because I was busy up until almost the very last minute, bringing other women's babies into the world.

I had always considered birth a natural function of the female body and I had looked on it with a purely professional eye. I knew from actual experiences that the event of birth was never pleasant, the only variation being that some cases were worse than others. A few nights before my baby was born I was called to the quarters of the hospital gatekeeper whose old-fashioned wife had rejected our obstetrical services, preferring the assistance of midwives. The old man begged me to hurry, telling me as we crossed the courtyard that the child had been delivered but that the women could not get the placenta. I examined the moribund mother and found that it wasn't the placenta at all. They had been tugging at the uterus which, in their rough manipulations, they had succeeded in pulling down and inverting.

From earliest medical college days I had disliked delivery cases, although my training in obstetrics had been exceptionally thorough and, heaven knows, since coming to China I had not lacked practical experience. Once I delivered as many as nine babies in one day. Each time the nurse handed me my "baby bag," always within reach and packed with the forceps, the bandages, the rubber sheets and gloves, the antiseptic fluid, the chloroform, and the syringes, I prayed that it would be my last labor case. It never was.

My own child was born on August 5, 1897, in the children's ward which I had built in the compound of the Soochow Woman's Hospital. I realized from my hemorrhagic condition, even before Dr. Polk and Dr. Poindexter were aware of it, that mine was a placenta praevia case, and I understood only too well what that meant. I had attended hundreds of these dangerous deliveries and I knew just what to expect, what should be done. They could not give me an anesthetic because that would increase the danger to mother and child, but if the doctors had not moved with such sure swiftness I would have died. I was conscious of each movement, and when a doctor's arm shot through the placenta to take the baby I suffered more than mere physical pain. I suffered the mental anguish that comes from too accurate a knowledge. Although my life hung in the balance for days both mother and baby survived. As a mother I forgot the momentary misery in the joy of the child; as a physician I remembered. The child was a girl, and we named her Elizabeth for my friend, Dr. Elizabeth Yates.

CHAPTER XI

The Big Miss Fee

I HAD ALWAYS KNOWN THAT MOTHERHOOD USUALLY ENTAILED sacrifices, but until Elizabeth's birth I had not realized how one's whole philosophy might be changed by a child. If Elizabeth's visit with us had not been so brief I might have been content to relinquish my practice and stay at home. I do not know. But I do know that if it had not been for Elizabeth I would have left undone many of the things that have been chalked up to my credit. I doubt if I would have contributed so much time and effort in later years to helping the children of China, both Chinese and foreign, if it had not been for her memory; nor would I have sought so hard to keep my days and nights filled with activity.

Because of this, I must tell you a little of Elizabeth and of the five short years she was with us. At her birth the Chinese had brought us red eggs, symbol of good luck, and during her short life they were always her friends and willing followers.

Siau Sih Bah (Little Snow White) they called her and on more formal occasions *Fee Doo Siau Tia* (The Big Miss Fee). (The Chinese character most closely resembling Fearn is "Fee" and the "big" always is used to designate the first born.) As soon as she was able to toddle The Big Miss Fee, who was about as big as a minute, made daily visits to the hospital wards, her small hands filled with flowers which she would present to the Chinese patients one by one. Proudly they would tuck them behind their ears and wear them all day long.

Often she would take her half-pint freezer to the wards, and sitting on the floor she would freeze ice-cream vigorously for as many as were brave enough to eat it. Fortunately for us, the Chinese at that time had an aversion for ice and a great fear of putting anything cold in their stomachs; otherwise our milk and ice bills would have been enormous.

She was well-named Little Snow White. She was fair of skin, blonde of hair and dressed always in white from head to toe. Only once do I remember her being adorned with many colors. She had always wanted a parasol and as she always got what she wanted, eventually she had one—a white parasol. She was terribly pleased with it and holding it straight up in front of her nose she would parade around the compound by the hour. This Ming Tse, her constant companion, could not bear and she pestered her mother until she, too, possessed a parasol. But Ming Tse's was a vivid one in red, green and purple, and as it quite captured Elizabeth's fancy there was a speedy exchange.

Elizabeth was not the first foreign child born in the children's ward, nor in the mission hospital compound, but it so happened that all during her lifetime she was one of two or three white children on the premises and of a necessity her playmates were Chinese. She played mostly with the sons and daughters of the native preachers and teachers, her favorite playmates being Ming Tse and Ming Tse's little sister Ming Li. We called Ming Tse the regular boarder because she took all of her meals with us; Ming Li, the irregular boarder because she ate only one meal a day—and it might be any meal—at our table.

In 1900, our life in China was briefly interrupted, and Elizabeth said good-by to her Chinese friends as she, my husband, and I sailed for our first furlough to the United States. From the very beginning, our journey was productive of out-of-the-way experiences, which my husband said were due to my "magnetic attraction for adventure."

Nothing happened on the trip from Shanghai to Japan, but no sooner had we left Nagasaki harbor than the steamer returned to her moorings. A steerage passenger had been found dead in his bunk. There was furious excitement among the Japanese. Innumerable Japanese doctors took possession of the ship; held consultations. The dead man's glands were microscopically examined and bacilli "resembling those of plague" were found. His body was cremated in the ship's furnace, and for two weeks we sat in the shadow of Papenheim Rock.

At last the yellow flag of quarantine came down and we went on our way rejoicing. But the day before we reached Honolulu, another death occurred among the steerage passengers. Again we were subjected to merciless examination and again bacilli "resembling those of plague" were found in the glands of the deceased. Again the yellow flag waved from our masthead. It was blisteringly hot; the ice machine broke down, the meat spoiled and we had no fresh fruit or vegetables, that being before the day of refrigeration. No one was allowed to come out to see us and for awhile it looked as if we actually might become a "plague ship" in good earnest.

We begged to be allowed to go on our way, to spend the last days of quarantine at sea. At first this request was denied, but quite unexpectedly one night when we had given up all hope of ever leaving we heard the sweetest music—the creaking of coal scows and the singing of the stevedores as they filled the ship's bunkers. It sounded to us like angels' voices. We saw ahead freedom and the cool, blue sea.

We dropped anchor in San Francisco Bay, only to weigh it again and sail across to Angel Island where we were put ashore. Above our luckless heads floated the too, too familiar flag. A Japanese woman had died a few days out of Honolulu!

For two weeks everything possible was done for our comfort, but oh, the dreariness of those primitive unfinished quarters! The arrival of the "plague ship" created a country-wide excitement. Telegrams, papers, books, toys for the children, tons of sweets and fruits came to us from interested friends and relatives, but while they helped to relieve the tedium of those interminable weeks, we were far too tired and restless to be philosophical about it.

Among the passengers on the ship was a Salvation Army officer who was making all speed homeward in the hope that she might reach there before her expected confinement. But she had reckoned without her hosts! Two weeks in Nagasaki, ten days in Honolulu and now two weeks on Angel Island had brought the day unpleasantly near. She had a *kyphos* (hunchback), and the quarantine officer, expecting trouble, asked me to take the case if the birth should occur on the island. And sure enough, the night before quarantine was over, the baby was born.

The following day the island was invaded by customs men, who for our convenience came to examine the baggage. Newspaper reporters and armed men of both Federal and State governments came in crowds to see that none of us stole ashore. I was pointed out to the reporters who had heard of the child's birth as the physician in charge of the case.

Among other questions I was asked the name of the baby. I replied flippantly, "Why of course there's only one possible name—Angelina Quarantina."

To my utter horror, the next day's papers appeared with headlines inches high of the birth on the plague ship, *Nippon Maru,* of "Angelina Quarantina."

While we were enjoying a delightful furlough, visiting my old home and seeing friends and relatives, China was in a state of upheaval. We had hardly left before rumors of trouble filled the land. Then news came from Peking of the coup d'etat which launched the Boxer Uprising, and eventually involved nearly every nation of the civilized world.

As we did not return to China until the worst was over, the story of that fearful, blind revolt against the foreigners' hold on the country has no place here. We read of the siege of the

Peking Legations and of the atrocities committed against Europeans; then came the rumor that the Legation had been assaulted, taken, and all the inhabitants massacred. Soochow we heard was in chaos; Shanghai was preparing defense. First the British, then the French, Americans, and Germans sent troops to quell the uprising; they entered Peking and the Royal Family fled to Sianfu. Finally, with sighs of relief and hope, we read that negotiations between the powers and China were under way.

Officials all over the Empire were setting about the prodigious task of reducing to order the seething, frightened, unruly mass of people. We received a cable from my old friend Tao Tai Jen, Governor of Soochow Province, imploring us to return. He felt that because we had worked so long among the people, our presence would have a stabilizing influence. Needless to say his appeal did not fall on deaf ears. We returned as speedily as possible.

I shall not forget that return. As our boat reached the city gate, we stared in horror. Seventy-five wooden buckets hung from the circle of the gate's arch, and from each bucket dangled a queue. Seventy-five decapitated heads hung from that gate. Nothing more was needed to make us realize the ghastliness of the trouble we had escaped.

We made a point of going about the city every day and as we passed along the streets we were received with eager words of welcome. The beggars on the street, the officials in their chairs, the shopkeepers from their doorsteps all cried delightedly, "All is well, the foreigners have returned." And when they realized that we both were physicians and that the hospitals were to be opened at once, we did not have to wait many days before we had more work than we could do. All the officials called without delay, offering us their friendship and protection although assuring us that the latter was not needed.

We found the hospital chapel full of soldiers and there were more at Buffington College. They had been there all summer, but at my husband's explanation that we needed the rooms for patients they were removed, all but one young official who stayed on—indefinitely it seemed to me. But at last he too was gone.

The joyous welcome was all very well; but with the exception of our friend, Mr. Pilley, who had returned with us, my husband and I and our small daughter were the only foreigners in the city. Terrible things had happened; equally terrible things might happen again. We were alone, utterly unprotected, and always before my eyes were those seventy-five limp queues, hanging from those seventy-five buckets. In the good daylight I endured it very well but when night fell and the city gates were locked I could not help the terror that came over me. Many a long night I lay awake, wide-eyed in the darkness, listening, listening.

Just at this inauspicious time I was sent on a case which came near to frightening me out of my "six ghosts and three spirits." There was still a current of unrest among the population, so, although by this time I spoke Chinese fairly well, I made a practice of taking my nurse-interpreter with me when I went to unfamiliar houses. As usual it was late at night when I was called out. It was a case of opium poisoning and when I reached the place I found that the woman had died before I had even been sent for.

We were led into the room of the dead and the door locked behind us. The husband's attitude was definitely threatening and I was chilled with terror when he said,

"You preach the gospel of the resurrection of the dead. Now bring my wife back to life."

It seemed to me that hours passed before my interpreter succeeded in explaining the doctrine of the resurrection as it is preached, and even then I was almost forced into giving a hypodermic, although I assured the man of its absolute futility.

My Days of Strength

Shaking with fear I sat there beside the dead woman while those two Chinese endlessly discussed the principles of Christianity, and wondered what was ever going to get us out of that ghastly room, and whether there was anything that could. If the dead woman had sat up in bed, or got up and walked, it would not have surprised me in the least, the whole experience was so gruesome and unreal.

How good the night air felt when at last we were allowed to leave that house; how sweet the fragrance of flowers behind a wall, and how glad I was to smell the filth of the alleyways!

Gradually other Europeans returned, but our five months of isolation in that walled city of nearly a million inhabitants is a memory which still brings an unpleasant chill to my heart.

Throughout this unsettled period, and later, when life had resumed a normal aspect, Elizabeth continued to develop as an individual. She early acquired very definite characteristics and particular interests. She was, for one thing, inordinately fond of the ragged urchins who played in and near our compound, bringing them in from the streets to have the midday meal with her. Her hospitality knew no bounds. One day when her tiffin party had grown to such enormous dimensions that it was impossible to crowd all the guests around our table we held a consultation with her and told her she could continue her daily tiffins on the one condition that she ask only as many guests as her special table would seat. She agreed. The table seated six and she almost always asked ten.

Like most foreign children born and raised in China she spoke the language of that country with greater fluency than she did her own and her tiffin parties were noisy affairs as chopsticks clicked and flew to hungry mouths and childish voices sing-songed in chatter. These poor, hungry street children impressed Elizabeth from her earliest baby days and it was because of Elizabeth that each year for twenty-four years, in Soochow and later in Shanghai, I had a Christmas tree with gifts for exactly one hundred raggedy-raggedies. It happened this way:

It was at the close of summer and a week or so before her death. I was dressing to go to a dinner at the home of Mr. C. C. Clark, the Commissioner of Customs, and as usual I had been detained by an unexpected sick call and was late. Elizabeth came in and begged me to write a letter to Santa Claus. I told her that I was busy, that Christmas was a long way off and that tomorrow would do. She was insistent so I gave in, dropped everything and sat down and wrote the letter then and there. Perhaps I remembered the disappointment of that far-off Christmas in the yellow fever year in Holly Springs when I was not even permitted to speak of Santa Claus.

She asked for a few things for herself; her principal request was that Santa bring a tree into our dining room on Christmas morning. She wanted it loaded with presents, not for herself but for one hundred of the little street urchins who played outside our compound gates and along the canal banks, whom she called her raggedy-raggedies.

We had the tree that Christmas—but without Elizabeth—and from that time on, as long as I had a home or a hospital, I gave a similar party with a tree and presents of clothing and toys for the raggedy-raggedies. In Shanghai, years later, I had two Christmas trees, one early in the morning for the Chinese and another in the afternoon for the foreigners, children of our friends. After closing my hospital in 1926 I contributed a sum commensurate with the amount expended for the trees and presents, and "Elizabeth's raggedy-raggedies" continued to receive some sort of Christmas cheer.

But never will I forget that first tree. Beautiful pines grow all around the Soochow countryside and dot the hillsides. We dug up one of the loveliest and loaded it with decorations—tinsel, fragile ornaments, popcorn and hundreds of candles. A few weeks before Christmas we sent the native Bible women of the

hospital, who knew all the families in our vicinity, into the
various homes where they listed the names, ages and sex of
the children. Thus we were able to provide suitable presents
for each—wadded garments, shoes, mittens, scarves, winter
hoods; a red bag containing sweets, cakes, an apple and an
orange, and most important of all, a toy.

The Bible women collected the children and herded them
into the house in one great group. They marched silently into
the parlor, awed by being in a foreign devil's house, as for
most of them it was their first visit. They were frightened
almost out of their "six ghosts and three spirits" when the doors
were thrown open and they saw, standing in the very center
of the room, the most miraculous tree—on fire! They made a
concerted rush for the door, screaming their fears. If the nurses
and attendants hadn't barred their way and calmed them I'm
afraid the Christmas tree celebration would have ended then
and there. They were persuaded back into the room and soon
their natural curiosity overcame their fright and they left,
hugging their precious presents.

It was the next year just at Christmas that Mr. Jeremiah
Jenks, who had been sent out by the United States government to work with the Chinese government in establishing a
monetary basis which would stabilize exchange, came to visit
us. He was so impressed with "Elizabeth's tree" and our work
that he asked if he might make a contribution. We welcomed
it. He gave us fifty dollars (American) and from that day
until his death he made a similar contribution every year to
the raggedy-raggedy tree.

If I am making Elizabeth sound too much like perfection I
am not painting an exactly true picture. She was like any other
little girl of her age, very sweet and unspoiled, it is true, but
at times very naughty. When she was three years old she
learned to ride a donkey and her favorite trick was to escape
from the watchful donkey-boy, who was responsible for her

Some of Elizabeth's Chinese Christian playmates at the Soochow Woman's Hospital.

Elizabeth's "Old Mother" and amah.

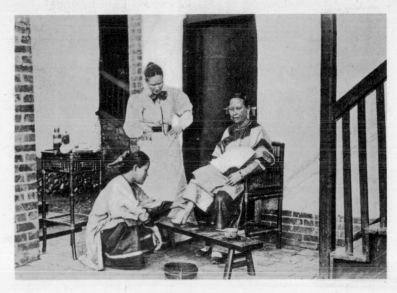

Unbinding Chinese feet.

Jetty at the Soochow Woman's Hospital compound.
The Chinese called it "The Heaven Given Place."

safety, and go streaking through the streets, broad-brimmed white hat dangling down her back, lines clutched in one hand. It was a source of great annoyance to the Boy, who would run after her, shrieking, *"Siau Sih Bah," "Siau Sih Bah"* (Little Snow White, Little Snow White), and of great amusement to the townspeople who would add their voices to his with cries of *"Le tse, le tse."* (Coming, coming.)

For punishment on all occasions Elizabeth was sent to the *Lan Nyung Kan* or "manikin room," so called because of the papier-mâché figure kept there for use in student anatomy courses; dissection in those days being strictly taboo. At breakfast one morning Elizabeth had been particularly annoying, doing the innumerable things a child can do to the irritation of grown-ups, carelessly spilling food, dropping spoons, overturning her milk. Her father scolded her. I scolded her, quite losing my temper. Finally in a burst of fury she reached over and deliberately emptied her cocoa cup over the centerpiece. Then, without a word, she climbed down from her high chair and walked out of the room, through the hall and into the manikin room. Later I followed her and we sat there together, consoling each other.

When Elizabeth had reached her first birthday she had been given a rag doll just her size and dressed in one of her dresses. Her name was Janey-Jane and she was the direct descendant of at least forty other Janey-Janes. The original had come across the seas with one of the first missionary families but eventually every little girl in all the mission compounds scattered over that vast country had a Janey-Jane, cut from the same pattern. Elizabeth's was her inseparable companion.

Elizabeth, Janey-Jane, Dr. Fearn, and I went to Kuling, high in the mountains, for a respite from the heat the summer of 1902. Elizabeth loved the gorgeous sunsets and always at sundown she was in a nervous state of excitement. She begged me to stay with her then to watch what she called "the opening of the gates of the sky." We returned to Soochow late in August and Elizabeth, never before sick a day in her life, fell ill with dysentery.

As I returned from my daily visits to patients one afternoon amah came to me. "Our baby is sick," she said.

"What is it?" I asked. She answered, *"Doo li za"* (diarrhea). But it wasn't, it was amoebic dysentery. Three days later she died in my arms as I sat in a rocking-chair by the window, just as the gates of the sky opened.

Ten years later Vedder discovered emetine as a specific cure for amoebic dysentery.

I was in a perfect frenzy after her death. I could not understand why death had passed by the beggars in their torn and filthy rags, the underfed who often went without their daily *san woen van*, the mentally afflicted, chained in some courtyard, and laid indiscriminate hands on my child, so protected, so well and so lovely. I decided that there must be some reason and until I found it—if ever I should—I could do no less than try to help those poor unfortunates, Elizabeth's beloved raggedy-raggedies.

It seemed that our lives were made up of tragedies. During Elizabeth's illness cholera had raged all around us, one of the seven similar epidemics I battled. One Sunday after a very hard day my husband and I had just gone to our room when I was called to attend the wife of one of our highest officials. Dr. Fearn went with me to my sedan chair and as we reached the door we were almost knocked over by a friend who had rushed to the hospital for help. He asked Dr. Fearn to come quickly, to see what he could do about saving the women and children who had been crushed when a temple fell. It was a feast day, the birthday of the god of the forest, and all the women and children of the neighborhood had assembled in this temple to celebrate the occasion. The stone beam, which supported that part of the temple built over the canal, had suddenly given way and all were dropped into the water, the swirling mass of human beings pinned under the debris of the temple.

Dr. Fearn went at once, taking with him all the hospital boys and the entire supply of bandages and splints. It was too late; some forty or fifty women and children were dragged out dead from the wreck; only four lived.

The people were frantic and begged my husband to bring the dead back to life. At midnight when I returned from my call I met litter after litter of the dead, and the grief of those who followed was heart-rending.

I had never been more unhappy in my heart, never happier in my work than at this time. We actually were accomplishing some of the things we had set out to do so long ago. During this period (1902-1907) the change in the attitude of the people toward surgery was surprising. It used to be that we had to cajole and connive to get them to let us perform the slightest operation; now they fairly beset us to do things that were nearly impossible. We had almost succeeded in rolling away that last obstacle; soon we should have dissecting taught in our medical college.

We had long ago outgrown the curtained hall which had served as our first medical college. By 1902 we were well on our way with a new building, already nearly fifty students were enrolled, and they were all from wealthy and hitherto decidedly anti-foreign families. I even had several applications from official families to take their daughters as medical students.

I celebrated the end of my first decade of medicine in China simultaneously with the beginning of a new social order in Soochow. In 1903, for the first time in the history of that ancient city, foreign ladies were invited to pay a social call on the wife of the highest official. My old friend the Tao Tai Jen had been succeeded by En Show, as Governor of the Province. Ever since turning over the regular hospital work to Dr. Polk I had continued my private practice. By this time my reputation was assured and I held an exalted position in the eyes of the Chinese. Immediately on his arrival En Show paid me an official visit along with all the other high and mighties. Soon afterward he invited Bishop Galloway's wife, Dr. Polk, Mrs. W. B. Nance, Mrs. J. D. Trawick, Mrs. C. C. Clark, and a few others, to call with me on Lady En at the official residence. The sedan chairs, winding through the city on their way to the yamen, made quite a formidable procession.

The visit was such a success that a few days later Lady En requested the privilege of returning the calls of her foreign friends. Her request, naturally, was granted, and she was introduced to the intricacies of a foreign home, from drawing room to kitchen.

She was inspecting my house when she stopped suddenly, entranced, before a kitchen range.

"What is that?" she asked.

When told that it was a stove, used for cooking the meals, she replied, "I have one of those. It is in the ceremonial hall with all our treasures; no one knows how to use it."

So my first ten years in China ended. I had witnessed many undreamed-of accomplishments, but I rejoiced principally that the barriers which surrounded the women of China were slowly but surely breaking down.

CHAPTER XII

The Foreign Devils Move In

C HINA WAS OPENED AT THE POINT OF PETER PARKER'S HYPO-
dermic needle." These oft-quoted words have a large
measure of truth in them. I spent seven years as a lay worker
employed by the Board of Missions, and in the face of all criticism leveled against missionaries in China, some of it un-
doubtedly justified, I feel that I cannot do less than pay a
tribute to medical missions. I agree with Dr. H. S. Wainwright
who said that as a means of affording tangible evidence of
the beneficent character of the Christian religion, of disarming
prejudice and quieting suspicion, of gaining access to hostile
regions, and as an auxiliary to evangelical work, medical missions have played an invaluable part.

Entrance to Tientsin, the great emporium of North China,
was accomplished when Dr. MacKenzie and Dr. Irwin saved
the life of the Viceroy's wife when she lay at the point of death.
A few days afterwards the doctors were called before Li Hung-
chang and other dignitaries and requested to perform a surgical operation in their presence, to display the powers and
possibilities of Western surgery. The skill of these men pro-
foundly influenced Li Hung-chang in favor of Christian civilization. When one realizes that so short a time ago as the period
of the Boxer troubles, even the Empress Dowager and the
majority of her court firmly believed that the foreigners were
barbarians from inconsiderable small islands and unworthy of
equality with the ancient Chinese civilization, one begins to
grasp the importance of this introduction of scientific methods
to Chinese understanding.

My Days of Strength

Dr. N. H. Allen, a young physician sent out by the American Presbyterian Mission Board for Korea, was called in to treat Prince Ik, the King's nephew, who had been seriously injured. He found thirteen native doctors trying to stanch the wounds by filling them with wax. Unwillingly standing aside for the young missionary, they looked on with amazement while he tied arteries and sewed up the gaping wounds. In a few moments a revolution was effected in the medical methods of the kingdom, and at the same time incalculable vantage ground was gained for the introduction of the gospel. The prince whose life was saved, said to Dr. Allen,

"Our people cannot believe that you come from America. They insist that you must have dropped from Heaven for this very crisis."

No doubt heaven did have something to do with it, for that was the beginning of missionary work in the Hermit Kingdom.

Missions, especially medical missions, have paved the way not only for Christianity but for commerce as well. In nearly every case where new territory has been opened up for trade, medical work has been the entering wedge. Trade and commerce have followed, not preceded the missionary. And in this pioneering, women have shown the most praiseworthy zeal and courage. In countries where homes and harems are barred to every alien male, it was possible for women doctors to penetrate the screen and alleviate suffering which had perhaps been patiently and hopelessly endured for years. To America belongs the credit and honor of inaugurating the women's medical work.

Years ago women in heathen lands were so inaccessible that peculiar devices were resorted to to preserve their seclusion and at the same time make possible the attendance of a male physician. Sometimes the patient was entirely screened and communications were made through servants. Occasionally a hand was thrust from behind a curtain for a doctor to examine the pulse. Ingenuity reached a climax when Dr. Wainwright, calling to see his patient, was handed a string, the other end of which was tied to the wrist of the patient upstairs. The poor man was expected to feel her pulse and diagnose the case through the string.

The missionary physician might well rest his claim on the relief he brings to human misery. Certainly it justifies all sacrifices. Without sufficient food, clothing, or shelter, and with absolutely no sanitary knowledge, uncivilized people as a rule are physically weak and therefore easy victims of innumerable diseases. Pestilences, unchecked, sweep away thousands of them. Their awful suffering is not only unrelieved but increased by the revolting practices of ignorance and superstition in the treatment of disease. No hellish lictor with boiling cauldrons, red-hot pans, fiery arrows, knives, claws or spikes of iron and bubbling filth, in the infernal regions of Dante's imagination, nor the hells of the efflorescent conceptions of the modern Buddhist, can exceed the ruthless cruelty of the "Medicine Man," nor the horrors actually perpetrated by him on thousands of ignorant people.

Of course, one cannot place China among the uncivilized nations, but her ignorance of sanitation is beyond belief. It frequently seemed to me that the continued existence of the Chinese was nothing short of a miracle, explainable only by the theory of germ saturation. Presumably the Chinese enjoy comparative immunity so that a few million germs, more or less, count for nothing. The weakest go to the wall, obeying the relentless laws of survival.

There is much yet to be done in China, for the great mass of people still know less than nothing of sanitation or antiseptics. The fetid canals are still used for every conceivable household purpose; they wash the rice in them and empty the slops in them. Those with contagious diseases, such as tubercu-

losis, live and eat and sleep in the same room with the rest
of the family.

I remember being called once to see a member of the Governor's household. While I was there the inevitable tea was
brought in. This, the Governor explained to me, was the best
he had, and went on to say, with much bowing and smiling,
that he had opened the box expressly in my honor. It had the
fragrance of hyacinths, jasmine, sweet peas and violets all at
once. The aroma was so lovely, and so like that of a bouquet
of sweet, fresh flowers, that I drank it with relish, although I
strongly suspected that it had been made with canal water
and seasoned with the refuse of the land. The next day I called
again, and when the tea was brought in there was some ob-
struction in the spout of the teapot. To my consternation, the
charming old Governor picked it up, and putting the spout
to his lips blew gustily through it into the tea. Even though
he poured and handed me a cup with all the grace of a Chester-
field, my doctor's training rose up within me and forbade me
drink that tea!

But forty-four years have wrought great changes. Gone are
the two hospitals in Soochow where I spent the first fourteen
years of my life in China. In their place today stands a substantial, up-to-date three-story building, with every possible
device to facilitate the work of the staff and add to the comfort
of the patients. It even has a roof garden with cubicles for the
tuberculosis patients. The foreign doctor no longer has to beg
the privilege of saving a life. On the contrary, no operation is
too serious; sufferers are not frightened away; and entreaties
for help now come from the patients. The people of Soochow
have been fortunate in the men who came to work among them.
Dr. W. H. Park, during forty years of service, paved the way
for today's results. He and his wife worked without stint, and
won their reward in the touching gratitude and affection of the

Chinese. Dr. John A. Snell, who succeeded Dr. Park, was a brilliant surgeon, loved and trusted by the people.

But there is still in China much suffering which the Western world no longer experiences, misery that reminds one of the far-off days when plagues depopulated vast sections of Europe and the people fled from their homes in search of safety, only to find the pestilence following them however far they went. Every year there are thousands of homeless in China, living on the scanty charity of the State, the insufficient help of the Red Cross and the missionaries. It seems that it will be an endless battle to slay the maggots of disease eating at the life of this great nation.

But there is one curse of China for which the West is all too responsible—opium.

The seed of the poppy plant, introduced by the Arabs, was used in the eighth century in China as a medicinal soporific. It is mentioned in poetry dating back to the Sung Dynasty in the tenth century. Much later the Chinese were taught the use of tobacco, in the preparation of which opium and certain other drugs were used. The Emperor attempted to check the growth of the habit by Imperial Edict, but the only result was that eventually the tobacco was discarded and the opium smoked alone.

Great Britain and the other European countries dealt in the contraband extensively during the eighteenth century. After 1810 America was tarred with the same brush. To be sure, our government disavowed all responsibility for those dealing in opium traffic, and there were many honest merchants who had no part in the trade, but unscrupulous men in every country made fortunes. The Chinese government made repeated efforts to restrict and abolish the traffic, but the avarice of Chinese officials and the foreign traders, and the ease with which opium could be smuggled into China through the hundreds of small bays along the southern coast, made the efforts worse than useless. Generally speaking the Americans smuggled Turkish opium, the British that grown in India.

Before the so-called "Opium War" between Great Britain and China, opium was a not inconsiderable part of American imports into China, and supplied perhaps one-third of the total imports from all the countries trading with the Empire. In addition, it was grown on a large scale in China.

A long series of disagreements, in which the opium traffic played only a minor part, led to the "Opium War." Subsequently the traffic was legalized by treaty because both Chinese and British officials felt that a complete prohibition was impossible. This was in 1840. The traffic grew. So did the production in China. So did the opposition until finally in 1907 the Indian and Chinese governments made an agreement by which Indian exports of opium to China would be reduced ten per cent of the amount then exported each year, and China would reduce the area under opium cultivation proportionately. A wave of enthusiasm for opium suppression swept over China. By 1911 the growth of opium in the empire was practically at an end.

Then came the confusion following the establishment of the Republic; opium growing revived because the military chiefs found it profitable. Nevertheless the steady reduction of the export to China by the Indian government continued. Since March 31, 1917, not an ounce of Indian opium has been shipped to China legally, and on that date, too, opium ceased to be a legally importable product in China.

But opium is still produced and smuggled into the country in huge amounts. An added misfortune is the smuggling of opium derivatives, morphine and heroin, in appalling proportions. The business of growing or dealing in this drug is highly profitable. No one knows how much opium is grown in China now. Although public opinion is strongly on the side of complete prohibition and government authorities have tried from time to time to make this opinion effective, governmental authority has been too weak to accomplish very much. Government officials have also, in many cases, been at the bottom of the business, although foreigners must also bear the stigma of having accumulated vast fortunes from the narcotic traffic.

The bare mention of the word opium brings to my mind such vivid pictures of tragedies that I have witnessed, such fearful destruction of life, morals, self-respect, health and prosperity, such wretchedness and degradation, destitution and suffering, that my heart grows heavy as I write. No words of mine can describe this awful curse of China. Happy, wealthy homes have been made destitute, wives and children have been sold, thefts and murders committed that opium might be obtained.

I think the least unhappy experience I had with an opium addict concerned an old postman who was dismissed from the service because of his slavery to the habit. When he found himself without work and without money, he consented to enter the hospital to see if we could cure him. After a month he was discharged, looking fat and well, and in response to our questions as to his future prospects, he smilingly assured us that he had a profession very like that of a gentleman. He would "buy fish and sell it in a basket on the street." From postman to fish vendor seemed to us rather a "Dutch" promotion.

But the last time I saw him he was holding a responsible position in the very office from which he had been dismissed in disgrace. Certainly he looked a very different man from the poor wretch who used to come with the mail at dusk, and pressing his gray emaciated face against the windowpane, cry in Chinese,

"Faster, Doctor, faster! The night has come, the road is long, and beset with terrors, and my heart is filled with fear."

Men and women with the opium habit were never taken

into the wards of the Soochow Hospital unless they came of their own accord and asked to be cured. I found it useless to attempt the cure of an unwilling subject. At that, countless cases found their way to us for cure. Some were tragic, others amusing. I remember one official in particular who wanted the cure and who had taken several steps in the right direction, but never had quite the courage to go all the way. Back he would go to his pipe.

I finally induced him to make one last try. In my firmest and sweetest tones I told him of a new and painless method. It really was new for I'd just thought it up; we'd tried almost everything on him. After strenuous coaxing on my part he consented and was given our best room and two bottles of medicine. Painstakingly I told him what to do and had him repeat the instructions regarding the bottles over and over until there was no danger of his forgetting or confusing them. Then, I left him in the charge of a private nurse, telling him we'd talk about the cure later, when he had finished his preparatory medicine.

At the end of four weeks I went back. "What about the cure?" he asked.

"Why, you are cured," I answered, "and you've done it yourself." I explained.

I had given him two bottles of medicine, one white and one pink. There was a solution of opium in the white bottle, a harmless colored water in the pink. I had asked him to take one teaspoonful from the white at short intervals and after each internal dose replace the amount taken from the white bottle with a teaspoonful of the pink bottle mixture. Then, when both bottles were empty, he was to send for me. He had followed instructions and for a week or more he had been spooning out doses of the harmless water and hadn't even missed the opium.

Truth compels me to admit that this was our easiest cure and most unusual.

Across the street from the Woman's Hospital in Soochow an opium-dealer kept a small shop and lived there with his wife and child. He cooked his opium daily in a huge copper kettle. One day, as was his custom, after the opium had cooked to the correct consistency, he set it out to cool on a low stool just beside the door.

Before returning to his duties in the shop he stopped to pat the head of his two-year-old child, playing in the street. Soon the sweet smell emanating from the kettle attracted the child, and she toddled over to it. She dipped tiny fingers in the sticky mess, then put them to her mouth. She liked the sweet taste, and fingers traveled back and forth from kettle to mouth several times.

Later when the mother went to look for the child she found her lying beside the pot, practically dead.

They brought the mother and the child to the hospital, the mother in an agonizing state of grief. But we could do nothing. The child died. The sorrowing father continued to cook his opium in the little shop across the street.

In 1844 when the Manchu Dynasty came to the throne an Imperial Edict was issued forbidding women to bind their feet or those of their daughters. So far as I know it was never obeyed at all, and it was not until China awoke to the need of reform in the days following the Boxer Rebellion that this particular evil of Chinese life came to an end.

The missions had been exerting pressure in this direction for many years. Of all the work the missions have done, nothing, to my mind, has been more productive of good results than the efforts of the Anti-footbinding Society. Nowadays the up-to-the-minute Chinese man desires a bride with a Western education and *dah kyak*, large feet!

Shortly after I settled in Soochow a woman came into the

clinic to ask me to amputate her toes. Her feet had been bound in such a way as to make walking extremely painful, but as the toes were in tolerably good condition, I refused to amputate them unless she would agree to unbind her own feet and those of her daughter. She would not agree to these terms under any circumstances. She got down on her knees and begged to have the toes amputated. When I remained adamant she departed in a towering rage, asserting that the gods would do for her what I had refused. Whether they did or not I never heard.

In the footbinding process many a child's life was sacrificed. *Fo-yung* (Happy Sound) was brought to us by the Chinese slave owner who had purchased her for sixty dollars (Mexican). Her feet had been bound and then in the very cold weather they became frost-bitten. When she arrived at the hospital they were in such a dreadful state from neglect that I decided the only way to save her life was to amputate both the legs, just below the knee. We were sure she would die, but she didn't. She soon became quite a favorite patient and stayed with us a long time because her Chinese owner, deciding she would be a total loss to him, was willing to leave her in our hands. We kept her for several years; we could not bear the thought of her return to a home where she was not wanted, or to the worse misery of a Chinese refuge. I once visited such an institution and never had I seen such squalor and general loathsomeness. It is impossible to describe. Later we found a place for her in a school, but not all the little Fo-yungs with bound feet had happy endings to their stories.

I was intensely interested in anti-footbinding propaganda and did everything in my power to aid and further the cause. When Mrs. Archibald Little, a pioneer in this work, came to Soochow I was delighted to give her a reception in my house. The hour set for the entertainment was three o'clock in the afternoon but by eleven an enormous crowd, of officials, all the leading gentry of the city, and Manchu ladies precariously balanced on their imitation small feet, filled the street. Incidentally, although the Manchus were able to force the Chinese men to wear the queue, they could do nothing with their own women who, while not binding their feet, wore their silk or satin shoes raised on wood blocked in imitation of the bound feet. The ladies came in coats embroidered in precious stones, wearing elaborate headdresses, their fingers and wrists heavily laden with jade and diamonds. They were followed by a mighty army of amahs bearing silver wash basins, face cloths, tea pots and all of the paraphernalia of a perfect lady, not forgetting silver water pipes and tobacco pouches.

Our hearts dropped to the bottom of our boots as we watched the crowd grow. Willingly, but anxiously because of a limited larder, hurried preparations were made for an impromptu meal. It is in such emergencies that the Chinese cook rises to show what he can do. Strange and mysterious are his methods; what he does not possess, he begs, borrows, or steals (it is wisest not to ask) and lo, he has worked his own version of the miracle of the loaves and fishes! In place of a well-ordered tea party to which some three or four hundred guests were invited, we had a reception which lasted five or six hours, commencing at eleven o'clock in the morning.

When the last cups of tea were set down, we adjourned to the church to listen to the lecture. Mrs. Little succeeded marvelously in keeping her audience interested, although to tell you the truth the proceedings often were interrupted by the ubiquitous amahs who padded around the church with hot face cloths, pots of tea and pipes, seeking to sooth their mistresses excited nerves.

But she aroused their enthusiasm, and during the evening a formal petition was sent in by the husbands and local officials asking that the lecture be repeated so that the men might hear the "wonderful foreign woman speak on a subject so important to every man."

Other meetings were held in Soochow and at one a fashionably dressed lady arose. In a bored voice she said:

"I am sick and weary. I am tired of hearing of my feet. I shall unbind them and join your society."

Although this was not what one might call a gracious capitulation, still capitulation it was, and a start, and many other ladies followed her example. Mrs. Little truly deserves a monument, for her initiative and tireless efforts were largely responsible for the abolition of footbinding in China.

It is a custom which originated many centuries ago, through the chance remark of an emperor whose favorite concubine was an exquisite dancer.

"Your feet are like golden lotus petals," he said, and immediately all the court ladies tried to crush their feet into shoes even smaller than the petals. The fashion spread from the court throughout the country, just as did that of wearing corsets when Catherine de Medici invented them. It has taken a little longer to correct the footbinding than the corset-wearing habit (and that hasn't entirely disappeared), but China is an old country and things move slowly there.

Chapter XIII

The Fire-Wheel Carriage and Other Developments

BEFORE THE OPENING OF THE FIRST SHOP FOR THE SALE OF FOR-
eign goods, a soap and cigarette shop, soap was an unknown article in Soochow. Women washed the clothes with the
aid of a huge stone and a vast expenditure of energy. They
would squat along the banks of the canal with their baskets of
soiled clothes, hammering them with a brick and scrubbing,
while they chatted with a neighbor on the right who was washing rice, and one on the left who was washing the containers of
the night-soil, all clubbily using the same water within easy
conversational distance of each other.

The introduction of soap created tremendous excitement,
excelled only by the arrival of another foreign innovation—the
"fire-wheel carriage."

The Chinese made dire threats against the Shanghai-Nanking
Railway and against the men who were to put it through the
countryside. They were in the grip of a paralyzing fear. The
task of the engineers, aside from having to cope with the
antagonism of the population, was a stupendous one, and it was
a great moment for the Europeans when the survey for the
road actually began.

Work on the Shanghai-Nanking Railway began in 1904. The
first engineer to come to Soochow was Mr. Graves W. Eves,
who, with his charming young wife, took up residence in the
houseboat, "Sunbeam," near the Tsong Mung, where the railway station now stands. Mr. Eves was the chief engineer for the

road from Shanghai to Soochow, while Mr. Frank Grove was in charge from Soochow to Chingkiang. During the survey of the road the "Sunbeam," and a larger boat, housing the unmarried engineers, were yulohed on to a given point where they awaited the return of the surveyors after their day's work. I often went with Mr. and Mrs. Eves on these surveys and the engineers on their return would relate the amusing incidents of the day.

The theodolite was an object of unfailing interest and terror to the Chinese. Great tact and much ingenuity were required when it was necessary to get a line through a house. But money makes a strong appeal in any language and when it was known that holes made through houses were repaired immediately and the owner generously remunerated into the bargain, buildings sprang up overnight in the surveyors' pathway, simply waiting to be looked through and paid for.

The actual ground-breaking was a great event. Never before had there been such a gathering. All the elite of the country were there, as well as business men representing every nationality in China. The curiosity of the Chinese country people surpassed their fear of the railway and an enormous crowd gathered to watch the strange spectacle of a spade thrust into the ground by Mr. King King-pow. Then Mr. A. H. Collinson, chief engineer, asked for my unofficial blessing and I too thrust a spade into the earth. For this slight effort a small silver spade, a replica of the one actually used in the breaking of the sod, was given to me and it is still a treasured possession.

Engineers tell wild tales of the difficulties they encountered in building railways in China. It was almost like putting a railway through a wilderness, with bad roads or no roads at all, and a superstitious and hostile people to deal with. But the Chinese reactions to the coming of the mysterious "foreign-dragon" were many and varied. During the process of construction a stray water-buffalo was killed, and when the terror-stricken owner

was asked what valuation he placed on the animal, he answered
he would pay whatever the railway authorities saw fit to
charge.

Not only animals, but people, were killed along that road
before it was opened to traffic. The Chinese, having overcome
their initial panic, found it a wonderfully direct route from
town to town, not, like the path through the rice fields, broken
by unbridged streams. When night fell many of them simply
lay down on the broken stone ballast (a Chinese of the coolie
class can sleep anywhere and at anytime), placed their heads on
the rail which was just the height of a Chinese pillow, and
slumbered blissfully, until a construction train came along to
decapitate them!

The railway promised to be even faster than the old foot-
boats and I, for one, was delighted with the coming of the
"fire-wheel carriage." Usually we traveled over the waterways of
China in houseboats or yuloh boats or we were carried across the
fields in sedan chairs. There were always four coolies to carry
the chair, two to do the actual work and two, running alongside,
to relieve them. The chair was slung from one pair to the other
without any interruption in the running. But when it was a
matter of life or death and speed was of paramount importance
we went in foot-boats, so called because the oars were pushed
with the feet, the rower sitting in front, the passenger sitting or
reclining in a cramped position behind him. The foot-boats, in
reality primitive canoes, were easily capsized, so you could
change your position only with the greatest patience and
caution. It was a frightfully uncomfortable way to travel but
it was fast and many were the times I foot-boated it from village to village and from patient to patient, along the creeks and
canals that crisscross China.

Mrs. Eves and I were the first women to make the trip by train
from Soochow to Shanghai. We were the only passengers, besides Mr. Collinson, and we rode on a dinky flat-car, the fore-

runner of the compartment-cars that later were to run along the same tracks. The journey took only a little more than three hours. What a difference from that first trip of mine from Shanghai to Soochow, when we traveled for three days and three nights!

Hand cars preceded us to make sure that there had been no tampering with the rails. Railway bolts and nuts, to say nothing of fishplates and spikes, were worth many coppers to any Chinese; nor was it an unusual event for the train to meet a water-buffalo head on, in which case the cowcatcher did its work according to tradition. Mr. Eves had promised his wife and me the exciting experience of a trip to Shanghai lashed to that cowcatcher, but when the time arrived he changed his mind and forbade the expedition as being too dangerous.

It was not many moons before the "fire-carriage" became so popular that traffic was seriously disturbed. This plethora of patronage which threatened to clog the wheels of transportation reminded me of a notice I once saw in Philadelphia on the door of a free medical clinic, "Closed on account of sickness."

My husband and I each had a part in this enterprise. He was appointed railway physician, which meant that all the wives and children fell to my lot. But the friends I made among the railway people more than compensated for the additional work.

The work in Soochow included attendance upon European and Chinese representatives of the Chinese Maritime Customs as well as of the Shanghai-Nanking Railway. The Customs concession was outside the Foo-meng, the city gate nearest our compound. It consisted of a group of substantial and very handsome office and residential buildings for members of the foreign staff. The many Chinese workers were boarded out in Chinese homes. The Shanghai-Nanking Railway Concession had similar quarters just outside the Tsaung-meng, the most important gate of the city and the most distant from us. When the Europeans were very ill we took them into our own home but as a general thing we supplied them with trained nurses and cared for them in their homes.

Few people are aware of the immense importance of the Customs Service. Historically, it goes back to 1842 before which time China had no fixed tariff rates. For many years it was the one sure source of income for the Chinese government. Nominally it has always been a department of the government, but actually since 1854 it has been under the control of foreigners. At that time, at the close of the Taiping Rebellion, Consul Alcock inaugurated foreign supervision to minimize confusion and insure integrity of management. But since 1928, when new treaties were signed giving China full power to fix her own tariff rates, a determined effort has been made to increase the Chinese proportion of the personnel.

It seemed to me in the days when my husband was Customs physician, that there were plenty of Chinese already employed by the service. The Customs service station, as I have said, was located at some distance from the Foo-meng and there were two ways, neither of them quick, by which we could go to the long list of waiting Customs patients. We could either walk to a boat or go along the wall to the city gate and from there be ferried across to the station. It meant an expenditure of time and energy but I was able to be of real assistance by taking charge of the women and children. Never before or since have I met so many confinement cases in such a record breaking short space of time!

It was during the autumn of 1905 that we began to hear disquieting rumors of trouble in Shanghai, fomented apparently by students who had been educated abroad, particularly in Japan. The outcome of the Russo-Japanese war had a decided effect on the Chinese psychology. It strengthened the underlying resentment against foreign control; if a small Asiatic power could be victorious in arms, why then should China with greater resources, greater man power, and far greater land area, be kept under the thumbs of Westerners? Formerly it had been the literati who influenced public opinion but in 1905 it was the students who swayed their countrymen and summoned them to action.

The first evidence of the new attitude was the boycott of the American trade in retaliation for the restriction of Chinese immigration to the United States. The government was not behind the boycott, but the movement was popular and students kept the people in a turmoil until the Chinese traders found they were losing too much by it and turned cold shoulders on the agitation.

But Shanghai particularly was in a state of ferment and only a slight excuse was needed for the city to explode again. The excuse came when some women were brought before the Mixed Court and charged with kidnapping girls for unlawful purposes. To the Chinese the Mixed Court in the Shanghai Settlement was decidedly a sore spot. They regarded the regulation that a consular assessor should be a party to the judgment in every case as an infringement of their sovereign rights. There had been arguments about the presence of Municipal Police in the courtroom and about the custody of women prisoners. Prisoners of the Mixed Court usually were taken to the Municipal Gaol as the Council considered that the cells of the Mixed Court Gaol were not fit for the housing of women prisoners; but the Tao tai strenuously objected to the women being sent to the Municipal Gaol because of the Chinese prejudice against handing over women to the custody of foreigners.

On the occasion of the arrest of the three women the British assessor ordered them removed to the Municipal Gaol pending trial. The Chinese magistrates objected and ordered them taken to the cells in the Mixed Court. A free-for-all followed between the police and the court runners before the police succeeded in getting the women and girls into their van. That was as far as they got, however, for the runners had barred the gates of the prison yard. The magistrate refused to have them opened and summarily dismissed court. After he had gone home, the gates were opened and the prisoners removed to the more commodious and sanitary Municipal Gaol.

The news of the episode spread quickly and lost nothing in repetition. Excitement was intense. Chinese authorities demanded an apology from the British assessor and the dismissal of the inspector and policemen concerned in the case. The case was further complicated by the fact that the leader of the three women was the widow of an official of Szechuan Province. Protests were made against such treatment of a Chinese lady of official rank.

Then the diplomatic corps in Peking stepped in with an order for the women's release on the ground that, as the Mixed Court had been closed by the order of the Tao tai, there was no court in which the women could be tried and it was unfair to keep them in custody indefinitely.

Meanwhile, the Shanghai Chinese had worked themselves up to fever heat. A general strike was threatened; they refused to pay municipal taxes; and there was an exodus of Chinese from the settlements. Chiefly because of violent propaganda, the mob daily grew more uncontrolled.

Unrest prevailed throughout the country. The Boxer uprising was still vivid in our minds, and also in the minds of the Chinese; only a small spark was needed to start a conflagration which might have far-reaching results. All foreign residents in the interior were called to the Treaty Ports. While we had been expecting something of the sort, it was startling to receive from our Consul-general in Shanghai the following message:

"All foreigners requested come Shanghai at once. Serious conditions existing. Riots."

We left at once. When we arrived at Shanghai and our houseboat was tied up at the Garden Bridge we were confronted by guards with guns and bayonets. Shanghai was a changed city.

My Days of Strength

One could feel tension in the air; the crowds in the streets were not the usual joyous, busy throngs, but an excited, threatening mob, sullen and resentful, kept under control for the moment by the armed patrols which guarded the streets on all sides. One breathed danger in the very atmosphere, and I was reminded horribly of the sight which had met me on my return to Soochow—the seventy-five swinging buckets with their gruesome contents and dangling queues.

What was coming? Would the small body of volunteers and the forces landed so hurriedly be able to control the mob? What if the mob broke loose? Futile speculations raced through my mind as we drove up Nanking Road escorted by a company of marines between a double line of blue jackets, all with fixed bayonets.

My husband and I were called into service immediately, but I cannot remember clearly the details of the night following our arrival. I only know that it was hectic. Relief work was organized and first aid instructions given. The city was under martial law and every man, woman and child, knew where to seek refuge at a given signal in case of emergency. Shanghai at that time had an excellent volunteer corps but it was far too small to afford protection except in a limited number of localities.

The whole foreign population was on guard that night. Word had reached us that the city was to be burned and that at a gunshot signal fires, previously prepared, were to be lighted simultaneously in hundreds of widely separated sections, thus making it impossible for the fire brigade to answer all the calls. Men did police duty around their own homes, keeping a strict lookout for incendiaries. Indoors, the women watched, and waited for the signal which meant they were to seek safety in the segregation center to which they had been assigned, where there would be armed protection. There were nightmarish hours when the worst seemed bound to happen. But for some reason

136

these plans failed to materialize and after a long and anxious night, morning found the city anything but a mass of cinders and ash.

That day several automobiles were demolished, among others the British vice consul's, which was set on fire in the middle of Nanking Road. Some of the men, unable to reach home in any other way, were seen tearing up Nanking Road on a fire engine.

One woman started to market but was turned back by a guard at the bridge and reached her home just as the surrounding streets filled with a mass of howling and raging Chinese. Garden gates were slammed shut hastily, and shutters closed and bolted. Everywhere women and children were scurrying to shelter before the mob came upon them. Men were torn from rickshaws and the clothing wrenched from their backs. Others emerged from fights with heads bleeding.

It was unnerving to see men kneeling on seats of brokers' traps, keeping the crowds away with loaded guns. Dr. J. W. Jackson, a British physician with whom I was to work in later years, was dragged from his carriage, his watch snatched from his pocket, and his head badly bashed, although he was not seriously injured. It was all terrifying, especially to a woman alone, who could only peep from behind closed shutters and wonder what she would do if the mob should burst into the garden and attack the house.

I do not remember just how long the trouble remained acute. It was throttled almost immediately in Shanghai, for the pickets landed from warships were able to disperse the crowds almost at once.

The aftermath of this affair was a meeting between the Chinese and officials of the Municipal Council. The question of the presence of the Municipal Police at the Mixed Courts was settled, and it was decided that women prisoners should be housed there, with the stipulation that suitable quarters be provided for them, and that the premises should be frequently inspected by the Municipal Health Officer.

The trouble was over for the time being and after a few weeks we returned to Soochow and three years of steady, routine work.

Again I took the place of Dr. Margaret Polk at the Soochow Woman's Hospital, while she went on a much needed holiday trip to America. My capable assistant doctor was Zak Foh-me who had been a neophyte nurse on that long ago September day of 1893 when I had my first glimpse of Soochow and the hospital. Three years later she was one of the first students graduated from my co-educational medical school.

Nothing extraordinary marked our days except for the plans my husband and I made for our first journey around the world, then a great event. The chief item of interest in connection with the hospital during these last Soochow days was the medical school graduation in 1904. This was a grand occasion. His Excellency En Show, Governor of the Province and ruler of twenty million people, presented the diplomas and sat on the platform with forty-eight other high Chinese officials, all gorgeously arrayed in satin and peacock feathers. We had come a long, long way from that first graduation in 1896.

The most important event of a personal nature was when the parents of twenty-seven better class babies, representing nine different nationalities, that I had delivered during the year 1906-1907 presented me with a silver cup engraved with the names of the babies. I have kept the cup, but the babies are scattered all over the world.

My Soochow days were drawing to a close. Dr. Fearn and I, before setting out on our globe-girdling tour, had decided that we would leave Soochow and China for all time and establish our home in America.

CHAPTER XIV

At the Eight Fairy Bridge

M<small>Y HUSBAND RESIGNED FROM THE MISSIONARY BOARD AND WE</small> said good-by to China forever, or so we thought, and returned to America to spend the remainder of our days. But his heart was in China and I was more than willing to go back. So, in the face of many splendid opportunities in the United States, Dr. Fearn accepted an invitation to act as business manager of the Associated Protestant Missions in China. This time Shanghai, not Soochow, was to be our home.

I must have been very young when I first read the travels of Marco Polo. I remember that I would sit for hours, entranced by his descriptions of the glories of that country, the Land of the Lotus Eater. It was a land of enchantment, dazzling my eyes with the gleam of gems, of rubies and sapphires and pearls, jasper and jade. I read of garments of richest texture, of satin and silk embroidered with pearls. In fancy I wandered through the palaces of marble, and journeyed over the wondrous bridges that spanned the rivers; I marveled at the ten thousand sacred horses and mares of Kublai Khan and the rich appointments of his palace; and with the shrewd, quick-eyed Italian I traveled through the rich and fertile lands of the great Khan.

But Marco Polo, with all his tales of the wealth of gold and silver and copper, only skimmed the surface of that immense country. The marvels of China continue, in a different form, for present-day enterprise is beginning to uncover vast subterranean veins of unexplored wealth; of iron, coal and other minerals which are more valuable to the modern world than the jewels and gold of Kublai Khan's time.

My Days of Strength

And the port of entry to this country of treasure; this country of contrasts, of culture and crudities, of riches and poverty, is Shanghai.

The old Shanghai was first mentioned in history two thousand years ago under its original name of "Hu," indicating that it began as a fishing village. In 1280 A.D. the Chinese renamed it Shanghai or "Upper Sea" and by that time it was well on its way to being a thriving commercial port. It was not until 1843 that it was opened to foreign trade, as one of the five treaty ports acquired by the British at the end of the "Opium War." In Canton, Amoy, Foochow, Ningpo and Shanghai, foreign merchants and their families were allowed "to reside for the purpose of carrying on their mercantile pursuits, without molestation or restraint."

The other nations were not slow to take advantage of this opening wedge, and soon the settlement included American, French and English. By 1849 the number of foreign residents had increased from fifty to one hundred and seventy-five. They suffered many inconveniences, much discomfort and the intermittent hostility of their hosts. It was several years before the actual boundaries of the settlement were determined, and longer before satisfactory protection and efficient sanitation could be provided.

The Bund was originally a muddy road, used as a tow path by the Chinese. Today it is a handsome street with a wide sweep of greensward separating it from the smaller jetties that fringe the busy Whangpoo, burstingly alive with every kind of river life.

Shanghai has a fascination of which I was conscious when I first saw the city, when the one word that expressed my feeling for it was the word I cabled to my mother—"Delight." Perhaps it is bred of a subconscious excitement in the thought that here East meets West in a jumble of co-operation, misunderstanding, struggle, friendship; here they go their separate ways side by side.

Shanghai is a city of hustling, bustling, hurrying, scurrying, jostling millions; a city of noise and confusion, tramcars clanging gongs, motor cars tooting horns, coolies sing-songing their interminable "ah ye—ah—yees." Chinese men walk the streets dressed in their traditional long silk gowns, blue cotton ones, or in the latest Western style. Some Chinese women are beautifully dressed, with smart waved heads, silk stockings and high-heeled shoes, and some cling to the divided skirts and embroidered jackets of tradition. There are Japanese, Indians, Annamites and Europeans, a conglomeration of every nationality under the sun.

The traffic—foot, rickshaw, hand cart, wheelbarrow, bicycle, motor car, bus, tramcar—is stupendous. Occasionally a passage has to be cleared for a patrol of mounted Sikhs on beautifully groomed horses, carrying lances from whose tips float red and white pennons. They are on their way to head some parade, a picturesque and colorful sight. There are crowds everywhere, not only hurrying and jostling crowds moving about the streets, but silent, gaping crowds. What many Chinese do I have never been able to fathom, not in all my years in China. They stand in groups and stare at nothing or everything. They never seem to be doing anything or going anywhere. They are content to stand still and stare, to meditate perhaps, to obstruct traffic certainly.

There can be no comparison from an artistic standpoint between Shanghai and Soochow. Shanghai, the one-time mud flat which the Chinese ironically sold or leased to the "foreign devils" as their segregation quarter, was a swampy waste, a hot bed of malaria, undrained and uncultivated, its only road a wheelbarrow track. Good enough for the foreigner, the "outside barbarian," to live in and, hopeful thought, to die in. But out of this the "foreign devil" evolved a sumptuous city.

My Days of Strength

In the early days of the century when we moved from Soochow to Shanghai, via Europe and America, the city had few large buildings, an occasional automobile and a population of only two hundred and seventy-five thousand, including both Chinese and foreigners. Now it is a city of nearly four million. Many of the organizations with which my life was to be concerned were either in their embryonic stages or were just amoeboid ideas. But the present city was germinating, more rapidly than we then realized.

Our new home was situated in Rue Palikao, number one hundred and twenty-two. The Chinese designated it as *Pah Sien-jau*, or "At the Eight Fairy Bridge." The missionaries called it Poverty Flat. It was one of the first mission houses built in Shanghai, a large, rambling eight-room house in the same compound with old Trinity Church. We were in the French Concession, only a block or two from the race course and from Nanking Road, which the Chinese called *Tai Ma Loo* (Great Horse Road). We were rather uncomfortably close to the native city but once we were inside the garden gate the charm of the place made us forget its disadvantages.

We had so many rooms we didn't need that I furnished a few for the missionaries who came to Shanghai from Korea and the interior, and as long as we lived "At the Eight Fairy Bridge" the visiting missionaries were always welcome.

Before we left Soochow we had been loaded down with silver, gifts from our friend the Governor and other high Chinese officials, and from customs and railway patients we had known there. The silver cups and platters, candelabra and bowls were really quite beautiful; I had them advantageously displayed in the living room. I remember soon after we opened our home to the traveling missionaries, a couple came from a primitive hill station in Korea. The wife examined my lovely collection and then said, "Oh, Mrs. Fearn, how do you keep your pewter so bright?"

142

I didn't correct her. It would have been too difficult to explain how a poor missionary family had annexed all that gorgeous silver.

The missionaries sometimes stayed overnight, at other times for weeks or months. They came to have their babies, to have typhoid fever, diphtheria or malaria. In those days missionaries had to pay their own medical bills and their salaries were small —$500 a year if single, $700 a year if married.

One time a woman from an interior mission came to Shanghai to stay with me for a few days. She was taken suddenly ill and called in an English doctor, an old friend. The doctor came now and then but he was callous toward missionaries, knowing how little money they had. One day, a month or so after the woman's arrival, I heard steps on the stairs and walking out into the hall came face to face with her doctor. He beamed broadly at me.

"And how is Mrs. ———, may I ask?"

"You may," I said, "and I will tell you; she is dead and buried."

That's the only time I've ever been really annoyed with another doctor.

I was practically a stranger in Shanghai, and after the first excitement of settling a new home had subsided I found that I missed Soochow and my own work with a poignancy that made me restless and dissatisfied. A period of apparently aimless drifting was opening for me, although I was never without some work to do. For several years I was to expend my energy on various activities without finding the one channel into which they could flow with complete satisfaction. It was a new experience for me and not wholly a happy one.

I was drafted immediately to help at the "Door of Hope," a rescue home for Chinese girls who had run away from enforced lives of slavery and prostitution. Its story is really remarkable. One Christmas morning just at the turn of the century Miss

C. Bonnel was riding through the streets of Shanghai in her rickshaw when she saw a little slave girl being dragged, screaming and kicking, along the pavement. She was trying futilely to fight her way free from her burly captor. Miss Bonnel decided then and there that she would devote her life to freeing these girls who so obviously wanted to be free. After a time she persuaded the Mixed Court to promise her that if any girl could escape from a brothel and find her way to the tiny room on Hankow Road, she would be safe. Once there her owner could not touch her.

These girls, poor little waifs or in many cases mere babies who had been sold into slavery by elder brothers and fathers, ran away by the score, found Miss Bonnel's room and dashed through the always open doorway into the waiting arms of the amah. Often the irate owner was following close behind but he dared not step over that doorsill.

The "Door of Hope" had long ago outgrown this one small room when I arrived in Shanghai. It had merged with an institution known as the "Slave Refuge," founded by Deaconess Maude Henderson, which had as its object the rescue of slave girls rather than of prostitutes.

The girls came to us brutally beaten and cruelly mistreated. Almost all of them were found to be horribly diseased. I made daily visits to the home to give them treatments, for their venereal infections, bind up their broken bones, their suppurating sores, their mutilated bodies. They were dreadful to look upon. But after they had regained their health in some measure they were given an education, training in an occupation such as cooking, sewing or embroidery, and husbands were found for them. Now the "Door of Hope" is a flourishing institution and no Chinese girl is disgraced if she has been an inmate of it; many graduate from there into good marriages.

Very soon after I came to Shanghai, I offered to contribute my services as clinician to the Margaret Williamson Hospital for the Chinese. The hospital, in Chinese territory, was for women only. It was equipped with about one hundred beds and a staff of Chinese nurses under the direction of an American trained nurse. Dr. Elizabeth Reifsnyder and her associate, Dr. Emily Garner, were in charge. Both these women were regular missionaries and excellent doctors and I welcomed the opportunity to be of assistance to them.

The clinic was open in the afternoon from twelve-thirty until six, and treated from one hundred to five hundred patients daily, the number being regulated by the weather. On rainy days, when they could not work in the fields, the women came in droves. It was grinding, heartbreaking work, but the next best thing to work of my own and infinitely better than idleness. People in all sorts of trouble came to us, but malaria was our greatest and most frequent problem. The poorer classes especially, with their lack of cleanliness and sanitation of any sort, were hopelessly susceptible to this disease. Before the advent of the foreigner with his "white medicine" (quinine), they had no means of combating it and long indeed was the death roll. There were days when it seemed as if every woman who took her seat before me simply pointed a finger upward—"Heaven has called me!" A silent evidence of their hopelessness, for they had no word for malaria.

My hours at the office were busy ones. I opened boils, amputated fingers, rescued flesh-imbedded needles with magnets, applied applications to sore eyes, pulled teeth. I remember one old woman who came to the clinic and had five teeth pulled without once closing her mouth. The teeth were loose and the extraction was done without anesthetic.

I think that one of my most amusing experiences was reducing three dislocated jaws in one hour. One old woman had dislocated her jaw yawning, the second had hers done for her by an irate son-in-law, and the third woman's "just happened" while she was eating her breakfast.

My Days of Strength

I think of scabies when I think of Margaret Williamson days. Scabies were my particular horror and even now when I get a whiff of sulphur ointment I'm back again at the clinic, treating a long line of patients afflicted with skin diseases. Skin diseases and sore eyes were prevalent all over China in those days. They still are. There were a good many cases of trachoma, blepharitis marginalis, and pterygium, which is often confused by the laity with cataract because both end in blindness.

The Chinese who came to the Margaret Williamson clinic had about as much idea of cleanliness as the ones I had left behind me in Soochow. In the middle of the day, on my way to the hospital, I would find the ordure being removed casually from the streets and gutters; the native city was innocent of the most primitive sanitation, a forcing house for smallpox or worse.

The horn-rip cases were our worst. Before being brought to us, they were frequently treated with cow-dung plasters, a common device of native therapeutics. I remember one particularly awful horn-rip case that was brought to me. A twelve-year-old girl was tending a water-buffalo in the fields across the creek when the buffalo, usually a friendly animal, especially with children, ran amuck. The child, frightened, started running and screaming toward her home. The buffalo, ramping in pursuit, caught her with his horn and ripped the abdomen open from the pelvis. The father, who was working near by, rushed to her side. He found her on the ground, her bowels gored out. He stuffed them back and packed the wound with cow-dung from a handy heap and brought her to us. We cleaned her up as well as possible and, because of the odor, as quickly as we could, and made an attempt to replace the bowels. She died a victim of tetanus as well as the goring.

Theoretically I was to do only clinic work at the Margaret Williamson Hospital but actually I performed many emergency operations. I could not escape, it seemed, from my predestined task of bringing babies into the world.

At the Eight Fairy Bridge

Once a man, greatly agitated, rushed into the room accompanying a litter which held his wife, who was obviously enceinte and, I feared, dying. Only with difficulty was I able to drag his story from him bit by bit. Between gesticulations and tears he told me that his wife was expecting a baby at almost any minute. He loved his wife so very dearly that just to help her he had lowered himself to the humiliating work of peeling vegetables. That afternoon as he sat outside the door scraping sweet potatoes with a long knife, which was sharpened down both sides to a fine point, his wife had playfully taunted him about doing "amah-coolie pidgin" (the most menial tasks) and then had run from him as quickly as her heavy body would let her. Just as playfully he had pursued her, brandishing the knife. She had turned unexpectedly, and unintentionally he had run the knife, to the hilt, into the abdomen.

Would I save her? Could I save the child?

I said I would try, and made speedy preparations for a Caesarean. The mother died. I took the child from the uterus in what at first seemed to be the second stage of asphyxia, but quickly discovered that the baby was dead. Then I noticed a tiny red spot on its breast; performing a post-mortem I discovered that the heart had been pierced by the knife. The father's playful gesture had lost him his wife and a son, for the knife had entered not only the mother's abdomen but the uterus and fetal heart.

A Chinese widower without progeny always made all haste to get himself another wife. Dr. Fearn's Number One Boy came to him a day or two after his wife's death. He wanted to borrow three hundred dollars for burial expenses. My husband remonstrated with him.

"Surely," he said, "you can get a simple funeral costing much less. Must you spend so much money and go so deeply into debt?"

"Oh, yes," replied the Boy, "one hundred dollars can do

funeral, plenty good. Two hundred dollars must payee, catchee new wife."

Sterility is the worst possible thing that can befall a Chinese wife. Her chief mission in life is to multiply and replenish. They came to the clinic in hundreds, begging me to help them, promising to give me anything they had, which usually was nothing. In a few cases I could help. If the husband were sterile or if disease had ravaged the woman, leaving her sterile, then, of course, treatment was useless. But often, if I could persuade them to undergo slight operations, I could help them. Many times it was necessary merely to straighten a retroverted or anteverted uterus. One woman whose tilted uterus I put back in its proper place later gave birth to several children. After each birth, to show her gratitude, she presented me with a handsome pair of roosters.

Once a woman from a very poor family came to the clinic leading her prospective daughter-in-law, a girl of about thirteen.

"What is the matter with her? She is sick and cannot work."

A simple examination revealed that the girl was pregnant. I explained this, expecting the old woman to fly into a rage. To my surprise she took the news calmly.

"Now," she grinned toothlessly, "we won't have to spend all that money on a wedding."

It was the custom of the Chinese of the poorer classes to send the bride-to-be to the groom's family as soon as she was old enough to help with the work, in the fields or in the house. In that way, as far as both families were concerned, a liability was converted into an asset. Human nature being what it is, it often turned out that she was even less of a liability and saved her in-laws the cost of an elaborate wedding; fond as the Chinese are of weddings and funerals, only virgins in China rate weddings with all the trimmings. But there are no illegitimate babies in China.

Until I crossed the threshold of the Margaret Williamson

Hospital it had been a long time since I'd walked into a well-equipped laboratory. In Soochow, our laboratory facilities were practically primitive and, lacking other assistance, we made our diagnosis from symptoms. I had always had a sort of sixth sense for it, however, and my diagnosis, often given in the face of concerted opposition, usually was correct. Don't ask me how or why. It is one of the many mysteries I've never been able to solve.

I was vacationing one summer at Mokanshan, a cool mountain resort above Hangchow. One of the missionaries, a woman from Ningpo, had her leg in a cast. Her husband, a doctor, had diagnosed it as tuberculosis of the bone. So certain was he that there was no chance of saving the leg that he was leaving immediately for Shanghai to get the proper instruments for amputation. He asked me to take the case until his return and to prepare his wife for operation. I agreed.

I didn't think it was tuberculosis of the bone, so as soon as he was out of sight I took the liberty of removing the cast. One whiff and I knew I was right. I could tell by the smell that it was rheumatoid arthritis; there was no mistaking that acidulous odor. The doctor returned, slightly surprised. I begged him to let me have the patient for just two days longer. I promised I would watch her every minute. He consented. I gave her 120 grains of sodium salicylate, closely observing her heart reactions. At the end of two days there was no pain. I lessened the doses. At the end of the week she was up and walking on two legs. She is still walking.

We were careful at the clinic to assuage the fears of the Chinese patients who were easily frightened. For instance, we never used the stethoscope on them until they had complete confidence in us. Then they didn't mind the *ting-ting ḳasan* (listening instrument). At first the X-ray apparatus frightened them almost to death. But far more frightened than the Chinese ever thought of being was the Japanese consul in Soochow.

My Days of Strength

I remember that we were very proud of our first X-ray equipment which was installed shortly before we left for America. Anxious to show it off to all the important people, we invited them to come one afternoon and view this wonderful machine. One of the doctors explained the workings.

"You can see the heart beat," he said. "Try it."

The Chinese governor popped himself into the frame at once and posed there, pleased as a small child. The Japanese consul, however, refused, nor could we persuade him. Perhaps he thought that his heart might be read.

In spite of the modern conveniences and equipment the Margaret Williamson clinic was the saddest place in the world; not even in Soochow had I seen so much suffering. Here I had only the sorrow of observing their ills, seldom the joy of watching their recovery, for there were few opportunities to follow the clinic cases through. The patients came, were given medicine or treatment, and wandered away, save for a few special cases kept under observation. In respect to my clinic work, Shanghai was like Soochow—the same Chinese patients, the same diseases, the same overpowering scents. But I knew that there was another Shanghai if I could only find it.

In a previous chapter I spoke of a few of the horrors of opium and the attempts made to reduce its import and export. I was intensely interested in the opium question and when the International Opium Conference was held in Shanghai in February of 1909 I welcomed the opportunity to sit in on the proceedings as an unofficial observer. I never missed a meeting.

The invitation came to me through an old friend, Mr. Frank Carl, the brother of Kate Carl, the American artist, who achieved the impossible by painting the portrait of the old Empress Dowager, Tzu-hsi. Mr. Carl was an official delegate, representing the Chinese customs which naturally was very much concerned with the problem.

Regulations were adopted by all the nations to aid China

in her fight against this dangerous drug. Locally, the movement was received with enthusiasm. Dives in the native city already had been closed and steps were being taken by the council to cancel licenses of the opium divans in the International Settlement. Then came another swift change of government, and with the coming of the Republic the cultivation of the poppy was condoned rather than discountenanced; it was a source of revenue. There are now stringent laws for opium suppression, and various anti-opium organizations carry on vigorous crusades to arouse the people to its evils. Nevertheless, the sickly-sweet smell of opium continues to impregnate the Shanghai atmosphere.

This conference was directly responsible for the widening of both my interests and my circle of friends. While it was still going on I gave the first of a long list of semi-diplomatic affairs, and started on my career as a Shanghai hostess. I had always loved big parties, but I hadn't had much chance to entertain on a large scale in the mission compounds of Soochow and Shanghai, I remember that I gave an afternoon reception to all the delegates. Mrs. Harry de Gray, whose husband was for many years the chairman of the Shanghai Municipal Council, helped me receive such distinguished men as Viceroy Taun Feng, China's representative; The Right Reverend Charles H. Brent, Bishop of the Philippines and Chairman of the Conference; Sir Cecil Clementi-Smith, the Senior British delegate; Mr. W. L. Mackenzie King, later Canadian Labor Minister; Mr. L. O. Ratard, the French Consul-General; Tao Tai Yu Yaching; Dr. Hamilton Wright, one of the Americans; Mr. R. Laidlaw, Member of Parliament; Minister A. A. de Jongh of Holland; and Sir Alexander Hosie, whose wife, Lady Dorothea Hosie, daughter of the great Confucian scholar, Professor William Edward Soothill, later became one of my closest friends. There were many others whose names I have long since forgotten.

My Days of Strength

The cosmopolitan character of the social life of the city held a strong fascination for me, as it does for most people who go there; so when a note came from the secretary of the American Women's Club, inviting me to join them, I hailed the idea with eagerness. The club, now in existence for over forty years, was the outgrowth of a small reading circle founded by five American women in 1898. Its purpose, among other things, was to knit the American community in Shanghai more closely together.

I was elected corresponding secretary almost immediately and felt that here at last was something to interest me, some specific work for me to do. The activities of the club were so far-reaching I hoped to be able to use up a little of my pent-up energy. It did occupy the greater part of my spare hours for many years, especially later when I was elected president, an office to which I was returned several times.

But my days were not yet complete and I was not happy. I wanted more work, particularly work that had more meaning for me.

CHAPTER XV

Pestilence and Prestige

IT WAS IN THE SPRING OF 1909 THAT THE GREAT HUAI RIVER
flooded the country. The distress that seized that part of
China was so terrible that the whole world waked suddenly
to the realization of her exigency. Enormous quantities of
grain, flour and money poured into the country, most of it
through the agency of the Red Cross.

My husband was sent with two young men to Anhui Province. They took food and money and they stayed for weeks,
directing the work of draining the soil, building temporary
dams and levees until expert engineers arrived to install the
permanent structures. They distributed food and paid the wages
of those who were able to labor for their own living.

At first the people seemed a hopeless lot; spineless and
amorphous as jellyfish. What had they to live for? Famine,
plague or death. That had been the fate of their fathers. It
was theirs. It would be the fate of their children. They were
too exhausted to try to save themselves. Dying mothers sat with
their dead babies in their arms, waiting the grim call for themselves. They gnawed bark stripped from trees, and stared with
dull eyes at those who tried to help them.

No matter how hard the rescuers worked, no matter how
heroically the missionaries toiled, the numbers they could save
were pitifully and tragically few compared with the thousands
who could not be reached in time.

I spent a week with my husband and his two companions
in a queer little three-room bungalow, surrounded by a mud-
floored veranda which was piled to the ceiling with cases of

copper cash. Here these three men labored like heroes to "save life." They lived with fewer personal possessions than soldiers in action. I remember that there were three shaving mugs which were also called into service for tea and coffee, and one cup and saucer, a most effete touch, which fell to my lot by courtesy.

A year later there was a repetition of the same condition—the Huai River had not yet been brought under control—and the three went back to take up once more their work among the destitute, the dying and the dead.

The horror of it is that even as I write the same tragedy goes on in China. In the past the Chinese have talked a great deal about their sovereign rights, unequal treaties, extraterritoriality, but until lately they themselves have done little to lessen the sufferings of their own people. Now, however, there is no question but that they are fully aware of their responsibilities. Under the present regime, at least until the current "Trouble," dams and dykes were being built, although it is often impossible to keep them in good repair. It takes a great deal of money, and money is needed for a thousand other important operations, chief among them the vanquishing of the war lords, the bandits and the ubiquitous Japanese. Year after year flood, pestilence and famine continue to do their worst among the unfortunate country people.

The small farmers in the districts subject to flood and drought live from hand to mouth in any case. They live in rickety one-room shacks; they till their fields the same way their ancestors did thousands of years before. They have only themselves to rely on for protection of their property against roaming bandits and robber gangs. They are taxed literally both coming and going, for there are duties to be paid when they go into a town to trade and duties on everything they bring out with them.

When there are floods hundreds of these over-taxed victims

are driven from their homes. I have seen them toiling along the roads, trundling their household goods in wheelbarrows, with an old mother riding on top, perhaps, and half a dozen children trailing close along beside. Where they are going they do not know, but certainly to a life little better than that from which they have fled.

These conditions have existed as long, or nearly as long, as China herself. China is old and vast and slow to move—but she is moving. Napoleon said, "China is a sleeping giant. Let her sleep!"

Nearly two thousand years before our era there was a drought which lasted seven years; there were tremendous floods of the Yellow River which the Chinese claim has its origin in the sea of stars but which has overflowed so many times it has come to be called China's Sorrow; there was a famine and great loss of life. Droughts and floods have alternated unceasingly and there are only a few years at the most when some part of the country has not been visited by one or another of these catastrophes.

Suffering at these times is greatly augmented by the inadequate communication between one part of the country and another. The road system is abominable and very little, until recently, was done to improve it. Even now many "highways" are merely narrow, rutted paths. The railway mileage is entirely insufficient, considering the immensity of the country. China's telegraph system is incredibly antiquated, a fact that has infinitely tragic implications. When that monstrous cataclysm took place in Kansu, when it was said "the mountains walked," it was three months before the news that three million had perished reached Peking, only a thousand miles away! It was estimated that one out of every three in the province was a taxpayer and after the earthquake they were short one million taxpayers.

In the days before the foreign devils came to China, with

their Western ideas of organization, their trained doctors and missionaries, the little help given these sufferers was of the most ineffectual kind. Even now, such help as we can get to them through the missionary societies, the Red Cross and other organizations, seems hardly more than a drop in the bucket when one of these devastating calamities swoops down upon a district. But it is something to know that much is being done, that the "sleeping giant" is now fully awake to his responsibilities. Of that giant I prophesy great things.

During the period of the 1909 flood, while my husband was away, giving his time and skill and strength to aid the flood victims, I remained unwillingly in Shanghai, my feeling of uselessness and discontent mitigated somewhat by the friendship and hospitality of my new friends. In my search for some object in life, I offered my services for the relief work being organized for the epidemic of pneumonic plague raging in Manchuria. My luck deserted me. My services were accepted but I was required to take the serum treatment before starting on my journey. And before this course was finished, I received a telegram that my place had been filled by a doctor on the spot who already had been primed with the serum.

In sheer desperation I turned to civic affairs in Shanghai.

It was early in 1910, I think, that four of America's largest battleships, commonly called the "Big Four," visited Shanghai. It was bitterly cold and it rained endlessly. Sailors coming ashore on leave were forced to take refuge in the Broadway Bar for shelter, to sit wet and dripping in the parks, or to give up shore leave and return to the battleships. At that time the only institution in Shanghai which catered to seamen was the Hanbury Institute, a British "Sailors' Snug Harbor" whose accommodations were totally inadequate for such an influx.

Something should be done to remedy this situation, I thought, but what? Then came the inspiration. Sympathy of the leading American citizens was easily enlisted. At once Consul

General Amos P. Wilder and others entered enthusiastically into my plan for opening a shelter, with restaurant attached, for the sailors.

We rented an empty building on Nanking Road and worked like demons to get it equipped and opened immediately. Comfortable chairs, books, magazines, newspapers, a piano, a phonograph, two big stoves and the necessary fuel were all contributed by the Americans. British friends lent assistance and within forty-eight hours we had the place in full swing with Sam Joe, a Chinese *compradore* (provision merchant or caterer) who had spent many years in America and who had been with Dewey in the Battle of Manila Bay, grilling the beefsteaks for the grateful sailors.

We had been warned that there might be trouble; that sailors were rough and we were weak women. Up until eleven o'clock each night two or more members of the American Women's Club were always on hand to see that all went well and to act as hostesses. The place was patrolled, but never once in all the time the fleet remained in port was there a suggestion of drunkenness or disorder. It was a tremendous success.

During those ten hectic days, eight thousand sailors patronized the place. They slept on the floors, in the long chairs and on the fifteen or twenty beds prepared in an upstairs room. Those who occupied the chairs and the floor had only the heat from the two stoves which were kept red hot all night long to keep them warm.

We lived in a blaze of glory. Later we had the pleasure of knowing that our hasty effort to give some sort of hospitable shelter to our sailors led directly to the building of the present Navy Y.M.C.A.

After this burst of energy the American Women's Club had the temerity to tackle the Shanghai Municipal Council. We wanted sheds for the rickshaw pullers, whose average working life is about three years. When they were not busy they sat in the pouring rain, drenched to the skin, or else on some near-by doorstep, sowing the seeds of tuberculosis, the disease to which many thousands of them succumb each year. Honesty compels me to admit that our requests did not meet with the spontaneous approval of the Council. Whether they resented our interference or not I do not know; our proposals were shelved politely but firmly.

Ultimately, however, the matter was reconsidered, and today the rickshaw coolies have not only their protective sheds in the principal streets of Shanghai but a large and well-equipped clinic-center. It was Mr. George Matheson of the Rickshaw Mission who succeeded in accomplishing this.

I went to Japan during the summer of 1910 for a little recreation but was immediately involved in a huge practice. There was little rest for an obstetrician in Nikko that summer and I could not leave my expectant mothers when the Shanghai Municipal Council wrote asking me to return and act as mediator for them among the Chinese.

Bubonic plague, carried by rats from the ships, was threatening Shanghai. The authorities were afraid it might get a foothold in some of the congested Chinese sections. The consequences then would be disastrous. They wanted me to join in the house-to-house inspection and talk the Chinese into making their houses rat-proof by filling in the space between the floor and the ground with concrete. However, once Chinese objection was overcome, the campaign moved along successfully without my assistance and the plague disappeared, thanks to the quick and effective work of the settlement's health department.

After delivering dozens of babies to foreign missionary and diplomatic mothers in Japan, I returned to Shanghai and another scheme of the American Women's Club. It was to segregate the houses of ill-fame and eliminate the licensing of prostitutes. This, said the Council, was a proposal which would have far-reaching results and was not to be undertaken lightly, particularly, we were informed, not to be undertaken lightly by *women*. So that was also shelved for a time, but we have lived to see most of our reforms adopted.

Almost from my very first days in Shanghai I had been drawn to the foreign prostitutes, or they to me. They came to see me when they were sick and I could not turn them away. I treated their diseases, delivered their babies, helped them when they were in trouble. I was the only woman physician in Shanghai at that time, except for the few missionary doctors who were too busy with their own work among the Chinese to take on any additional burdens.

The Foreign Women's Rescue Home had been founded by a number of philanthropic British and American women with the idea of reclaiming the foreign prostitutes, many of whom, having grown old in their profession, were left stranded and unwanted in Shanghai. In those days many women of that type flocked to the Orient. Some ran away from strict homes looking for work and the only jobs they could find were the ones that were always open to them. Others were brought out to China under false pretenses. They were usually poor and ignorant, a hopeless lot.

I contributed my services as a physician to the Foreign Rescue Home, sometimes taking one of the girls into my own house during her pregnancy. Often a missionary, who had come down to Shanghai from the interior to have her baby, would be in the next room. It did not matter to me; they were both women who needed care. Many of those we helped stayed reclaimed but others, I must admit, wandered back to their old life as soon as they were cured of their ills or delivered of their babies.

And so in spite of, perhaps because of, my friendship with these women I joined in the campaign of the American Women's Club. But before this abortive attempt of ours the

United States Court for China had already taken steps to put the disorderly houses in order.

One of the most epoch-making events in the life of the American community in Shanghai and of the Americans throughout China was the establishment of this court. It came about in 1906 as the result of an act of Congress, dated June thirtieth of that year. The first judge to be appointed was Lebbeus Redman Wilfley of St. Louis, a dear friend of mine, who had been serving as Attorney General in the Philippines. By the United States' treaties with China in 1844 and 1858, American citizens in China were accorded extraterritoriality, as are most of the European nations represented there. This simply means that while living in China they are not under the laws or jurisdiction of that country, but subject only to the laws and jurisdiction of the United States or whatever their country may be.

Until 1906 the only courts for the trial of Americans were the Consular Courts. They served very well while the American community was a small one, but with its rapid growth and the great increase of American interests in China, these Consular Courts were inadequate to the needs of the changing situation.

The establishment of the United States Court for China created consternation among a considerable portion of the American community, whose activities were of such nature as to be open to serious interference by a stricter enforcement of the laws of the United States. Since the Boxer troubles of 1900 and the Russo-Japanese War of 1904-1905, Shanghai had been the scene of operations for numerous undesirable foreigners of all nationalities, including a great many Americans. It was a paradise for adventurers, among whom were the organizers as well as the victims of the white-slave traffic.

Shyster lawyers, gamblers, ladies of easy virtue, riffraff of every kind, ranging from those who manipulated shady operations down to the garden variety of bum, had fattened on the flesh of poor Shanghai. Now this scum of civilization received word that the long arm of American law was reaching out for them. Their feelings were outraged; events soon justified their apprehension.

The first act of the new judge was to announce that only Americans who could pass an examination in law, and moreover, who could furnish proof of good moral character, would be allowed to practice in the American Court. Here was a bomb shell! A storm of protest was raised by the so-called American legal fraternity but to no avail. Examinations were held; only two passed and were admitted to the court. These two men were the late Mr. T. R. Jernigan and Mr. Stirling Fessenden. The latter subsequently became Chairman of the Municipal Council, and still later the Secretary-General of the Council.

Attention was next turned to the houses of ill-fame. It was thought that most of these were owned and operated by American women. So many of this class were, or claimed to be, of American origin that up and down the China coast the foreign demi-mondaine were spoken of as "American Girls." This reputed monopoly of prostitution was not a pleasant condition for the decent American element to contemplate and it was generally felt that something drastic should be done. When the court opened there were eight bordellos in Shanghai known as "American Houses."

Complaints were filed in the court against the keepers of these brothels and there was so much excitement that the conservative British-owned *North-China Daily News*, the leading daily paper, issued an extra.

When the case came up for trial most people were surprised to find that four of the "Madams" successfully established their nationality as other than American. It later developed that one other "keeper" who accepted American jurisdiction and pleaded guilty, was also non-American.

The residents of the bagnios who were not Americans immediately rushed to their consulates to register their citizenship in order to escape actions which they thought might be taken against them. At that time any American woman's nationality was changed by marriage and several of the local celebrities who were of American nationality took prompt matrimonial steps to ensure continuance of their activities in Shanghai. The whole town was convulsed with mirth when the following advertisement appeared:

> "Wanted—a husband. Will pay $1000.
> No Americans need apply."

No houses actually were closed by action of the court, but all ceased to operate as "American Houses," and many American girls left town. So the canard of an "American Monopoly" was exposed, and the light ladies of Shanghai lost their profitable trade name.

Judge Wilfley did not escape the criticism inevitable in such an efficacious house-cleaning. While the new court was taking action one of the local newspapers became quite rabid in its comment on the proceedings of the court and published statements which the Judge considered libelous. The editor of the *Gazette* was a British subject, and action against the paper had to be taken in the British Court. Judge Wilfley made his complaint to the British Crown Advocate who filed a charge against the editor, alleging criminal libel. The case was tried in the British Court, the defendant found guilty and sentenced to a short term of imprisonment.

This case created intense excitement. It was the sole topic of conversation everywhere. Shanghai society was rocked to the very foundations, much as it was a decade later when the question of septic tanks and cesspools came up for heated discussion at every dinner party.

I remember a tiffin party I attended at the home of Sir Edward Pearce, the Chairman of the Municipal Council, while the excitement was at its height.

"It's a rotten state of affairs," said one man, "when the Judge of the United States Court has to defend himself against such charges."

I protested that any charges brought against Judge Wilfley *must* be the most arrant lies.

"I have it on good authority," said the man, "that the editor's lawyer has a safe packed with letters the Judge has written to the 'American girls.' They're letters of the most incriminating character."

He spoke with such assurance that I was simply crushed.

Judge Wilfley came to tea later that afternoon. When I saw him standing there before me, I felt that I could not bear to have people dragging his fine, honest name in the mud and whispering scandal behind his back.

"I must tell you what they are saying about you," I burst out—"what they said about you at tiffin today!"

I told him the whole story and when I had finished he said, pounding the table with each word,

"Let them talk. I'm not afraid of the devil himself."

By sentencing any number of swindlers and gamblers to terms of imprisonment, the Judge made it clear what the fate of this class of offender would be. In the case of the demi-mondaine, this resulted in a general exodus—for the time being. One report had it that the girls were given a fixed time to leave town, but that was without foundation of fact. When the "Madams" were arrested, rumors flew round that the girls also would be prosecuted and many left of their own accord and with speed, to drift back later.

Naturally all this cleaning of the Augean Stable in Shanghai was not allowed to go unchallenged. The pickings had been too good for the criminal element not to put up a fight, and the result was an attempt in 1908 to impeach Judge Wilfley. President Roosevelt exonerated him at the request of Secretary of State Rost, and highly recommended the work of the court.

By his courageous honesty Judge Wilfley did much to build up American prestige. In a conglomerate foreign settlement like Shanghai, that almost indefinable quality, prestige, is of great importance, and the dominant personalities of each separate community within the settlement have a tremendous influence on its rise and fall.

CHAPTER XVI

The Dragon Flag Comes Down

ONE MORNING LATE IN THE YEAR 1911 I WOKE WITH THAT curious suspended feeling one has when the whole earth breathlessly waits for the approaching thunderstorm or when a ship's engines stop in mid-ocean. The city was uncannily quiet. None of the usual early morning hubbub of coolies, rickshaw men, merchants slamming open shops, women going to market, or children running to play—only a vast discomposing stillness.

"What is it?" I asked my husband. "What's the matter? Something's up."

"If you ask me," he replied, "I should say that something is down."

As usual he was right.

The Manchu government, like Humpty Dumpty, had had a great fall. Only yesterday the Dragon Flag had floated over housetops, gutters and alleyways. Today the white flag of the Revolution took its place. From doorsteps, from bamboo poles, from lines strung across the streets, from official gates, from houses, from shops, hundreds of white flags hung down, as limp as the week's wash hung out to dry.

The upheaval which brought the long reign of the Manchus to an inglorious end had been threatening for some time. Revolution had broken out in Hankow, but had been promptly suppressed by the Imperialist forces. For a moment it had seemed that the Empire was safe, but the tide was too strong to be turned back. Between October ninth, when the outbreak occurred in Hankow, and November fourth, when Shanghai

165

went bloodlessly over to the Revolution, provinces and cities declared their independence of the Manchu yoke. By the end of the year a provisional republican government under President Yuan Shih-kai was functioning from Nanking.

China has always been rich soil for secret societies, and for years these societies had been plotting and propagandizing against the government. After the deaths of the Emperor and Empress Dowager in 1908, within a few hours of each other, revolutionary activity had grown rapidly. The new Emperor, Hsüan T'ung, was no more than a baby, and his Regent was not only a weak man but obstinately obstructive to reforms and changes. Poverty and distress among the people was terrible, and I suppose many of them had the feeling that they could not be much worse off under a new form of government than they were under the old.

Our house as I have said, was near one of the bridges connecting Frenchtown with the native city and on all these bridges the revolutionary army had stationed two men. As each rickshaw came up, the coolie was stopped by one of the soldiers while the other, armed with a pair of big shears, neatly removed the coolie's queue and flung it with disdain across the shafts of the rickshaw. The coolies danced up and down in rage at the indignity.

"If we lose the insignia of our nationality on this," one of them said to me, "there is no reason why we shall not lose our heads on the next bridge." The queue was the badge of loyalty to the Manchu Government. Deprived of it one literally was a man without a country.

I sympathized with the cogency of his reasoning as I stood at my window and gazed upon the spectacle of hundreds of rickshaws with amputated queues dangling from their shafts.

Many stories of daring and courage came out of the Revolution, but not one, I think, is more remarkable than the episode of "Sowerby's Light Brigade." It happened in the early days of the Revolution, in far off Shensi, and the hero was Mr. Arthur de Carle Sowerby, big-game hunter, explorer and, until recently, editor of *The China Journal*.

Certain groups of missionaries of the English Baptist Mission had been cut off from the outside world by the anarchy which the Revolution let loose in Shensi Province. No word had been received beyond the news that part of the Mission Station at Sianfu had been destroyed and a number of foreign children and adults killed. The gravest anxiety was felt for the safety of the other missionaries, who had not been heard from since the outbreak of the trouble.

Mr. Sowerby was at Taiyüanfu, the capital of Shansi, where he had been outfitting an expedition for exploration into Mongolia and Manchuria. Being familiar with Shansi he offered to organize and lead a company to rescue the missionaries, or at least learn their fate. He got together a group of eight men and a boy of seventeen, and rode off into the interior.

For six or seven weeks the party was lost to sight. Then they emerged triumphantly at the railway head at Honanfu, the present Loyang, in Honan Province. They had journeyed nearly one thousand miles. With them came a train nearly two miles long composed of carts, litters, sedan chairs, pack-mules and ponies, with thirty-nine foreign missionaries and numerous Chinese.

During this amazing trek, on the way from Dianfu to Honanfu, the party had been alarmed one late afternoon by the sound of guns coming ever closer. In the rough mountain country of Honan, safe shelter is difficult to find at best and with darkness coming on almost impossible. While they were hesitating as to the wisest course to take, they were met by the Revolutionary Army in full retreat before the advancing Imperialist forces, some twenty thousand strong.

Mr. Sowerby found a deserted inn or two where the members

of his party could spend the night, and set off himself to interview the Revolutionary general.

At dawn he proceeded to ride through the Imperialist lines, which could be seen in the gray light advancing over the distant hilltops. He coolly ignored the danger he ran of being shot by the approaching troops and, on reaching the Imperialist lines, demanded to be taken to the commanding general.

I have no idea what the Chinese thought of this solitary horseman, perhaps that he bore a charmed life, but they brought him before the commander. Whereupon Mr. Sowerby asked him point blank to postpone further attack until he rode his party through safely.

The audacity of the request probably took the general's breath away, but Mr. Sowerby's assured bearing, coupled with the prestige which foreigners had in those days, won the general's assent and he said that he would call his men into bivouac for twenty-four hours.

As the Revolutionary general had already agreed to the same terms, Mr. Sowerby returned, well content, to his party of refugees. In the morning, while the two armies lay watching them on either side, Mr. Sowerby brought his expedition safely through the lines.

While they were still in the wild, almost deserted country of North Shensi, working their way to the capital, Sianfu, along the narrow mountain paths which are the only highways in that part of the world, they approached a walled town named Ichun. It straddled the road leading along the top of the mountain ridge, with deep impassable defiles on either side. Several of the party had left the caravan to shoot deer that had been seen off the road and Mr. Sowerby was left practically alone in the vanguard. As they topped the low rise, they came unexpectedly into full view of the town wall.

To their horror they saw that the wall was manned by hundreds of Chinese shouting and gesticulating in their direction.

Many were wearing black turbans, the insignia of the dread Ko Lao Rui, or Elder Brother Society, the members of which, for all practical purposes, were bandits. They were armed with rifles, guns, spears and swords, and the situation looked hopeless. It was impossible to turn back. There was no way around the town; the only road to safety lay right through it.

Mr. Sowerby was as cool in this emergency as he had been when caught between the advancing and the retreating armies. Raising his empty hand as a sign of friendship, he rode straight up to the gate of the town where he informed the robber chieftain who he and his party were, and asked to be allowed to proceed without molestation.

During his conference at the gate with the black-turbaned bandit, guns were leveled at him from every direction. Angry voices cried, "Shoot! Shoot!"

Fortunately there was wiser counsel among the leaders, who agreed finally to allow the party to enter the town in safety. As they marched through the streets, a guard was lined up three deep on either side, with loaded rifles pointed in case of treachery. I imagine that many prayers of thankfulness went up as the refugees filed out the gate on the opposite side of Ichun.

Afterward it was learned that Ichun had been frightened by the sound of shots fired by the deer-hunting party. They supposed it presaged an attack by a large force of foreign troops, for a rumor had been circulated that such a force was on its way from the capital to avenge murders that had taken place in Ichun.

Later I talked with one of the men who had been there and he told me that Mr. Sowerby's action in riding up to the gate was the bravest thing he ever saw, for it looked as though he were riding to certain death.

Although Mr. Sowerby received the written thanks of British, American and Swedish governments, since nationals of all three countries were among the missionaries rescued, he received no other recognition for this remarkable achievement, which seems to me a rather sad commentary on the way honors are dealt out.

After the first Revolution came a period of peace and accomplishment. The Mixed Court, which previously had given so much trouble, was reorganized with the Consular Body taking charge. The extension of the court's powers caused some slight displeasure on the part of the Republican authorities as there was no appeal from its judgments. There were other changes: the solar calendar was adopted; an institution for the Chinese blind was founded by Dr. John Fryer; committees met to devise means for helping the rickshaw coolies.

But modern ideas were seeping in through the many publications and societies which sprang up all over China. The members of the Kuomintang were dissatisfied with President Yuan and accused him of planning to make himself dictator. Seditious articles urged the people to rise and overthrow his government.

By July, 1913, China was ripe for what is now generally called the second Revolution. It really was more of a rebellion, as it was a revolt against the government established by Yuan Shih-kai. Actually it affected Shanghai a great deal more than had the Revolution of 1911. The Settlements were put into a state of defense. The bridges forming the natural boundaries between them and the Chinese city were picketed by armed forces, and huge barricades were erected at strategic points. Every possible precaution was taken, but as it turned out no actual fighting took place within the limits of Shanghai.

We were very close to the main current, however, and likely to be dragged into it at any time, for the main object of both armies was primarily the Arsenal, and secondly Shanghai.

Our house on the Rue Palikao was situated on the border between the French Concession and the West Gate of the

Native City, exactly in the thick of the fight. From early dawn, and even through the night, we watched ceaseless streams of refugees from the neighboring villages through which the devastating armies had passed, pouring into the city for protection.

Never in my wildest dreams had I imagined the horror which marked the advance of the hordes of Chinese riffraff, called by courtesy soldiers. There is a Chinese saying, "You don't make nails out of good iron; you don't make soldiers out of good men." These men were not only undisciplined, but they were encouraged to sack, pillage, and rob the villages and towns through which they passed, loot being the sop to Cerberus in lieu of wages.

I shall never forget the sight of those refugees—young women with babies at their breasts, old men and women hobbling along under the impetus of a dreadful fear, small children running beside their parents, crying with hunger and weariness—or the pathetic look of the few household goods they had managed to heap on their wheelbarrows or that they carried in their hands and on their backs.

Work at the clinic at the Margaret Williamson Hospital still formed my chief daily occupation, and the hospital lay under the eaves of the arsenal. We were surrounded from morning till night and from night till morning by these milling masses of miserable refugees. They were homeless, starving, sick, and many were wounded by the merciless shot and shell which fell on the roads along which they fled to safety. There were fifty or sixty thousand of them. Many already were suffering from disease. There was no possible means of sanitation. Wounds went undressed. Scores died in the streets from wounds, from illness, from sheer exhaustion. Their presence was a menace to the whole population, both Chinese and foreign, unless an immense and efficient organization promptly took measures to care for them.

A Central Relief Committee was formed at once by the heads

of all the big Hongs, both Chinese and foreign, with smaller relief committees under it. Being on the central committee, the only woman member, I had at last plenty to do. There was no time now for vain searching after the unknown. The known was here at hand, too close at hand to be pleasant.

Much as we wanted to help these unfortunates, it must be admitted that our efforts were self-protective as well as altruistic. With these multitudes surrounding us on all sides, with new hordes approaching the city from all directions, and still more to come, the city was like a man caught in the midst of innumerable, crawling, voracious, giant ants whose lines extended into the unseen distance.

The first necessity was housing. I was fortunate to have placed at my disposal a large godown (warehouse) on Soochow Creek. This would accommodate five hundred men, women and children. The next problem was to introduce some order into the reigning chaos, and to find some way to control the starving five hundred who fell to my lot. Luckily for me Mr. Matheson offered his services and I welcomed him as a gift from God. It was rather like being helped by Ajax, for this gentle soul had a stentorian voice appropriate to his mighty stature, and I felt that if the crowd ignored my feeble tones Mr. Matheson could roar at them effectively. Moreover, he thoroughly understood the Chinese and had in return their love and confidence.

With problems of housing and sanitation solved after a fashion, we concentrated on the enormous task of providing food for that starving mob, many of whom had had nothing to eat for days.

The tenants of my godown were sorted out in families or groups of eight. Each person had enough floor space for a sleeping mat, and the entire floor was covered with these woebegone specimens of humanity.

Mr. Matheson's deep voice boomed, ordering them to remain

still, each on his own mat, and when the place was comparatively quiet, I told them that rice was coming, plenty for all. A wordless groan, an indescribable sound, swept through the godown.

"But," I added, raising my voice, "when it comes, if any dare to leave their mats, *the rice will be thrown into the creek.*"

We had decided that this threat was necessary if we were to thwart a wild stampede toward the rice kongs. If there were a rush, many of our five hundred charges might be seriously hurt.

Then the coolies came in sight carrying the four enormous jars, each big enough to hold two men, suspended between bamboo poles. The sight of the food within their reach was too much for those starving people. With screams and cries the whole crowd leaped to their feet and made for the rice. Even Mr. Matheson's voice was lost in the howling confusion. I simply stood still, in imminent danger of being trampled underfoot, and gave the situation up as lost.

It all happened in less time than it takes to tell it. Suddenly I heard, high above every other sound, a shrill, piping voice screaming insistently. There was something so terrible and arresting in the very thinness of the sound that even that mob paused a second to listen.

"Let be! Let be!" the voice cried. "The Foreign Devil means what she says and we shall get no rice! She will throw it into the canal!"

I stared in amazement at the place from where this feeble piping came, and saw a small emaciated boy, lame and in rags, who by the aid of his crutches had managed to climb to a table top. It was heartbreaking to see the tears roll down his twisted, terrified face while his sparrow-like throat gulped with sobs. His eyes, so big and haggard, were fixed with longing and terror on the big rice kongs, as he visualized the tragedy of watching their precious contents cast into the creek.

That pitiful little figure quieted the others as no authority of ours could do, and one by one they fell back and sank onto their mats. Both Mr. Matheson and I breathed freely again, and the distribution of food went on without hindrance.

One of the first undertakings of the Central Relief Committee was to find work for the refugees. Labor gangs were organized and somehow work was made to keep the able-bodied busy. One day, as I was inspecting a godown, I came across a man who seemed to me to be capable of working. He held a baby in his arms and four children were huddled around him. I asked why he was not working. He replied that he could not leave the children, and then broke into sobs. His wife had been hit by one of the stray shots that raked the roads to Shanghai. He had taken the baby from her arms and left her to die by the roadside, in order that the children might be saved.

These stray shots and spent bullets which still had power to kill fell not only on the roads around Shanghai but even within the Settlement. Once, during the bombardment from the Chinese warships I was walking from our front gate to the house when a bullet fell just in front of me. Instead of instantly bolting for safety, I stopped and dug it out of the ground in which it was imbedded and held it, hot though it still was, in my hand. I was aroused from my contemplation of it by the voice of my husband.

"Come in at once!" he called. "Don't be a damned fool!"

"Let me alone," I answered. "I'm perfectly safe." When bullets and shells were plopping like raindrops on the roof it seemed to me that one place was as good as any other.

Later these shells became a real menace to the Settlement. The Chinese warships were assisting in the defense of the Arsenal against the invading army and shells began falling promiscuously all over the place. Finally the captain of one of the British warships thought it high time to make some stringent inquiries. He found that the men-of-war lying off the

Arsenal had guns trained straight onto the Settlement. Others, supposed to be trained on the advancing army, had been sighted at low tide and not depressed when the tide rose. Thus, their shells fell miles behind the enemy. It was this almost inconceivable carelessness or stupidity which cost the lives of so many of the innocent country folk.

The exceedingly irate Britisher announced that he would retaliate by sinking their battleships unless the firing ceased immediately. The Chinese evidently thought discretion the better part of valor and to our intense relief the bombardment stopped, at least until the guns could be properly sighted.

In the meantime many of the residents of the outlying districts had taken refuge in the Astor House Hotel. I remember one afternoon, as we were having tea in the lounge, one of the gentlemen of our party was called to the telephone. In a moment we heard his loud, indignant voice.

"What! A shell in *my* drawing room! Impossible. . . ."

But the Chinese shells were no respecter of persons or places in those days.

One afternoon during the bombardment we were told that the children in the Mission Orphanage near the Arsenal were in grave danger. My husband and Mr. Joseph H. Black, then of the Standard Oil Company, went out to bring them into the comparative safety of our compound. They collected the terrified children and brought them back by the safest route possible. But it was a nerve-racking walk of about two hours and they darted under the eaves of the houses, under trees, crouched by the sides of grave mounds, seeking any slight shelter they could from the whizzing shells. When they reached us the children were a shivering mass of misery.

We put them in the chapel, on the floor and on benches, wherever there was available space, and when we brought them cakes and fruit we found them so exhausted by the terror they had experienced that they could not eat the food they so badly needed. They sobbed themselves to sleep, forlorn little creatures whose lives at best were none too happy.

Many and varied were the activities of our relief committee. Among others, caring for maternity cases was no small job. There were babies everywhere; babies on the pavement, babies in baskets, babies in packing cases—they seemed to multiply by the hundreds. Our maternity wards were full to overflowing, and still they came, into conditions that were appalling beyond expression. What would become of them? What use to save them?

We were all so busy that when night came, even if we had time then to rest for a few moments, we were too exhausted to sleep. But I admit that I loved it. It was a fight; it was excitement; and I reveled in it.

CHAPTER XVII

I Open My Sanatorium

I N JUNE, 1914, WANDERLUST AGAIN ATTACKED US. WITH MY OLD friend, Dr. Elizabeth Yates and her niece, Helen Chapman, we planned to cross Siberia and visit Norway and Sweden, after first giving our visitors a glimpse of the interior of China.

Our first stop was Chufu, the birthplace and burial place of Confucius. His grave is a simple mound outside the North gate, but near the center of town rises a magnificent temple dedicated to the memory and worship of the great teacher. There are many temples to Confucius all over China, but this, in his own home town, is the most beautiful. The roof is of yellow glazed tiles, the walls of vermilion stucco. There are courts of noble dimensions, giving it an air of spaciousness, and many buildings surround it, including a small pavilion erected on the site of the philosopher's favorite apricot tree. The place is serene and the spirit of ancient, timeless wisdom seems to hover over it always.

Tai-shan, China's holy mountain, is not far distant from Chufu. Its cloud-capped peak dominates the entire region, and dozens of legends have grown around it. For many, many centuries Tai-shan has been an object of worship in China, with temples, priests and sacrifices dedicated to her mysterious powers.

We made the steep and dangerous ascent of the holy mountain in sedan chairs which were very light, carried by bearers who were very strong, but who had a disconcerting habit of swinging the chair from one shoulder to the other when they grew weary. The sensation which comes from being swung over thousands of feet of precipitous depth is not pleasant.

Travel in China then was either by slow boat, with possessions and personal safety entrusted to wind, wave and kind providence, or, in the interior, which was not intersected by canals, by *shenza*, a bamboo reclining chair suspended between two mules, one in front and one at the back. Frequently the mules parted company and the occupant of the litter fell ignominiously between. Long trips in the extreme north were made on camels or on the tough little Manchurian ponies.

Traveling in the interior of China in 1914 was anything but comfortable. The inns where travelers of necessity stopped for the night were noisy, dirty and generally insect infested. The traveler's constant companion was a tin of Keating's Insect Powder. No one would think of traveling without his own food, bedding and personal servant who cooked the food, and made the beds. These were made up on the long, wide, brick ovens in which a fire was kept burning through the night; and one waxed hot or cold according to the temperature of the fire tender, who added fuel when the cold kept him from sleeping. I never linger over the memory of those nights on *kangs*.

We were in Moscow when the Crown Prince of Austria was shot. We arrived in Bergen on the day the Germans marched into Belgium.

We arrived in England filled with martial spirit along with the rest of the world, and tried to enlist. We were told that there were too many applicants; the best thing for us to do was to continue to New York and return with the Red Cross.

It seemed a long way to go simply to get back again but obediently we set off. The dangers of war were as nothing compared with the dangers from air and water that pursued us across the Atlantic. One night the ship was in such danger from storm and icebergs that we were ordered to the saloon at midnight to don life preservers. Two passengers died of seasickness during the voyage.

Eventually we landed in New York and at once sent in our applications and qualifications. As a matter of fact I was the only Dr. Fearn who applied. By that time my husband, having calmly considered the situation, decided that as he was still in the employ of the Mission Board and under obligation to them, it would be better to return to Shanghai before severing his connection with the board.

The answer to my application was disheartening. According to instructions from headquarters only men surgeons and women nurses could be accepted, a ruling which, to their great regret, disqualified me for service with the American Red Cross. I had a spasm of being very sorry for myself indeed, that I was a woman.

Sometime later I fell into conversation with a youngster just out of college who had had the luck to see service at the front, and I told him of my rejection and disappointment.

"Well, Dr. Fearn," he said, and a frown of deep thought creased his young brow, "the truth of the matter is, they don't need doctors and surgeons. What they really need is brains."

This tactful remark almost reconciled me to my sex.

We spent many restless weeks in America before returning to China. I still hoped that a kind fate would send me some war work to do, but on the way back to Shanghai, during those long days at sea when there was nothing to do but think, I decided definitely that once again I would practice medicine in good earnest.

I had never been an idler. I had been busy enough. But somehow I felt that I was not squeezing all that I could out of life. The several hours daily that I gave to the Margaret Williamson Hospital clinic, the vast amount of time and energy expended on the undertakings of the American Women's Club—all that was good. But nothing so far had satisfied that rankling sensation that something more important, to me at least, lay waiting around the corner; and I must find it or remain forever only half a person.

We returned to a changed Shanghai. In place of the society-loving, easy-going, pleasure-seeking city we had left several months before, we found a beehive buzzing with war activities. Amusements, except money-raisers for war relief, were abandoned.

In addition to my clinic, club and civic work, I had practiced medicine in a desultory way since coming to Shanghai seven years before, but now I opened an office and set about it whole-heartedly. I took an office on Jinkee Road, then known as Medical Lane. Dr. Margaret Polk severed her connection with the Mission Board and came to Shanghai to share the office with me, although we kept our respective practices separate.

I remember that on her trip from Soochow Dr. Polk's trunk was damaged. Dr. Polk, a rabid teetotaler, sent it to a Chinese shop to be repaired and in due course of time it was returned, and with it was a bill made out: "To Dr. Polk for one big drunk, two dollars."

Things like that were always happening to Dr. Polk, who was a very proper missionary doctor, devoting her days to good deeds and her spare time to committees. Dr. Frank Rawlinson, who was killed in the first Shanghai bombing on August 14, 1937, had been appointed head of the Moral Welfare Society of Soochow early in the century and he, in turn, named a committee to assist him, all men missionaries with the exception of Dr. Polk. The news of the formation of the committee was faithfully reported by the Chinese press. It read, "The committee consists of four adults and one adultress."

Dr. Polk and I worked for days getting our office ready. One night I stayed on long after she had gone. I gave the office a final, fond glance, closed and locked the door on the treatment room, arranged pencils in my treasured silver cup on the consultation room desk, and ran my hands lovingly over the freshly painted panelings of the waiting room. I had worked like a dog all day and I was tired, but I hated to leave, even for the few hours of much-needed sleep.

It was nearly midnight, and I dozed as I jogged along in my rickshaw to our new home and my bed two miles away at 119 Bubbling Well Road.

But not to bed! A man was waiting for me on the veranda steps.

"Quai, quai!" (Quickly, quickly!) he cried. No need to tell *me* why. I tried to shake the sleep from my eyes as I grabbed my "baby bag," awakened the nurse and started across the city to the native section. Our rickshaws bogged down in the rutted roads and we were none too soon.

My nurse had barely finished washing the woman when the baby was born. I held my hand on the uterus, pressing down to contract it when another came; while I was still holding and pressing the third baby squeezed out. I still felt that the uterus was not empty and sure enough, there was something hanging from it, a fourth baby. My first quadruplets!

The fourth, weighing only three-quarters of a pound, gasped and died. But the triplets are still living.

I soon won the name of "the twin and triplet doctor"; patients were warned by their friends not to seek my services—unless they wanted more than one baby at a time. I brought hundreds of twins and several triplets into the world, but never again quadruplets.

I have delivered children under almost every imaginable condition—dead babies from living mothers and vice versa. A Chinese woman, a cardiac patient, was pregnant. Her labor promised to be troublesome and Dr. Polk, whose patient she was, had injured her hand and could not manage the case alone. She asked me to stand by. While Dr. Polk was still talking to me about it a woman rushed into the office crying, "Quickly, doctor, it's Mrs. Yang." We rushed to the woman and found her cyanosed, lying back in a rattan chair. I applied the forceps and took the baby just as the mother died. While Dr. Polk resuscitated the first baby I hurriedly applied the forceps again and extracted the second child, still living although in the second stage of asphyxia.

Another time I was called to the home of a foreign woman, the wife of a missionary. She had just stepped into the tub to take a bath when her baby was born. She gave one agonizing scream and died—a heart attack. But the baby lived.

One of the strangest things connected with childbirth that has ever come to my attention occurred in Shanghai. The woman, a foreigner and the wife of a German specialist in Oriental diseases, had given birth to twins on three different occasions. She was pregnant for the fourth time. In June she gave birth to a pair of five-months-old twins. Four months later she gave birth to two full term children who lived and are still living. The general opinion of the doctors was that she had a double uterus.

The most frightened patient I ever had anywhere was a Chinese woman in a perfectly normal birth. She rolled and yelled, and when I delivered her she was astride the footboard of the bed, screaming at the top of her lungs, although the birth was by far the easiest of my entire six thousand and seventeen.

In Soochow I had had relatively few foreign patients and those were mostly missionaries or connected with the Customs or Railway—God-fearing, hard-working people. Now in Shanghai, having given up my clinic work, I was to have few Chinese patients and those only from the higher social order, but my foreigners were to come from all walks of life.

In Shanghai I had my first experience with adventurers and adventuresses. My clientele was catholic and included official and religious dignitaries, missionaries, the demi-mondaine, the rich and the poor. A physician takes what comes along. I walked right into an excellent practice. In fact it finally grew so large that I increased my charges in the hope of decreasing the work. It had just the opposite effect; more and more patients came, thinking no doubt that because I charged more I was just that much better.

An understanding heart is the first prerequisite of a doctor practicing medicine in Shanghai, for here one meets many tragedies. The foreigners who flock to that city, so often called "the Paris of the Orient," and especially the young ones, feel free to take chances. Shanghai seems at the other end of the world and so far away from home ties that these young men, and women too, burn all of their bridges and take liberties with their bodies as well as their money.

And so, instead of battling the ills resulting from filth, superstition and ignorance, I was now to fight the sicknesses of alcoholism, free and easy living, and the mental depression caused by financial and marital worries.

Those were busy days and equally busy nights for both Dr. Polk and me. Our practices were largely with women and children, who have a disconcerting way of developing ills past midnight. One night, especially, I shall never forget, because of its own particular awfulness and because it was another turning point in my life. In the early hours of the morning, after an unusually difficult confinement case, I stumbled out into the waiting rickshaw. The case was across the city from my home and the night was rainy and cold with that penetrating rawness I have found only in China. Owing to the zoning restrictions under which rickshaws are operated, I was forced to change several times. Each time the rain soaked me to the skin. When finally I crawled into bed I could not sleep.

With the coming of light I had an inspiration. It was obvious I could not go on like this with nothing but rickshaws available for my comings and goings. A car was the only answer. My spirits rose at the very thought. Of course I didn't have any money, but then I never had any money so that problem didn't worry me. I started thinking and my thoughts led me straight to Mr. C. H. Blake, one of the kindest-hearted and gruffest men God ever made. I would borrow the money from him and buy a Ford. Much comforted by the prospect I fell asleep.

Before dressing next morning I telephoned Mr. Blake and poured my tale of woe into his sympathetic ear.

"God in Heaven, woman!" he shouted. "Why didn't you say so before. Be ready in fifteen minutes."

He came. We bought the car, and later driving up Nanking Road I shrieked joyfully to all the friends I met.

"I've got a car. This is mine!"

It was quite a triumphal progress.

I loved that Ford for with its purchase the rebound came. My spirits soared, and with them my courage to tackle other problems. It was not many months before the car was paid for and I was well started on the upward road.

But all this time the seed of my pet idea was growing and growing. I wanted a hospital of my own. It became an obsession with me. I knew now, better than ever since encountering the snags in the way of a moderately successful private practice, the innumerable obstacles I must overcome before any such thing would be possible. But that did not prevent me from planning for it by day and dreaming of it by night until this wild idea became an integral part of my being.

In the suburbs of the city, in the French Concession, stood the residence of Mr. E. Gerecke, a German broker. The approach was a long, sweeping driveway, bordered on both sides by magnificent juniper trees set so closely together that they formed an effectual screen concealing the garden from the streets. The garden itself was a gem; the house was huge but homelike. It was far enough out in the country to be free from noise, or so I thought, and near enough to the heart of the city to be convenient as a sanatorium. Without even dreaming that

I might possibly possess it, I had mentally been fitting it up as a hospital for a long time.

With the outbreak of the war Mr. Gerecke fell on hard times. One day he casually mentioned that he'd like to lease his house.

"I'll take it," I said, not asking the rent, which I found out soon enough was four hundred taels a month, at that time about $300 in American money. It was a prohibitive price for one as impecunious as I. According to my husband, I was "singularly lacking in common sense." It was, he concluded gloomily, "just another case of a fool 'rushing in where angels fear to tread.'"

I was in a state of rapture over my acquisition and would let no suggestion of forthcoming trouble ruffle my contentment. In the midst of winding up his own affairs preparatory to leaving for France, where he was to join the staff of the hospital for the Chinese labor division of the British Army, my husband smothered his doubts and took time out to give me invaluable assistance in the preliminary arrangements.

Mr. and Mrs. Gerecke did everything they could to help. They were dear people and the only shadow that fell on my pleasure was the thought that my good luck was due to their misfortune. I remember one day, as my husband, Mr. Gerecke and I were standing on the doorstep, two beautiful police dogs came romping up to us.

"Have you included these in your lease, Annie?" my husband asked.

"No, no!" Mr. Gerecke said hastily. "Zees dogs zay go to Kuling, but if you will like, I vill gif you one of zees dogs' kittens."

The Gereckes, with all their worldly goods except the concert grand piano in the huge music room and a few heavy pieces of furniture, moved out of the house at nine o'clock on the night of November 30, 1916. The next morning at dawn I moved in.

My great adventure had begun.

185

My Days of Strength

Two patients were staying in my house on Bubbling Well Road. By ten o'clock accommodations were ready for them and they were brought to the new sanatorium in ambulances. Between dawn and noon a small army of servants managed, by a magic known only to Chinese servants, to settle two rooms for my patients, to work wonders with the veranda and to bring the culinary department into running order. That afternoon I gave a party.

It happened that just at this time a noted pianist was passing through Shanghai, so I had scattered indiscriminate invitations to friends to drop in at five to hear the music and incidentally see the garden and as much of the house as had been put in order. About two hundred people came. They listened to the music, wandered through the house and garden, congratulated me and said everything was perfect, and finally drifted homeward.

For me the aftermath of that housewarming was deep despair. I had not seen the house, except in the most casual way, before deciding to take it. That day I had had a series of calamitous disappointments. By the time the last of my guests had departed I was limp and ragged with exhaustion, both mental and physical.

Out of the ten bedrooms at the disposal of patients, four were en suite, with no other entrance than through an adjoining room. I had horrible visions of stretchers being carried through rooms occupied by patients. There was no suitable room on the ground floor for a private office. I suddenly, and too late, awakened to the realization that beds, quantities of bed and table linen, towels, furniture, hospital accouterments, dishes, kitchen utensils, thousands of things, had to be purchased, and I had no money.

Where could I put the patients who had engaged rooms for the following week? How was I to manage the dietary kitchen, the very heart of a sanatorium such as I hoped to make mine?

186

Who would I get for nurses? Must I depend on a kind providence and a few waifs and strays, wanderers to and from the Russian front?

Now I saw only too clearly how precipitate I had been. Lying there, sleepless and nerve-racked, I remembered the repeated warnings my friend, Mrs. John Cromarty, had given me. She had been the matron of the Victoria Nursing Home and her experience should have made me listen. When I had babbled of the advantages of the country, she had reminded me of one of the almost inevitable accompaniments to country life.

Barking dogs! That awful night after the party I listened to them for hours, yowling and yapping and howling at the moon. And that was only the first of many similar nights.

The mornings, when I could get up and do something about it, brought better courage. Few people knew of my worries but one who did was my friend, Major Hilton Johnson of the Shanghai Municipal Council. One day when I was discussing some large but inevitable expense with him he said gently that I really had no cause for worry; my credit in Shanghai was unlimited. The knowledge that I was believed in to such an extent comforted me considerably.

Mrs. Cromarty, realizing that warnings did no good, was an angel of mercy, giving me practical advice. My friends among the doctors gave me wise counsel, and I found that by buying in small quantities, a bed at a time, I could avoid excessive outlay of expenditure and keep from running too deeply into debt. Everything I bought was of the best for I never believed in wasting money on makeshifts, and gradually my little plant grew into a well-organized, well-equipped, smoothly running sanatorium. But certainly I had never dreamed how many bills there would always be to pay.

In lieu of an office I placed my desk in an alcove in the entrance hall, well away from the staircase, and well lighted by a large bay window. I had my telephone by my side, bookcases behind me, and a Herring Hall combination safe within easy reach of my hand. At the start that safe was as empty as Old Mother Hubbard's famous cupboard, but I sat there with great bravado and paid bills. I often wonder now what I paid them with.

Despite the bills I throve on the knowledge that I was responsible for the success or failure of this enterprise, and that what once had been a wild, impossible dream was now a reality. I vowed that no matter what obstacles were ahead I would make this thing a success.

One night, almost on the stroke of twelve, I was awakened by the ringing of the telephone bell beside my bed. At the other end was Mr. Gerecke. Under stress of some excitement, he offered me the house as it stood, except for the grand piano which belonged to his wife, and for half the price he had previously quoted. The Germans had been notified that by three o'clock on the following day all German property in the French Concession would be confiscated by the French. He offered me the option until next day noon, stipulating that out of the purchase price I must remit the sum of $36,000 (gold) to the firm of Schultz and Ruckaber of New York, paying the remainder into his account in the Deutsche Asiatische Bank in Shanghai.

My husband, sitting up in his bed not three feet away, could hear every word of Mr. Gerecke's excited conversation, but before he could interrupt I said,

"Done, I'll take it."

I hung up the receiver and looked defiantly at my sorely worried husband.

"Annie, are you mad?" he protested. "Where *are* you going to get the money? And if you do get it how in heaven's name are you going to send thirty-six thousand dollars into the United States to be paid to a German firm?"

"Well, I can try," I said.

At eleven o'clock the next morning I had been the rounds of

the banks. I had been to the telephone company and to several personal friends. They had all referred flatteringly to my personal credit but no one would risk lending money to be paid to a German. I was as far from my goal as the North Pole is from the South and my option expired in an hour. I was about to give up, to my husband's great relief, when I had a brain wave.

A few minutes later I was in the drawing room of my old friend, Tang Shao-yi, one of China's great men and former Premier of the Provisional Republic.* I told him my story, my words tumbling over each other in my eagerness, and I ended by announcing that I must have the sum within fifteen minutes.

"Where are you going to get it?" he asked.

"From you," I said.

"Ai yah!" He sat up very straight.

"We have no time to talk about it, Mr. Tang," I said. "You know the place and you know me. We can arrange all the gruesome details this afternoon or tomorrow. Only now, this minute, I must have the money, if it's only for today!"

Five minutes before my option expired we arrived at the Deutsche Asiatische Bank. Mr. Tang's check was accepted and I had my property. The deed, insurance policies and other documents were handed over to me. Everything was in order and the deeds were registered promptly in the land office of the American Consulate.

The first part of my contract I had met, but the almost insurmountable obstacle to closing the deal was the transference of the money to the United States. Nine times I cabled the thirty-six thousand dollars across the Pacific and nine times it was cabled back to me. Schultz and Ruckaber were blacklisted and no one dared receive the money for them. After spending a small fortune in cables I had another belated in-

* In October, 1938, Tang Shao-yi was assassinated at his home in Shanghai by Chinese who believed, erroneously, that he was pro-Japanese.

spiration and cabled it to my sister without a word of explanation. In time a letter followed, relieving her of her bewilderment, and the transaction was completed.

The very day the deeds were registered with the American Consulate, an official from the French Municipal Council called on me. After the usual amenities he asked if I were Mr. Gerecke's tenant.

"No, I'm not the tenant, I'm the owner of this property," I said, trying unsuccessfully to conceal my pride.

He seemed surprised but he certainly was no more surprised than I at finding myself the owner of this magnificent estate.

"And when did you buy it, Madame?"

I told him.

"Ah! And may I ask why you bought it, Madame? How much you paid, and why there is no record of this sale at the French Consulate?"

I showed him the deeds and the tax receipt and explained that the suddenness of the transaction accounted for my apparent irregularities. He apologized for having troubled me and rose to go.

"Just a moment, please," I said. "You called on me as Mr. Gerecke's tenant and I would like to know the reason why?"

He replied it was to notify me that he was my landlord and that all money for rent should be paid to the French Municipal Council.

"Then it is true you have taken over all the German properties in Frenchtown?"

He shrugged and smiled charmingly. "Mr. Gerecke had very good judgment to sell you this place so suddenment. And you, Madame, the good fortune to buy at that moneys. So beautiful! So *magnifique!*"

Two weeks later my husband left for France and in addition to the burdens I voluntarily had heaped upon my shoulders there was that of not knowing what was happening to him.

For months I did not even know where he was, and even then the news was reduced to the barest facts.

Many times during that period I was truly thankful for any work or worry that would occupy my mind to the exclusion of useless wonderings as to how he fared.

CHAPTER XVIII

Trouble at No. 30 Pichon Loo

I WANTED MY HOSPITAL TO BE PERFECT, WHATEVER IT COST. I
wanted it as different from the whitewashed walls, straw-
mattressed and red-blanketed beds of the Soochow Hospital as
it possibly could be. The General Hospital, the Victoria Nursing Home, the Isolation Hospital and those that appeared and
disappeared sporadically were the only hospitals in all that
huge city of Shanghai, aside from the few operated solely for
the benefit of the Chinese, and I felt that mine would fill a real
need.

But all sorts of outside factors gnawed at the perfection of
my particular paradise, The Fearn Sanatorium. As the hospital
lay within the limits of the French Concession, it was not long
before I made the acquaintance of the French Police. We had
lived in Frenchtown when our home was at the Eighth Fairy
Bridge, but now I discovered that although a private person
may go for years without ever coming in contact with the forces
of law and order, the head of an institution, no matter how
small, runs into diverse difficulties, directly or indirectly in-
volving the police.

Shortly after the sanatorium opened I was perturbed to find
that the refuse carts which were supposed to collect the garbage
were ignoring Number 30 Route Pichon. This went on for
three days. Mademoiselle, my French nurse, wrote twice to the
Municipal Council, notifying them of the omission, but both
notes were disregarded. Finally the Number One Boy placed
the refuse outside the south wall of our property.

The following day the gardener was subpœnaed. Highly

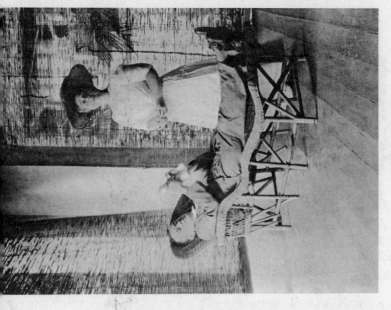

With my husband at our home at the Eight Fairy Bridge.

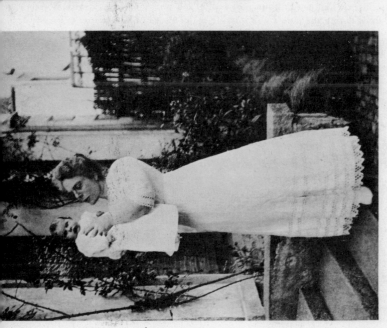

With one of my 6,017 babies.

Wheelbarrows are used to transport coolies and amahs. Myself and Mrs. Wilbur Estes, during the time I was working at the Margaret Williamson Clinic.

I am driven in state to call on a patient. The patient's husband is driving the donkey.

indignant, I went to the French Mixed Court. When he was called to the witness stand I stood near by.

The magistrate opened the case by saying that my servant had been rude to the garbage coolies. Before the gardener had a chance to speak I said that I did not doubt it, that I did not vouch for the unfailing courtesy of my servants any more than he could for that of the garbage collectors.

"Madame, your boys also have been rude to my policemen," he said.

"Very likely," I answered, "but the conduct of the police is not always above reproach." I drew a long breath and went on. "This is beside the point and I will not pay a five dollar fine because your coolies refuse to remove my garbage. Coolies are paid to do that."

A tall gentleman dressed in gray, the prosecuting attorney, rose and spoke fiercely and quickly. Unfortunately he spoke in French and I could understand only an occasional word. When I thought he had gone on long enough, I held up my hand for him to stop. He subsided courteously and with a polite bow took his seat.

"And," I continued, "the Council really ought to pay me for my inconvenience. I intend to see that there are no flies in my hospital."

I turned to the prosecuting attorney. "Have you anything more to say?" I asked.

"I beg the pardon of Madame," he replied, rising and bowing deeply, "but as yet I have had nothing to say."

"Then I shall go," I replied with hauteur, and motioning to the gardener to follow me, I left the courtroom.

But that was not the end of it. The following morning as I was stepping into my car, the gardener and a policeman came running, the latter having another order for the gardener's appearance in court. I was furiously annoyed.

"Stay here," I commanded the gardener. I drove at once to

the French Mixed Court and stormed into the judge's chambers where I demanded to know the reason why my gardener had received another summons when the case had been settled.

The judge looked as alarmed as though a bomb had burst.

"It is all settled," I went on wrathfully, "unless I decide to bring suit for damages against the French Municipal Council."

"But Madame," he remonstrated, "you have dismissed the case with such suddenment that I had no time to make the judgment. The gardener must come to receive it."

I joined in the laugh at my expense, shook hands and went home.

Some little time after this one of the patients in the hospital was a girl who had attempted suicide. She had taken mercuric chloride and all night the doctors fought to save her life. With the morning came hope and three policemen who marched in solemnly and ranged themselves by my desk.

"Dr. Fearn," said one, "as this is your first experience with us in a case of this kind, before you say anything we would like to remind you that it is well for you to stand in with the police. Also, before you say anything, I would mention the fact that the punishment given an attempted suicide is two years in prison."

I bowed gravely in acknowledgment of the majesty of the law while my heart beat in double-quick time.

"We know," continued the policeman, "that Miss —— is here and we have strong suspicion of the cause. What can you tell us about it?"

Praying silently that I would say the right thing, I answered, "Only that it was not with the intention of taking her life that she took the poison. It was in an hysterical attempt to frighten her friend into giving her the thing she wanted."

"That is your considered opinion?"

I repeated it fervently.

The leader jotted down some notes in a little book, bowed

to me, we shook hands all around, and the three marched out as solemnly as they had entered.

A man came to the hospital once, ostensibly for undisturbed quiet. "No visitors," he had growled. After he had been with us for some time, the doctor discharged him as cured, but the day he was to leave, my three friends of the police appeared before me.

"Here we are again, Dr. Fearn," the spokesman said.

"What now?" I asked with a sinking heart.

"We have a warrant for the arrest of one of your patients," he said, and gave me the name of the gentleman who had requested rest. They informed me that he had, among other indiscretions, stolen a motor car, and had come to my sanatorium to evade the law.

I sent for Miss Beane, my head nurse, who escorted the policemen to the patient's room. As they walked in the gentleman said just one word, "damn!" and getting out of bed began pulling on his trousers.

One habit of the police force caused me serious annoyance. The Annamite policemen were drilled regularly in a vacant lot next to my hospital and the noise had driven several patients away. In despair I finally called on the French Consul-general, M. Wilden (later the French Minister to China), to ask him, if possible, to change the drill ground to a place far away from my property. Few things could be more fatal to a hospital than a noisy neighborhood.

The noise stopped that very day. He was so nice about it that I told him my other worries.

The terrible dogs whose incessant barking had formed a noisy background to my first night there had never stopped barking; I was at my wit's end to think of some way of getting rid of them. Every Chinese city is cursed with hundreds of *wonks* (ownerless mongrels) who roam the streets, making the nights hideous, but Shanghai is less harassed than most. I simply was paying one of the penalties for being on the outskirts of the city.

M. Wilden was extremely sympathetic and told me that at the first sound of a dog barking I was to telephone to the nearest police station and say that it was the Consul-general's order that any barking dog should be captured and impounded. He promised that he would inform the police and instruct them to pay immediate attention to calls from my sanatorium.

How the police did it I do not know, but in less than a week we were enjoying the comfort of noiseless nights. Perhaps word circulated among the city's dogs that that part of Frenchtown was unhealthy.

Another brush with the authorities turned out to be amusing, but it might have been a tragedy. We were re-tarring the macadamized drive from the house to the gate and in melting the tar the overhanging branches of the tree caught fire. A small rustic pavilion on a knoll facing the door of the sanatorium was soon in flames.

The hospital was full, and I put in a frantic call for the fire department to come immediately. To my horror, a calm voice at the other end of the line informed me that they could not possibly come as the head of the department was out and they must await his instructions.

The entire hospital staff went to work and succeeded in extinguishing the fire with the garden hose. Half an hour later, when we might have been burned to cinders for all they knew, the fire department telephoned, asking if we still needed help.

The fire department scored heavily later on. When my cottage for the nurses was built, the Chinese owner of the property next door had been extremely kind in allowing the contractors to cart material across his property, thus saving a tremendous amount of wear and tear on my macadamized drive. I was duly appreciative of his courtesy and did not fail to give expression to my gratitude. Then he suddenly decided to build a magnificent residence on the lot and, although he had plenty of ground, bang up against my tiny cottage.

That was bad enough, but one morning I discovered to my dismay that he was erecting a bamboo fence, thirty feet high and nearly two hundred feet long, upon our boundary line. I rushed over and inquired, in the friendliest manner possible at the moment, the reason for this fence.

"I am a very nervous man," he replied, "and I can't see a nurse or a hospital without at once feeling ill. Nor do I like windows overlooking my garden."

I begged and pleaded but the bamboo fence went up and stayed up.

Various members of his large family became ill; we received emergency calls at all hours of the day and night. Our nearness in case of sickness was a godsend to him.

Typhoons came and blew the fence down on my cottage; eaves and gutters were broken; the wind whistled through the bamboo with the noise of shrieking demons and rocked it to and fro with creakings and groanings all through the night. The nurses could not sleep; the patients complained bitterly and left the hospital.

Then my neighbor, Mr. En Fu, brought his son to us for an appendectomy. During the operation the distracted father sat by my side in the little alcove-office. I rejoiced with him when the operation was safely over. As he left he clasped my hands warmly.

"I can never thank you enough, Dr. Fearn, for all your kindness," he said. "If there is ever anything I can do, don't hesitate to call on me." I nodded silently toward the fence.

"Oh, that," he said, "is impossible. I am sorry but that is a different matter."

When I heard that he was leaving for England and would be gone two years I begged for the temporary removal of the fence. After I had signed papers, promising to replace it or produce a satisfactory hedge in his absence, the fence was removed. I spent hundreds of dollars on tall shrubs and trees. It was a beautiful hedge but two years later my neighbor demanded his fence back.

I was desperate and furious and applied to my lawyer who merely suggested that I begin rebuilding the fence. I was much too desolate to be reassured by the twinkle in his eye.

Two days later, with an alarming clatter and a loud ringing of gongs, the fire department tore up to my door. Uniformed firemen rushed around, took measurements, inspected the grounds; then noisily and conspicuously they rushed out. From my sanatorium they drove next door where, with a great deal of official haranguing and noise, a similar performance took place.

My ingenious lawyer had applied for a permit to build a fence of the exact measurements of the original, the first application ever received, I suppose, for such a minor detail as a bamboo fence. The next day a written permit was issued for the erection of a fence not to exceed six feet nor to be placed any nearer my cottage than ten feet, for it constituted a fire hazard. That was the end of the fence.

On April 12, 1917, real disaster threatened me again. Mr. Tang Shao-yi informed me that by the end of the mouth he must have the money he had loaned me. Only a moment before I had been rejoicing; all the patients were doing well; most of the current bills were paid, and it was a glorious spring day. With Mr. Tang's message my heart sank.

I was determined that my hospital, on which I had expended so much energy, would not be relinquished without a struggle. I went to Mr. A. G. Stevens, manager of the Hongkong and Shanghai Banking Corporation. At first he shook his head. He had positive instructions from the Hongkong office not to make loans on real estate. He suggested that I see Mr. Edward Ezra, whose estate joined my property, and ask him to buy it and give me a five-year lease. If he declined I was to return to the bank.

"Until then," said Mr. Stevens, "do not worry."

Easy to say.

In the meantime it was necessary to know the exact value of the property, so Mr. Blake of the Standard Oil Company assigned the head architect of that company to make the appraisal. The result was 102,000 taels on the real estate alone. Mr. Stevens thought this too high and sent the bank appraiser. He was even more enthusiastic about the house and the property, and his appraisal, much to my delight, was several thousand taels higher than the first.

Mr. Ezra greeted me cordially but explained that as he was a British subject it would be exceedingly unwise for him to buy my property so soon after I had purchased it from a German. Sir Everard Frazer, the British Consul-general, had discouraged him about such a transaction, pointing out that if a Britisher came into possession of the place at this time no power on earth could make the purchase seem aboveboard to the British community.

I went back to Mr. Stevens; there was nothing else to do.

After examining the second appraisal and listening to my tale of woe the banker said, "That settles it, Dr. Fearn. We'll have to see you through. You can tell Mr. Tang that his money will be ready for him on June fourth and you may come with him on that day and bring the deeds with you."

A great weight rolled off my mind. To assure him of my appreciation I offered to relieve him of his appendix, free of charge, should he ever care to part with it.

"Thanks," he laughed, "but I still have it and I think I'll keep it."

On the appointed day I went with Mr. Tang to the bank and gave him my check for 86,000 taels. When Mr. Tang had gone Mr. Stevens turned to me.

"Now," he said, "let's have a talk. I don't suppose you have any assurance of being able to return this money in the near future?"

"Not the slightest," I replied with perfect honesty.

"Suppose you should die?"

"That would be your gain," I answered.

"But suppose you should fail in health; have typhoid for instance?"

I told him that with the assistance of Dr. Jackson, the members of his firm, and my nurses, I believed the hospital work would go on as if I were still at my post. He then said that my success had been phenomenal, and that as he had heard of my work and my hospital from all sides he was convinced that I was really an unusual woman. Therefore, and because he thought the sanatorium was needed, he had been willing to act in direct opposition to the head office and advance the money. He ended his talk by saying:

"Well, Dr. Fearn, all that I can say is I believe you are a natural financier."

"I hope," I said, "that is what my husband means when he calls me a 'born gambler.' "

Thus, with the aid of two loyal friends, Tang Shao-yi and the Hongkong and Shanghai Banking Corporation, I was able to buy my hospital and to keep it. Both were world prominent. Tang Shao-yi was one of the leading financiers in Shanghai at that time. Although retired from political life, he still acted as adviser to the government, collected Chinese porcelains, and was an ardent baseball fan.

For months after this crisis we sailed on the very crest of the waves of prosperity and popularity. Expenses were met, interest paid and small but regular payments were even being made on my overdraft. Success seemed so assured that, because of our inability to meet the demands for rooms, I decided to build. I wanted to add a wing, or even put up a separate building for maternity cases. I talked this over with Dr. Jackson who said, "No, not now."

"Wait awhile," he cautioned. "One never knows what may happen. It is just possible that a case may be brought in with an infectious disease. Other patients may be infected and lives might be lost, and then where would you be? Don't be in a hurry."

Our conversation took place on Friday, July 13, the day before the National French fete. That night, as a forerunner of the next day's celebration, the annual torchlight procession was held. A party of ten or twelve young people, after tennis on my lawn in the afternoon, went to join the throngs of sightseers. All day Saturday most of Shanghai stood in the blistering heat of the July sun, watching or taking part in the festivities.

Sunday morning I awoke at five. It was raining and I thought that as long as there were no serious cases I would spend the morning luxuriously in bed. I had just turned over with the comforting thought that here was one of my rare opportunities for a good rest when the night nurse brought me a note from Mr. Zankle, asking me to come at once to see his wife who was very ill.

I did and she was. From that moment until two o'clock the next morning I never stopped.

In an hour from the time I reached the Zankle home Mrs. Zankle was on her way to the Isolation Hospital. Scarlet fever! By night I had eleven cases in that hospital. Every doctor in town was clamoring for admittance for his patients, and by the following night there was no accommodation to be had there; every bed was full. Nearly all of the patients were residents of the fashionable Bubbling Well district. Whole families were down with the disease. Houses, even groups of houses, in that residential section were isolated under quarantine. It was an epidemic of a particularly virulent type of streptococcic scarlet fever.

From the very first the report was unaccountably circulated that the infection had started at my tennis party. The slender foundation for this rumor was that several of my guests were among the first to be attacked by the disease. The fact that they had gone from my house to spend the evening standing side by side with innumerable Chinese watching the procession was ignored. People lost their heads; they fairly went mad with excitement and fear. It was reported that I had thirty cases, all of whom were dying, and later that I myself had succumbed. This last rumor brought a telephone call from the undertaker. He was quite taken aback when I answered it in person and declared myself to be very much alive. The French librarian informed us that we must burn the books that we had taken from the library; on no account was a single book to be returned. My beloved sanatorium was called "The Pest House"!

And there was not a patient, not even a sore throat, in my place! The doctors all stood by me, but they couldn't stop those ridiculous and astounding stories. Dr. Jackson, as usual my stand-by, told me not to worry, that it would all blow over, but I had little heart to look to the future.

The hospital was closed for six weeks, partly because it was during the hot season when most of the people who could afford the sanatorium were away, but very largely because of those abominable stories. The expenses kept on. Again I was in desperate straits. The doctors and my patients gave me their undiminishing loyalty; if it had not been for them I think I should have given up. With the hospital empty many needed changes might have been made, but I didn't dare incur added expense when we were so wobbly financially. The only thing I could do was try to forget my own troubles by visiting the convalescing and the quarantined.

Trouble at No. 30 Pichon Loo

As Dr. Jackson had prophesied, it did blow over finally, although it nearly blew me over first. With the beginning of September we opened again, and the hospital was filled almost from the very first.

But the treasury was nearly empty, and if it had not been for Miss Christine England, one of my nurses, I don't know how we could have weathered that terrible summer. Miss England accompanied a convalescing patient of mine to Japan, and for her services the Fearn Sanatorium received ten dollars per day. That was all the actual cash I had to meet current expenses. At that it was not enough to pay the salaries of the nurses and the servants, and I was forced to increase my overdraft. In recognition of her assistance in keeping the wolf from the door Miss England was called "Wolf" and the name still sticks.

With the coming of cold weather I was faced with a coal situation that actually made my hair turn white. Coal at that time was thirty-two dollars (Mexican) or more a ton. Early in the summer I had ordered part of the winter's supply, several hundred tons. This coal reached Woosung where it was held up by the coal guild which had a monopoly on all coal brought to Shanghai. While this was an outrage on the part of the guild, we were at its mercy, and nothing could be done. In addition, they put a prohibitive price on the coal in spite of the fact that there was an abundance in Shanghai. All this meant that I had a coal bill of from eight hundred to one thousand dollars (Mexican) a month to meet and, as usual, I had no money.

Life was just one big trouble. Why had I ever elected to travel such a thorny path? But having started I had to go on, and there were compensations.

CHAPTER XIX

Mosquitoes and Menials

ONE OF MY NUMEROUS ACTIVITIES WAS AN ATTEMPT TO MAKE
Frenchtown as unhealthy for mosquitoes as my immediate neighborhood was for "wonks." The mosquito is the
major pest of Shanghai and the French Concession its strong-
hold. It lies on the edge of the Settlement, bordered by rice
fields which are flooded during the planting and growing
season. Here the mosquitoes find ideal breeding places, and
every breeze wafts them into the foreign occupied area.

The mosquito problem became so acute that when Frenchtown hosts invited guests to dinner they offered them, with
the customary cocktail, pillow cases into which they could slip
their feet and cover their legs from the annoying insects.

In 1918 we opened our campaign. Women of every nationality were marshaled for war against the enemy. Plans of
strategy were drawn up and proclaimed from the housetops.
Then the work began. Gutters and drains were cleaned and
drenched with kerosene; bamboo fence posts were examined
and a hole bored at the base of the top section to let the water
drain away, otherwise it would act as a cup and be a fine nursery for some mother mosquito; flowerpots and their saucers
were emptied daily and sprayed; puddles and ground drains
were inspected, and many unsuspected breeding places were
unearthed. A pond of stagnant water at the side of the hospital
drew so much attention that the Health Department of the
French Municipal Council ordered it filled in.

In the midst of our operations Dr. Alvin J. Cox, former
Director of the Bureau of Science in Manila, arrived in Shang-

hai. It was due to his persistent efforts that Manila had been practically freed from mosquitoes, so we made him our commander-in-chief for the duration of our mosquito war and his visit.

He gave us much useful information and even cabled to Manila ordering a shipment of Gambusia Affinis, top-water minnows commonly called mosquito fish. A wire sent from Manila advised us of the departure of the fish and suggested that we meet the steamer immediately upon arrival. The coming of these amazing fish caused quite a flutter among the anti-mosquito forces. Several flippant people wanted us to send a delegation of women with banners and a town band to meet them, but as the steamer arrived at midnight only Dr. Cox and I drove down to the wharf. A nursery of fine wire netting had been prepared for them in the Bethel Mission Hospital pond, but only twenty-one, out of the several hundred which had been shipped in a five-gallon kerosene tin, survived the hardships of the trip.

They were queer looking little things, about three-quarters of an inch long, all eyes and stomachs. But if they were not beautiful no one cared, for each peculiar looking stomach was guaranteed to dispose of five thousand mosquito larvae a day. And apart from this valuable attribute, we were also assured that the fish would reproduce like super guinea pigs. We planned the distribution of their progeny to all parts of the city, but we expected too much of them. They lay down on the job and died. We were told afterward that they would have died in winter in any case, as they could not have withstood the rigors of the Shanghai climate.

This was a woman's undertaking that seemingly had the whole-hearted support of the men. Our organization included representatives from the Shanghai Municipal Council Health Department, and Mr. Tillott, chief of the Health Department of the French Concession, also took a personal interest in our operations. Kerosene was donated in large quantities by the two municipal councils and by the leading oil companies. I was unsuspicious, therefore, of anything but the friendliest co-operation from the head of the Municipal Health Department, and I walked gaily into his office one morning, confident of the usual warm welcome. When I asked if one of the men in the department might be appointed to work with us permanently the very atmosphere congealed about me.

I sank into a chair and sat speechless while Dr. Davis walked the floor, pouring on my luckless head his official indignation and his private opinion of us for poaching on his preserves, for making a laughingstock of him and the work of the Health Department which had waged war for years against the ubiquitous mosquito.

"And now," roared the doctor, "now everybody's saying that since the women have taken hold of the matter something will be done!"

I wanted to walk out of the office, but for the moment I had lost the use of my legs. I sat still and listened, and realized that this meant the end of the mosquito campaign. With the head of the Municipal Health Department resenting our very existence our efforts would inevitably fail for lack of official support. We were forced to surrender and leave it to the men to rid Shanghai of the pest.

And now, no longer do the mosquitoes bother the residents of Shanghai; that is, those who find it convenient to stay high above the city in airplanes or balloons.

For many months we had been feeling that we were living on top of a powder keg. Under cover of the war, as early as 1915, Japan had made her impossible twenty-one demands on China. Although she did not succeed in enforcing an obedience that would automatically have stripped China of the last remnant of sovereignty, she did succeed in establishing herself in Kiaochow, which formerly had been leased to Germany.

To consolidate her position still further, secret treaties were made with Great Britain and France in which, in return for Japan's aid in Eastern submarine warfare, the two European nations promised to support Japan's claim in China. When these facts were publicized during the Peace Conference in 1919, the atmosphere grew thick with a sense of impending trouble. Strenuous efforts were made at Versailles to settle the question, but the Japanese continued to hold Kiaochow and the important Shantung railway zone, and the Chinese continued to protest vigorously but vainly.

An added cause of resentment lay in the fact that certain officials high in the government were supposed to have conceded Kiaochow in return for loans made them by Japan. When the Chinese delegates refused to sign the treaty of Versailles, their action received the acclaim of the Chinese people.

An explosion was bound to occur and did, on June 5, 1919. A group of students in Peking attacked and burned the house of Tsao Ju-lin, one of the pro-Japanese leaders. Some agitators were arrested and imprisoned, which only fanned the already mounting flame. The agitation spread beyond the student body, and a boycott of Japanese goods was started. Then Shanghai students went on a sympathetic strike and on that hot summer's day, in token of their agreement with the student strikers, the merchants closed their doors. Every shop in town put up its shutters, the telephone operators were called out, and even chauffeurs were threatened with such dire consequences if they refused to join the strike that they did not dare to ride beside their foreign "masters."

There were days when the electric light and water plants were threatened, but everything was organized should the strike reach that point. Volunteers were held in readiness to take over and operate the plants, and every precaution was taken against incendiarism or destruction of the works.

My Days of Strength

When my husband had been home on a short furlough from France I had asked him to send me a sample of "bully beef," my curiosity having been aroused by all that I had heard of it. He had arranged with the purser of the ship which had brought him and his coolies from France to send me a case, and the result was that I received not one but two cases which now were to prove a boon.

With every market closed, the question of food in such an establishment as mine naturally caused great anxiety. The sanatorium was crowded, and I was beginning to be seriously worried when the "bully beef" arrived. We rationed it sparingly, as we had no way of knowing how long the strike would last. I remember giving six precious tins to Dr. Jackson and Dr. F. M. Neild, as special marks of favor.

As usual, the foreigners accepted the situation with philosophic indifference to the inconveniences to which they were put. There was no resentment; for once we were in full sympathy with the Chinese, although we would have preferred to have them choose some other method of expressing their indignation against the Japanese.

Later, in April, 1920, the students united in declaring a second strike, as a protest against the Chinese government's entering into direct negotiations with Japan in regard to the return of Kiaochow. The strike became nation-wide, and for a time threatened to be as effective as the first. In Shanghai it led to a clash between soldiers and students, but in the end, owing to lack of public support, it was abandoned. This brought about a temporary loss of student prestige, and increased the effort of the officials to suppress the unions.

One of my worst worries throughout both strikes was that the servants might leave. There were rumors that this threatened, but all my servants remained loyally at their posts.

As a matter of fact, in all my years of experience with servants in China, I have found them singularly loyal and efficient, in

The Fearn Sanatorium at 30 Pichon Loo, Shanghai.

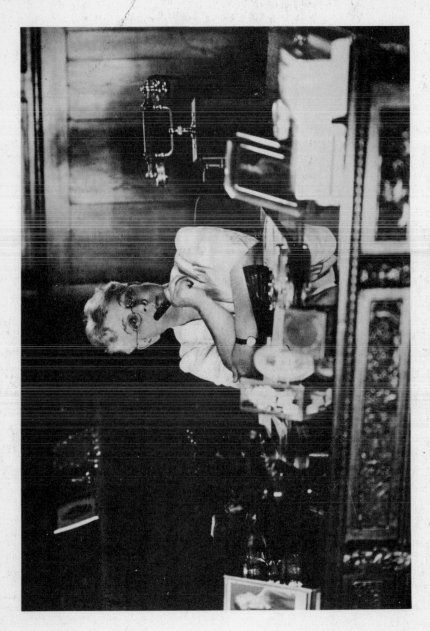

In lieu of an office, I placed my desk in an alcove in the entrance hall . . . .

their own way. I have heard a great deal of the so-called "rice" Christian but to my knowledge I have encountered only one example. He was the best boy, as far as work was concerned, that I have ever known, but I neither liked nor trusted him. My husband, on the other hand, thought him about ready for translation. He called himself a "cushion."

"I am a cushion," he would say, and it was a long time before I realized that he meant he was a Christian.

"I am a cushion," became a byword with me, much to my husband's distress, for he thought me exceedingly unjust.

My husband was home on furlough when one night about three o'clock the phone on the table between our beds rang. Picking up the receiver, I listened to a lengthy dissertation from the other end of the line.

"Police station! drunk! gambling!" I exclaimed at intervals, keeping one eye on my attentive husband. "Creating disturbances in the street! He's in jail! Very well, I'll tell him; he may do something about it in the morning. Good night." I banged back the receiver and drew the covers up around my head.

"What's all that about?" asked my husband.

"It's your 'cushion,'" I replied. "He's in jail and wants you to come, immediately, this minute, and get him out."

But he was such an unusually efficient servant that I kept him on, even after I discovered that he was running a gambling den in the servant's quarters where he was simply coining money, and incidentally burning my coal, now fifty dollars a ton, all night long.

He began to come on duty later and later every morning in spite of warnings and admonitions, and one morning when I appeared in the dining room at my usual hour, seven o'clock, there was no sign of the "cushion." I waited for him until eighty-thirty when he rushed in, buttoning up his long gown, and looking very busy indeed.

"Boy," I said, making an effort to control my temper. "You have been told repeatedly to be here by seven o'clock. . . ."

Before I could say another word he interrupted me.

"Dr. Fearn, I think I give you too much trouble. Suppose more better I stop."

"I quite agree with you," I said.

"All right, I stop."

A few minutes later various amahs began coming in, positively popeyed with excitement.

"The Number One Boy stop? Then what?"

The Boy sent messages to the effect that he had served me well for years. He had no work; what was to become of his wife, of his children?

"Tell him that's no concern of mine. Stopping was his idea."

The distressed cook and coolies came in to say that if "Number One" stopped they also would have to go. He had ordered it. It was *M'Fah* (had to be).

"All right," I said, "go."

I kept my face hidden behind the paper while they moaned that they did not want to go but it was *M'Fah, M'Fah*. I suppose they owed him money. As they trailed out the Boy himself appeared—to ask for his wages. I dropped the paper.

"Your what?" I demanded.

He gave me one look and fled.

Almost immediately the Number One Amah came rushing in to report that all the boys were *tanging* (tying up their bedding).

"Let them tang."

Then I was informed that all the coolies were *tanging*. Still later I learned that three of the cooks were *tanging*.

In half an hour quite an army of dejected boys, coolies and cooks were to be seen walking up Route Pichon while I faced the appalling situation—a house full of patients, an important operation set for that morning, and my large and efficient staff reduced to the old cook who had been with me for over twenty years, the chauffeur and the head gardener.

Collecting my wits I got busy on the telephone. With the able assistance of the Standard Oil "mess" who were at that time occupying the Blake house across the street, and with the help of other friends, I was able to corral a borrowed staff of boys and coolies sufficient for our immediate needs. No one but myself was conscious that there had been the slightest jar in the household machinery, and by night I had a complete new staff.

One of our boys we called "the boomerang." He was so eager to oblige that he never waited for the completion of an order.

"Go to my room, Boy, get the—" and he was off like a shot with no idea of what he was to get. On his rebound I would ask, "Did you get it?"

"My no savee what thing you wanchee, Mississee," he would reply sheepishly.

The Chinese servant is extraordinarily adaptable, and it is amazing how in a few short weeks they can master Occidental difficulties. The chauffeur, for instance, is a recent development who has replaced the old time *mafoo* (carriage driver). "Mississee, my can do chauffeur pidgin," proudly announces your former *mafoo*, your Number Two Cook, or your pantry coolie, as the case may be. Sometimes he is good, sometimes very bad, but good or bad he has had the courage to make the attempt and the intelligence to learn. Their accomplishments seem especially remarkable when one considers that the mechanical age has touched China but lightly and to most Chinese machinery is as mysterious as the minds of their gods.

I have already mentioned my old cook, who was with me for more than two decades. He was an example of the best in Chinese servants, loyal, quick, and after much training comparatively clean, and thoroughly efficient. No emergency was too great for him. He could cope with any problem. I have a vivid recollection of him, on a cold, raw Saturday when six guests I had invited for tiffin arrived just after the table had been cleared from the nurses' meal. I had issued the invitations casually a week before and forgotten about them completely. Twenty minutes after I had informed the cook that the guests, of whom he had known nothing, had arrived, we seven sat down to a delectable meal—fruit cocktail, oxtail soup, fried sole, broiled chicken, ice cream and coffee. The guests hadn't the slightest idea that their coming had been a surprise to the cook.

I think one of the most amusing stories of servants was told me by a friend. She was giving a tiffin party one day and had ordered celery, a special delicacy in Shanghai at that time, coming in only on a few cold-storage steamers. Shortly before her guests were due to arrive she entered the kitchen to find the Boy cheerfully scrubbing the celery with a toothbrush. She pounced on him and threw the celery into the sink with a scandalized demand for an instant explanation.

The Boy stared at her, amazed at this outburst.

"Mississee, you no wanchee makee so much bobbery," he protested. "I talkee you true, this no b'long your toothbrush, this b'long my toothbrush."

It was a little later, in the spring of 1923 I think, when Jane Addams visited Shanghai. She was welcomed for her work and entertained for herself; and as President of the American Women's Club it was my duty to introduce her at various lectures and other functions. When all the speech making was over a round of parties started. A huge luncheon was given by Mrs. Gardner Crane, another officer of the American Women's Club. Miss Addams, of course, sat at the right and I at the left of the hostess. To my dismay and Mrs. Crane's, her well-trained boys persisted in serving me first, ignoring repeated reprimands and instructions to serve Miss Addams first. After the guests had gone Mrs. Crane called the Boy to her.

"Boy, how fashion you have do this dreadful thing? You savvey any lady sitee my right must belong number one lady. You allee time have pay Dr. Fearn first, how fashion you have do this? Dr. Fearn have talkee you, I have talkee you. I no have any face, evelly man thinkee my no have any savvey Number One Boy."

The Boy replied, "My too savvey mississee. My no have makee mistake. Evelly man savvey suppose Dr. Fearn sitee table must pay she first. Evelly man savvey Dr. Fearn belong Shanghai number one lady."

The hostess evidently told this around as a good story for it was printed in *The China Press*. It came again to my ears at a luncheon as far away as New York when on November 11, 1928, the late George Bronson Rea and I shared honors at the Shanghai Tiffin Club, where nearly two hundred old Shanghai friends of mine assembled to welcome me home.

The experience which taught me the most in a short space of time about the proficiency of the Chinese servant was an accident that occurred at a tiffin party I gave for Mr. Charles Freer, one of the leading art experts of the world and the man who presented an unrivaled Whistler collection to the Smithsonian Institution. There were thirty or forty prominent business men present and I was extremely anxious to have the whole thing go off well.

Everything went smoothly until the fish course, when the boy serving the egg sauce, suddenly and without apparent reason or provocation, emptied the entire contents of the silver sauce bowl down the side of the guest of honor. Mr. Freer was in the midst of an animated account of his discovery of an ancient piece of Chinese pottery. Without the flicker of an eyelash he continued his discussion, talking brilliantly and holding his audience spellbound.

No one saw the accident except my embarrassed and horrified self. Without waiting for any orders from me, for I was

213

struck speechless, the boy left the room and noiselessly returned with a basin of water. He washed down the side of
the guest, removed his shoe and sock, and the handkerchief
from his overflowing pocket which he turned inside out and
scrubbed. He again left the room, only to return with a hot
iron and a small board and proceeded to press the pocket dry,
while Mr. Freer continued to hold the attention of the other
guests, who were, or pretended to be, utterly unaware of
the side show. In a few minutes the boy appeared again, replaced the now washed and ironed handkerchief in the pocket,
knelt down and silently indicated to Mr. Freer that his shoe
and sock were again in a wearable condition. I shall never
forget the sight of that naked foot as it was extended around
the chair leg while the boy first washed, dried, and then dressed
it. Mr. Freer continued to scintillate as he discussed Ko Yao
pottery and Whistler's paintings.

Mr. Freer never lost his equanimity. I, eventually, recovered
mine, and the tiffin party turned out to be a great success.

"I'm awfully sorry about that egg sauce," I said to Mr. Freer
as he was leaving. "If I'd had any idea you wanted to take it
with you I might have had it done up in a more portable form."

"The fact of the matter is, Dr. Fearn," he returned with the
utmost gravity, "that egg sauce was so delicious that rather than
miss it, I preferred to take it as I did."

That party was only one of many that I held in the music
room of my hospital which easily could be transformed into a
banquet hall to seat one hundred and twenty people. I was not
at all averse to taking advantage of it as an ideal place in
which to entertain.

When Shanghai was honored by the visit of three of the
shining lights of the medical world, Dr. G. E. de Scheinwitz,
Dr. John C. Clark, and Dr. E. F. Simpson, I invited one hundred doctors to meet them. Every nation was represented
except, I regret to say, the German. It was too soon after the

war for mutual pleasure in companionship. But it was a representative gathering of "the sheep and the goats" for there were at least eight women physicians present.

As my guests assembled in the lounge, to greet the three American men who stood for all that was finest in a profession which I honestly believed had done more than any other to rid the world of evils, I was flooded with a feeling of gratitude for all the good things I had been given—friendship, success, an honorable standing in an honorable profession.

CHAPTER XX

The Hospital of the Generous Queen

C HINESE NAMES HAVE ONLY ONE CHARACTER, ONE SYLLABLE, while ours have several. Immediately upon a foreigner's arrival in China, his Chinese friends set about correcting this mistake, and a suitable character with a sound similar to the first syllable of the Western name is found. My husband's proper Chinese name became *Fee Ung*, which meant, according to the inflection, either "Dirty Dish Water" or "Prominent Front Tooth." Mine, *Wuan Me-tu,* almost forgotten because of my more appropriate nickname of *Tai Foong*, had come to mean only Dr. Walter but its real meaning was "Queen, Generous and Virtuous."

I often teased my husband about the difference in our names, his so funny and mine so flattering, and although he said little I am sure that he resented it. Indeed, all of our married life was tinged by the merest shadow of a professional jealousy. He had a strong sense of masculine protectiveness, just under the surface, and he was never so completely himself as when helping the sick and the weak. But in marrying a woman who took life with both hands and people as she found them, this protective instinct was more or less frustrated. He would much rather have had his wife sit at home and be managed by him. For her devotion to duty as a doctor, however, he had only admiration.

And now we were to become rivals in good earnest. He returned from France on October 1, 1919, to take up at once his appointment as medical superintendent and director of the Shanghai General Hospital.

The Hospital of the Generous Queen

In 1862 Shanghai had only two hospitals for foreigners, the Shanghai Hospital and Dispensary and the Marine Hospital. These were insufficient as there was a great deal of illness, due to the stagnant pools, lack of proper drainage and the unsanitary habits of the Chinese population. At times the death rate was exceedingly high and there were frequent epidemics of cholera, smallpox and typhoid. There was urgent need of better hospital facilities, so shares were sold and the General Hospital came into being; but as years went by it was necessary for the Municipal Council to contribute to its upkeep.

In those early days Catholic nuns were the only foreign women available as nurses. The Sisters of Charity of St. Vincent de Paul served the General Hospital from 1862, when it was built, until 1912, when they withdrew and l'Institute des Sœurs Franciscaines continued the work, the Mother Superior sending out thirty sisters from Rome within two years. The first women Protestant missionary nurses did not come out to China until several years after my arrival there.

When the hospital was first built it was located between the West Gate and the Ningpo Joss House; later it was moved to Soochow Road. For many years the hospital suffered considerably from the locality in which it was situated. The wards and verandas of the old building faced the creek on Soochow Road, which had grown to be one of the noisiest streets of the Settlement. Immediately in front of the hospital buildings was a row of shops, occupied principally by ironmongers and blacksmiths, and the constant and unholy din rasped the nerves of the unfortunate patients. The incessant clamor of the hammering, the clanging of sheets of iron as they were unloaded from the boats tied up in the creek, combined with the shouts of the coolies and the ordinary street sounds to make the General Hospital a place to be avoided.

A reconstruction scheme had been under consideration for some time. My husband's appointment was a happy thought for all concerned, for his natural talent for organization had been fostered and his experience widened by his work at the hospital for the Chinese Labor Division of the British Army where they usually had as many as two thousand coolies to care for at one time. His new duties gave his ability an abundant scope, for it was a monstrous job.

The first thing he did was to order the shops pulled down and the wide space thus obtained in front of the hospital transformed into a garden of real beauty. Owing to my husband's cordial relations with the Municipal authorities, the police reduced the canal disturbance to a minimum. The shrieking sirens of the countless little launches were curbed and cargo sampans, loaded and unloaded by noisy crews, were allowed only within certain limits; and the police saw to it that there were no infringements on these new regulations. Changes within the hospital were soon as apparent as those wrought without, and it was not long before the board of directors and the Municipal Council realized that what hitherto had been an eyesore and a liability was fast becoming a beauty spot and an asset.

My husband had an apartment in the hospital, a corner suite on the fifth floor. The view from his window stretched out to that busiest of rivers, the Whangpoo, and over the surrounding city, of which the hospital seemed to be the center. At night it was like looking out over fairyland, with the lights of the tall buildings piercing the sky and the lower lights twinkling and blazing all around us.

When my husband became my professional rival I told him that I had no fear of him. His hospital was the largest in the Far East, but it was the most usual, it might be any hospital anywhere in the world; while mine, although it might be the smallest, certainly was the most unusual. I told him there was not another hospital like mine in the world. Laughingly he assured me that there wasn't; that there couldn't be anyone else quite so crazy as to attempt to run a hospital along the same extravagant lines.

We were friendly rivals, however, and I was genuinely glad to have his apartment to go to at night. It meant escaping from my own responsibilities for a few hours at least. He usually dined with me, or we dined out somewhere together, and returned to his rooms. At seven o'clock in the morning my car was at the door of the General Hospital and half an hour later I was at the other end of town at my desk in the Fearn Sanatorium with the day's work begun.

There were times late at night when, worn out from a hard day and worried about serious cases in my own hospital, the prospect of walking down those long corridors, with more sick all about me, filled my soul with rebellion. The sight of the white clad nuns moving silently from room to room, and the sounds of suffering which struck with deadly familiarity against my ears as the doors opened, made me long to live in an atmosphere of health, of peace, of freedom from the burdens and the heartaches of others. I was discouraged and wearied by living so constantly with the sick. Often I was tempted to turn around, march back to my car and drive to my own place, but to what? To the same thing. Life in one hospital is not cheerful; life in two I found at times to be almost unbearable.

So I thought when I was depressed but it took only an amusing incident, or even a silly one, to lift me out of my dispirited state.

I remember the time a confinement case was in the next room to that of one of our leading business men who had been taken ill at sea as he was returning from a visit in America. He had been brought to me directly from the steamer but by this time he was well on the road to recovery, and was able to sit up, wrapped in a woolly shawl his wife had sent him. Carrying the new-born infant to its bassinet, I passed the open door of his room and stepped inside for a moment to show him our latest arrival.

"Isn't it sweet?" I asked. Being the father of three his reply was prompt and paternal. "Oh, Doctor, do let me hold it!"

I had just placed the baby in his arms and seated myself in the rocking chair by the bed when his wife walked in, her first visit. He motioned me to keep silent, and holding the baby tenderly against his chest he glanced up at her in feigned embarrassment.

"My dear," he said, "just another case of mistaken diagnosis."

Mr. Stanley Wright, an official high in the customs, came all the way from Peking for an appendectomy in my hospital "because," he said, "I hear your cocktails are so good." They were good but they were served only to the patient's visitors and not to the patient himself. When he was about ready to leave Mr. Wright sent for the head nurse, Miss Mary Hood, who found him sitting up in bed, clad in a chiffon bed jacket, on his head a lace boudoir cap, and in his arms a doll about the size of a new-born child.

"Miss Hood," he said, severely, "I refuse to stay in a hospital three weeks and have nothing to show for it, not even a drink."

The doll, solemnly christened Stanley Hood Fearn and duly presented to us, was treasured as our mascot.

Not all of our patients were so playful.

One day one of Shanghai's foremost doctors came to the hospital to engage a room for a patient who had been stung by a poisonous insect while big-game hunting in Siam. The patient was young William B. Leeds, Jr., the son of the tin plate king. His elbow had become infected from the bite and as time passed it had grown worse. It had taken him days to get out of the jungle and an even longer time to come by ship from Siam to Shanghai. When he arrived at the Fearn Sanatorium he was in an extremely serious condition and at first we thought amputation was imperative.

The Hospital of the Generous Queen

Young Leeds was accompanied by his secretary-valet and by his pet monkey. The young man was so sick and so persuasive that against my better judgment I allowed the monkey to stay and let it have the run of the conservatory. When I told the gardener that the monkey had been let loose he was furious and frightened. In a little time the gardener stood before me, immensely pleased. He had been right. The monkey had completely wrecked the conservatory. It was a shambles; pots were broken and plants had been uprooted. The only plant he had respected was the Euphorbia Splendius, the thorn tree. He hadn't tackled that. Posthaste the monkey was dispatched to the custody of the Sikh doorkeeper at the Astor House Hotel.

A few days later the sanatorium was impregnated by an awful odor; no one could go near the conservatory, and the patients were complaining. We investigated and found that Mr. Leeds' pet monkey had dismembered our pet cat, torn it to shreds and buried the remains under a potted fern.

Eventually Mr. Leeds recovered. There was no need for an operation and when he was ready to resume his journey he was accompanied by one of my nurses, Miss Shultz, and by a Chinese nurse boy, Morgan. Miss Shultz saw him safely across the Pacific and Morgan took over from there, going with him to New York and on to Europe, staying with him for a year.

When the year's contract was up Morgan returned to the Fearn Sanatorium. He was happy to be home again. He said he liked it better than the palace where they had visited Mr. Leeds' mother who had married Prince Christopher of Greece.

I asked him to describe the palace.

"Oh, it was all right," he answered, "only it wasn't anything like this."

I could well believe him, especially at that particular time when my sanatorium seemed more like an insane asylum than an orderly hospital. I once said that I had trained in surgery and degenerated into obstetrics. But at this time I felt that I should have trained in psychiatry and opened a home for mental cases. In fact, I was told many times that I had missed my calling; that I should have run a home for d.t. cases, for I had a good control of them. When Morgan returned, I had just sent the wife of a judge and the aunt of a prominent Britisher to the Mental Ward of the Isolation Hospital and I had my hands full trying to handle a shell-shock case. I'm sure Morgan was right—the Fearn Sanatorium wasn't anything like that gracious Grecian palace.

My shell-shock patient was a Britisher, one of the largest breeders of fine horses in the world. He had come to Shanghai during the course of a long ocean voyage because traveling on the sea seemed to quiet him better than anything else. He was quite all right in Shanghai until he came down with pneumonia and was brought to my hospital. Even then he showed no signs of shock. After several weeks his doctor pronounced him cured and one morning he was permitted to dress and go out to the bank where he cashed a large check, made steamer reservations, and then returned to my hospital where he was to remain the few days until his ship sailed.

Although he was completely cured of pneumonia and had shown no visible sign of being mentally off-balance, I nevertheless kept a nurse with him every moment, night and day. His nurse, no bigger than a minute, sat by his bedside until dawn. That night there was a terrific storm. The patient, on retiring, had placed his roll of money beside a glass of water on the bed table. The thunder and forked-lighting, reminiscent of battles over no-man's land, awakened him with a start. He sat bolt upright and reached for his money, overturning the water glass which crashed to the floor. This sudden noise like a rifle report set him off. He was out of bed in a flash, a raving maniac. He rushed from the room and with the strength of a wild man snatched up the heavy beamed steps that led to the attic and heaved them into a window on the stairway, where they stuck. A large circular iron table stood in the hall and he picked that up and threw it over the railing, and went leaping and bounding down the stairs behind it.

I telephoned his doctor to come at once. He, with some magical words, lured the shell-shocked man back into the house where the nurse was waiting with a wet sheet which she wrapped around him. Together they soothed the patient and got him back into bed and he went to sleep, peaceful as a baby. I stayed awake all night trying to calm the other patients who were much too frightened to sleep.

The next morning the gardener came in with a wadded wet mass which turned out to be bank notes. For days afterward he kept finding water-soaked money in out of the way spots in the garden where the shell-shock victim had thrown it as he might have tossed a hand grenade. He left next day on a sea trip which took him up and down the China coast several times before he was adjudged sufficiently recovered to make the longer voyage to England.

Another slightly balmy patient who found his way into my hospital was the young son of a wealthy Chinese official who lived near by. The patient came to have a small tumor on his back removed, the most minor of operations. He was scared half to death and so sure was he that he would die that he had commanded twenty or more of his young friends to come and escort his body back to his ancestral resting place. He didn't die, so his friends escorted him home—across the street—to the accompaniment of popping champagne corks and much merriment all the way down my drive. The noise was so disturbing to the other patients that I prayed he might make a speedy trip to his ancestral home.

Then came the sulphuric acid episode of the Columbia Country Club, which disturbed our serenity for over a week and almost sent me to the mental ward. Seven young women went swimming one hot summer's day, the morning after a big dance at the club. The coolie whose duty it was to put a certain number of pounds of sulphuric acid into the pool every night had grown weary and gone home, leaving a 200-pound carboy of the acid on the scale by the side of the pool, thinking he'd be the first person on the spot in the morning. He wasn't. The seven young matrons were and first of all they wanted to weigh themselves. There were scales scattered all around but only the one with the acid on it appealed to them. They rushed the carboy and attempted to lift it. It crashed against the tiles and broke.

I was sitting at my desk that morning when the phone rang and a voice said, distractedly, "Get all your rooms ready. Something terrible has happened."

The receiver clicked before I could ask, "What?" and I'd just managed to phone the operating room when a procession of litters and chairs came through the front door, their occupants weeping hysterically and shedding water profusely as they were carried up the stairs. In a little while the husbands arrived, excited and incoherent. While we were wheeling the patients into the operating room there was more loud wailing, this time the children who were calling for their mothers.

None of the burns were fatal although for days we feared that several might have lost their eyesight. What started as tragedy ended humdrumly enough. One of the girls, a trained nurse, had urged the others to jump into the pool, away from the acid. This they had done, blinded though they were by the fumes.

It was the hottest day of the year and I spent it pouring oil on troubled waters, soothing worried relatives, warding off pending damage suits, placating the police, and providing lemonade for the parched and thirsty patients and their visitors. At midnight when the excitement had subsided my dietitian sank into the chair by my desk.

"Well, Dr. Fearn," she said, "your contribution was two cases of lemons." At that moment it seemed more like ten years of my life that I had donated to that day's troubles.

Difficult as I often felt my chosen life to be, it gave me far more joy and solid satisfaction than any other that I can imagine. I loved every inch of my hospital; it fulfilled my idea of what a small hospital should be more perfectly than I had even hoped. I have always considered that surroundings and atmosphere play a most important part in the care of the sick, particularly during their convalescence. I wanted nothing in my sanatorium that would jar or offend the taste of a patient, and I was content when people told me, as many did, that they "loved being there—it was just like home."

The patients' rooms were large, airy, and as dainty as I could make them with soft lights, silk eiderdowns, easy chairs, cheerful curtains and fresh flowers from the conservatory. Each room was decorated in harmony and in the summer the convalescent patients could sleep on the wide veranda and listen to the orioles and thrush who made their homes in the garden.

My music room was the greatest joy of all, and it soon became the custom to have concerts for the patients at five o'clock on one or two afternoons each week, that is if there were no seriously sick patients who might be annoyed. Doors were thrown open and in many cases beds were pushed into the halls so that the patients might hear better. Mrs. Gerecke's magnificent grand piano was used by several great musicians. When John McCormack, Carrie Jacobs Bond, Mabel Garrison and Edward Johnson visited Shanghai, they came to the sanatorium to play and sing for us.

Paci, the conductor of the Shanghai Municipal Orchestra and one of the greatest musicians I have ever known, played for my patients on numerous occasions, in fact, about once a week for over a year. Although he made a point of never appearing in public, except with his orchestra, he did this for me because he credited me with having saved his baby's life.

My Days of Strength

I had been sitting at my desk one day when the telephone rang. It was Paci, excited as only an Italian can be.

"Come at once and see my baby," he cried.

I tried to explain that I was no longer in active practice. I suggested several other doctors but it did no good. He insisted that I come and in the end I did.

I found the baby crying, unceasingly. Paci pacing the floor, weeping. The mother lying on the bed, sobbing. The baby, six months old, weighed exactly what it had weighed at birth.

I asked them to give the baby to me for two weeks and with more tears they agreed, although they were sure they'd never see the baby alive again. I almost thought so myself but by the end of two or three days the baby had stopped crying; at the end of the week she was gaining weight; by the end of two weeks there was a miraculous change. I had simply fed her properly. Maestro and Mme. Paci, at their wits' end, had been listening to friends and had been feeding the baby everything that was recommended, from olive oil to macaroni. Now, Miss Paci, still known in Shanghai as "Dr. Fearn's baby," is a most attractive young woman, a great linguist and a talented musician.

It is impossible to keep count of all "my babies"; they are scattered all over the world. Some are known as "Dr. Fearn's babies," others as "Dr. Walter's," but I am proud to claim them all. There is a charming woman in the American consular service in Japan who is called my first baby, although she is really the three hundredth by actual count. I first met her in the summer of 1895 in Nikko when I was called in a desperate attempt to save her life. She was then a few months old and nothing but skin and bones, one of the worst cases of rickets it has ever been my bad fortune to see. I gave her dialyzed iron. She responded immediately, and to this day she is called "Dr. Walter's Baby."

But to get back to my music room— The piano platform was used on Christmas for Elizabeth's tree which was always a big one, brilliantly illuminated and loaded with gifts for the patients, the children of patients and the servants, and for the raggedy-raggedies. Christmas can be a very dreary time for those who have to spend it on a sick bed so I always made an attempt to stimulate a holiday spirit by sending up a tiny Christmas tree on each breakfast tray, and a special tray to carry the gifts. After breakfast the servants came with their offspring and the raggedy-raggedies. There were toys and clothing for the children and a red envelope containing a month's wages for each servant. At eleven o'clock the children of the neighborhood and of the patients came to find more gifts under the tree. Husbands were invited to come and lunch with their wives, or the wives with their husbands as the case might be, and as for ourselves the breakfast table was stretched to the utmost limit. Presents were piled at each plate, at times higher than the head of the recipient, for the nurses always were remembered with affection at Christmas.

Thanksgiving was another gala day at the Fearn Sanatorium. I remember especially the Thanksgiving of 1925 when Ruth St. Denis, Ted Shawn, and the entire troupe of thirty Denishawn dancers (and mothers) then touring the Orient came out to tiffin at midday; stayed on to meet practically all Shanghai at a tea dance; and then remained to finish the last bite of turkey at supper.

As much as possible I tried to make the Fearn Sanatorium a home for visiting Americans. I observed all the national holidays in general and George Washington's Birthday in particular. For many years it was my custom to give a dinner on that day to which I invited all the foreign diplomats and their wives. At the same time, a few miles away at the Consulate, the Consul-general would entertain the leading American business men and their wives. Later we would all come together at the Washington Birthday Ball held in the Town Hall. The dinners, the balls and the hall are now things of the past.

It was at one of the first of these dinners that I asked Sir Everard Fraser, the British Consul-general, to propose the toast. I rapped for attention. He rose, lifted his glass and said, "To the memory of that grand old Englishman—George Washington."

For a second there was silence. Then we realized that Sir Everard was quite right—George Washington was an Englishman by birth and education, although an American by choice.

The music room served many purposes. The walls just as often resounded to the anguished wails of hungry babies as they did to the strains of the violin or the piano, for it was requisitioned as the night nursery. After the ten o'clock feed, a procession of coolies carrying dainty bassinets descended the stairs, followed by nurses bearing the babies who were deposited in this room for the peace of their mothers and other less interested patients. At one time there were eleven bassinets placed down the center of the room from which came forth varying sounds, from basso profundo to high treble, not always, if at all, in perfect harmony.

Among this particular consignment was the infant son of the leader of the Carlton orchestra. We promptly dubbed him the leader of the Fearn orchestra, for he was the first to wake and his deep bass certainly led all the others in his demand for instant attention. The Fearn orchestra became something of an institution. Callers dropped in, during the anything but silent watches of the night, to hear this attraction.

Another not so pleasant function of the music room was its use as an emergency operating room. Behind the piano was a couch, innocent looking enough but our best maternity bed, and upon it forty or fifty babies made their entrance into the world. One was the son of one of Shanghai's consuls. After the delivery the father remarked, "I've been in the diplomatic service all my life and my father before me, but never did I think my son would be thrust into it by being born in a drawing room."

The Hospital of the Generous Queen

Not only were the babies born in the music room but innumerable weddings were performed there. Weddings were our long suit. There was one particularly that meant a great deal to me, that of my niece, Fredonia, to Malcolm Moss in 1923. The happiest personal recollection I have of the room is in connection with my silver wedding anniversary in 1921, when various friends of assorted nationalities gave me a surprise party and an exquisite silver bowl. When I saw the bowl shining on an ebony stand I rushed to it, impetuously crying, "Is it mine, is it for me?"

"Not yet," said Mr. Edwin S. Cunningham, the American Consul-general, who was standing beside it. "Not yet, just wait a moment."

But when he had finished his little speech of presentation, my eyes were too blinded by tears to see the silver bowl.

The pride of my heart was my kitchen. I hadn't been in the Orient long before I discovered that diet was extremely important in the treatment of every disease, even more so than in America. When I started the sanatorium I determined that dietetics would have their proper place so I engaged a competent dietitian whose sole duty it was to supervise this department. The kitchen and its equipment were spotless; here my cook reigned supreme, a true "God of the Kitchen" with his army of "small cooks" or "larn pidgins." He always dressed in a spotless white coat and apron with a big white cap on his head. Kitchen cocktail parties, just at the hour when the hot rolls were taken out of the oven, soon came to be the fashion at Number 30 Route Pichon. This delighted the cook, who fairly swelled with pride as he watched the proceedings and collected kudos from the many visitors.

My dietitian watched the preparation of each tray, standing by with notebook and checking each item. Nothing was touched with the fingers; tongs and chopsticks were used for handling all food. I was immensely proud of these trays of silver plate,

229

all of the same pattern and highly polished. The individual tea and coffee services and the hot-water dishes were of sterling silver, and each tray had its own set of embroidered napery with napkins to match. A vase of flowers decorated each tray.

The trays themselves attracted a great deal of attention and nearly every day visitors would interrupt me at my work; dragging me from my desk they would announce, "We want to see the trays go up," and troop into the kitchen to watch.

At eleven every morning, after the heavy work was done, clean white aprons, coats, gowns and caps were distributed among the staff. Altogether, there were usually fifty servants on the place, and the house servants in their immaculate uniforms were a joy to behold. Of course, all of these luxuries cost money but I managed to get all of the bills paid, although there was never much of a profit.

There would have been even less of a profit if it had not been for Mrs. J. F. Spink, the wife of an American naval officer stationed at Chungking. She appeared one morning soon after I opened the hospital. "Unless," she said, "you have the services of an efficiency woman you will soon find your bark on the rocks."

She offered to work for nothing for a month and said she could save enough to pay her salary. She did. I soon found a tremendous difference in the household expenses and in the smoother running of the whole sanatorium.

The operating theater on the second floor was small but fitted with the most modern equipment and sterilizing appliances, and suitable for any operation. This room was in constant demand and, small though it was, some of the most difficult operations undertaken in Shanghai were performed in it. Most of the doctors in Shanghai used it at one time or another and no nationalities were barred.

Although the American flag flew over my sanatorium, it was as cosmopolitan as Shanghai itself. At one time, of my twelve trained nurses, two were American and the others Russian, Scotch, English, Swiss, Portuguese and Bohemian. The nationalities of my clientele varied quite as much. At one time, in sixteen beds I had sixteen patients of sixteen different nationalities.

My hospital *was* different. In the entire history of Shanghai there had never been one like it before, nor has there been one since.

One day as my husband was helping me struggle over my accounts he said, "Annie, if extravagance is a virtue you are indeed virtuous. The Chinese knew what they were about when they selected those particular characters to depict your name, for this is surely 'the hospital of the generous queen.'"

CHAPTER XXI

The White Russian Invasion

NEVER, NOT EVEN IN RUSSIA, HAD I SEEN SO MANY RUSSIANS AS poured into Shanghai in 1919. I found myself constantly repeating the expression of the April Baby in *Elizabeth and Her German Garden* as she displayed for her mother's admiration the litter of kittens which she held in her apron. "Such a much," said the April Baby, and it was such a much of Russians. They came in by the thousands, an interminable stream of refugees, ill-kept, ill-clad, hungry: men, women and children.

The shock of the onslaught paralyzed Shanghai for a time but recovery was rapid; the machinery of all the charitable organizations was set in motion and people worked overtime to meet the demands of these poor creatures. Soup kitchens were opened in every district, food being their most pressing need. There was not a man, woman or child in the city who was not stripped of every superfluous article of clothing for the White Russians. In the orgy of providing relief for the destitute even evening dresses, satin slippers, top hats and many amazing garments of ancient date were resurrected and offered upon the altar of charity.

Food shops found their stock depleted faster than re-orders could be filled as Shanghai rose to the occasion with its usual ability to meet emergencies. Every day and all day desperate cases came to our notice. It was heartbreaking to see the refugees, sometimes hours before the soup kitchens opened, hurling themselves at the gates in a hopeless hurry to reach the food. They brought receptacles of every description, empty jam

232

tins, jars, pots, anything they could find which would hold food for their hungry children.

Work was found for many but the great barrier of language prevented others from obtaining jobs. We soon discovered that there were parasites among the White Russians: men who were too lazy to work, and men who spent their food money on drink. Blankets and clothing were pawned. We learned that some went from soup kitchen to soup kitchen, waxing fat, while others starved. It was a problem to stop these abuses, but stopped they had to be, and drastic steps were taken.

The police helped keep order, especially around the food distribution centers where there was always a struggling mass of people, an ugly, vicious mob. Many had become so debased by hunger, misery and despair, that they had sunk to unbelievable depths of degradation. To make matters worse they had come through the arctic cold of Siberia, many of them clad in sheepskins, the filth of which defied description: hotbeds of disease.

Hundreds of the refugees were well born, of the highest Russian aristocracy. Driven from their homes by the Bolsheviks, they had fled for their very lives, only to find themselves in a strange country, helpless and homeless, often in rags and shivering for want of warm clothing and food, and without any means of subsistence other than the charity of strangers.

Shanghai had never entertained, though unwittingly, so many notables as in that year of the Russian onslaught. There were princesses, women and men of noble birth, some of them closely related to the Czar, and officers of crack regiments; the men were lucky if they found jobs as bodyguards and chauffeurs, and the women work as nurses. Despairingly they turned their hands to anything which came their way, thanking God for it.

In my professional capacity I was soon deeply involved in the problem of caring for our guests. Apparently the whole of Russia was about to become a mother.

The burning question was where to shelter these mothers and their pathetic infants. I went house-hunting and found a place far out on Avenue Joffre, the property of the Asia Banking Corporation. It was to be demolished, I was told. Forthwith I went to Mr. Robert Buchan, manager of the bank, and begged the use of it for my charity patients. With the generosity I always found to be typical of Shanghai, he put it at my disposal free of charge. It was large enough to lodge a small army and a long list of little Russians saw the light of day through its windows.

For the Community Christmas Tree Celebration, the American Women's Club employed Russian men to stand on the roof of the golf club, dressed in flowing angelic robes, wearing wings and wielding six-foot trumpets. They nearly froze while the community sang Christmas carols, but they were well paid and the Christmas spirit of the Settlement was anything but chilly. There was such a tremendous offering of food and clothing massed at the foot of the tree that trucks were necessary to remove the donations to the various points of distribution.

Two or three weeks after this, when the Reds advanced in Eastern Siberia, Admirals Stark and Beziore left Vladivostok with a fleet of warships carrying eight thousand refugees. They called first at Korean ports but when the Japanese refused them permission to land they were forced to continue their voyage southward. They were so sadly in need of fuel and coal that several ships were compelled to remain in Gensan, Korea, no matter how inhospitable their reception had been. The others, with the exception of one vessel lost during a storm at sea, reached Woosung, Shanghai's port, safely.

Here also they were given anything but a warm welcome. The Chinese authorities joined the Japanese in refusing requests to land, but three hundred and fifty orphans, sons of Russian officers, were taken off by the foreign residents whose sympathies were aroused by their plight. After considerable difficulty, arrangements were made to care for them. They were housed in a large unoccupied building on Bubbling Well Road, where they were instructed and supported for several years at the expense of the community. Helping the Russians soon became an obsession with us, until it appeared that shortly our positions would be reversed and we would be forced to ask help from them.

At this juncture, fortunately, a Central Relief Committee was formed under the auspices of the King's Daughters Society; the exsanguinated residents of Shanghai were implored to stop giving except through the Committee. Deserving cases were duly recorded, soup kitchen tickets were issued, clothing distributed, and the parasites and cheaters relegated to their proper places. Soon a suggestion of order was brought into the chaos, but only after the expenditure of herculean effort on the part of the Committee.

House-to-house begging was to be discouraged, we were told; those who needed help were to be sent to the Central Committee. We listened, of course, to all that was said but went on our way giving much as usual. I am afraid I was one of the chief offenders in this respect. Russians appeared at my door nightly and they were never turned away without a dinner and a dollar. I don't know where it would have ended if Miss Opal Powell, my dietitian at the time, had not evinced more backbone and vision than I. Without mentioning it to me, she managed to put a stop to it.

Then Russian doctors, my confreres, began coming to my desk, begging steerage passage money to Harbin. This meant forty dollars Mexican, or twenty dollars in American money. They came singly and in small groups, and they were *all* doctors. I was terrified, but having started on my charitable career I could not stop. I felt myself being carried swiftly into the whirlpool of bankruptcy, when Miss Powell again intervened. She pointed out in no uncertain terms just where I stood and, backed by her, I grew courageous and declared roundly that I would pay no more passages to Harbin.

No sooner had the worm turned than a young boy with an expression of angelic sweetness walked into the hall. He stood at my desk with the tears streaming from his eyes.

"Help me to Harbin," he cried, "to my mother. I want my mother."

I had always suspected that I had the backbone of an earthworm. Now I knew it, for I said,

"If the Central Relief Committee pays half, I will pay the rest, but only through the Committee. Take this note to Mr. H. O. White and tomorrow bring me his written reply. But remember I'll give you this money only through Mr. White; I shall pay it to him."

Apparently overwhelmed by gratitude, he rushed off with the note, presumably to find Mr. White. He appeared next morning and leaning over my desk with a beaming smile said, "Mr. White said it was quite all right; you can give me the money."

"But," I said, "I asked Mr. White to write me his decision. Where is the note?"

"Mr. White said a note was not necessary."

I rang up the Relief Committee and immediately got in touch with Mr. White. When I told him the circumstances he replied that he had received no note from me, nor had he seen the boy with the angelic face, who incidentally was an impostor well known to the police.

"For God's sake, Dr. Fearn, stop giving privately," he pleaded. "You are causing us no end of trouble. Give us whatever you feel you can. Let us do the work."

I repeated this conversation to the angel child who wanted his mother.

"That settles it," I concluded. "I shan't give you anything."

His expression changed alarmingly. Swiftly he sprang at me, and clutching me by the throat he shook me violently.

"Give me money," he screamed, "at once!"

Within reach of my hand was a call bell, used to summon the telephone boy. I pressed down on it hard, saying in strangled tones, "My police call!" The words were barely out of my mouth before the door at the other end of the lounge opened and in ran the telephone boy. At the same moment Miss Powell entered the lounge from the dining room.

The boy gave me a final, furious shake before releasing me. He rushed through the music room into the garden and thence, I suppose, into the safety of the streets, for I never saw him again.

A roll of bills, something like two thousand dollars (Mexican) was in plain sight in my open safe. How he had missed seeing it I do not know.

My isolated position, after this experience, made it seem advisable for me to engage two night watchmen. Their presence gave me a feeling of security, although when working at my desk at night I frequently had to awaken them as the sound of their snoring disturbed my concentration.

Of course, among the thousands of Russians who came to Shanghai, there were many who were the salt of the earth and deserving of the best we could give them. My spinelessness made me an easy prey and it must have been only the worst who found their way to me.

Now, the majority of White Russians have settled down and found places for themselves in the life of the community. As they are natural linguists the language difficulty has been overcome. Many of the girls are employed as salesgirls, stenographers, dressmakers and nurses. Charitable organizations have been able to send others to Australia or America where they have started new lives under more favorable conditions. However, there is that inevitable number which has drifted to the places of pleasure.

It was during the very early part of the Russian refugee invasion that there appeared among us a Russian woman of exceptional beauty. She made her appearance nightly at the Carlton café and other places of public entertainment, always dressed in gorgeous gowns. It was the day of the sheath, split up the side, and hers were slit to the extreme limit, fitting her slim young figure to perfection. Evidently she had an unending supply of evening gowns, most of them of sequins, blue, silver, gold and black, while underneath she wore tights of the same color as the gown. She was a mysterious and vastly intriguing figure; naturally Shanghai buzzed with rumors about her. When eventually we learned the truth she became even more a topic of conversation.

She was the mistress of the great White general, Ataman Semenov, who had sent her to Shanghai with his jewels and as much of his portable wealth as she could take with her. She was ablaze with gems from head to toe; I remember an anklet of perfect diamonds among other exquisite things. It was Semenov's desire that after a stay in Shanghai she should continue to Paris where he thought she would be safer. The fact that his reasons for shifting her about in this manner remained mysterious to the very end did not detract from the interest that centered around her. A good many people suspected that he simply wanted her out of the way of her successor, but we never knew.

She had been committed to the special care of a young Russian officer, tall, handsome and extremely charming. Of course, they fell in love.

During the last days of her sojourn in Shanghai she begged him unceasingly to accompany her to Paris. Realizing that not only his honor but his life would be the price he must pay for such an indiscretion, he refused.

Her steamer sailed at dawn; the night before her departure she made her last, impassioned plea in his room, some place on Broadway. He continued to say no, and to end what was a painful scene for them both, he turned to open the door for her to go, and was shot—in the back.

She fled to the ship. He was taken to the General Hospital where he steadily asserted that he had shot himself—in the back!

The bullet had penetrated the spinal column where it rested on the spinal cord. He was examined by many doctors but, while they all agreed that it was possible to remove the bullet, no one was willing to undertake the operation because of the patient's nationality. Paralysis of the lower extremities set in and in time became complete.

Then Semenov sent a well-known Russian surgeon from Harbin with instructions to operate. But according to the municipal laws governing the General Hospital, a consular certificate was necessary before a permit could be issued to operate there. As no Russian Consul was officiating in Shanghai at that time, things reached an impasse. Then I, being a free lance, offered my private hospital for the operation.

It was brilliantly performed. The Russian worked with the precision of an artist. I watched him make the incision down the median line, then with chisel and hammer chip away part of a vertebra, and with tiny forceps pick out the bullet which had rested so long upon the spinal cord that it had cut it almost in two. The surgeon held it up for us to see.

"The bullet," he said quietly. "Four months too late. He will never walk."

With expert swiftness he freshened the ends of the cord, slightly overlapped and united them and closed the wound. The patient was returned to bed and ordered kept on his face for a week. I can think of nothing like the noise he made except the bellow of a suffering bull. His groans and cries could be heard for blocks. The disturbance was so terrible that the hospital rapidly emptied and when I finally reported this state of affairs to the Russian surgeon, he said, "Turn him over, he will die anyway."

As the days passed, however, we noticed that the patient was beginning to move his toes, then his feet, and at last he could lift his legs. It was not very long before he was able to stand, and in time he learned to walk, first with crutches and then with a cane.

At last an order came from Semenov for him to join the lady of their affections in Paris. He left Shanghai with one of my Chinese nurse boys who wrote from every port, reporting his progress. Naturally we followed his journey with interest, wondering what sort of future awaited him in Paris. From the different ports we learned of his continued improvement, but the death he had escaped in Shanghai overtook him before he ever reached Paris and the woman he loved. Several days out from Marseilles he was taken ill with influenza, and on the very day that the ship docked he died.

Much later we learned that the lady, on her arrival in France, had been met by representatives of the Reds and relieved of all her wealth. From her position of prominence and riches as Semenov's mistress, she sank rapidly into the obscurity of the Parisian streets.

240

CHAPTER XXII

Rheumatics and Reunions

WHEN I WAS A VERY SMALL CHILD, ALONG WITH OTHER things I contracted rheumatic fever which left me with rheumatism and the bad heart I've carried with me all these years. Like most doctors, I had paid little attention to my own ills. While I prescribed countless times for rheumatic patients I, myself, had avoided or neglected the doses of sodium salicylate, the special diets and exercises, the orange juice and the good hot sun.

The damp climate of the China coast is conducive to rheumatism even if one is not already subject to this affliction. I remember one day shortly after I had come to Shanghai I received word that my old friend, Margaret Polk, was very ill in Soochow and I must come at once; she would have no other doctor. I started immediately, although I was suffering from a bad attack of sciatica.

The trip was tiresome and the twinges came with increasing intensity and frequency. I actually staggered into Dr. Polk's home, threw myself down on the bed with her, and for a few hours we enjoyed a comforting, companionable sickness. Then, remembering I was the doctor and not the patient, I jumped up and between pains began the business of diagnosis and prescription.

I'd gone for years without serious illness, although always on trips to Europe and America I had sought relief at all the spas I'd ever heard about. But now in the early spring of 1923 my old enemy, rheumatism, was again upon me. Finally, having recommended the cauldron of Japan to scores of patients, I decided to go there myself and try the curative sand baths and sun at Beppu. The night before leaving I dined with my old friends, Mr. and Mrs. H. E. Heacock, and when I told them of my plans Mr. Heacock instantly offered his assistance, Beppu being one of his favorite haunts.

He advised me against the foreign hotel, suggesting that I go to the Beppu Hotel where he always stayed and take the room he always occupied, number thirty-three, a corner room, free from mosquitoes and delightfully cool. He would cable, making reservation and arranging for someone to meet me at the station. For all this I was immensely and prematurely grateful.

Long after midnight I reached Beppu. I was tired and the station was dark and deserted. But when the train stopped, the first thing that met my eyes was a bow-legged porter, holding high over his head a yellow lantern bearing in large red letters the inscription, "Beppu Hotel." As I stepped down on the platform, he rushed up and relieved me of all my bags, while a torrential flow of perfectly unintelligible words fell from his lips, among which I frequently caught the one word, "Heacock."

He arranged everything and when I reached the hotel I found that the entire staff, from the most honorable proprietress to the most humble serving maids, had waited to welcome the friend of Heacock-San. They accompanied me to number thirty-three and I grew more and more impressed with the importance of that gentleman and of my importance by reason of his friendship.

I awoke with the rising sun and as I looked from my windows to the ocean below, I knew that Heacock-San had not misled me. A great quiet brooded beneath the reddening sky and over the sea, which lapped with the incoming tide almost against the foundations of the hotel. A lovely all-pervading sense of peace hung over the whole establishment. I felt that here I would get the rest I needed even more than I needed the cure for rheumatism.

I had often seen the advertisement of Kusatsu, "Hot Steam Baths! Uncommon to the world! Cures rheumatiz, stomachache, and various other diseases by the cold caught!" The same praises were due Beppu. The place is surrounded by geysers and natural cauldrons of boiling water; even the sands of the beach are hot beneath one's feet.

In all that city there were only two English-speaking persons. One of them, Mr. J. A. Turner, a Britisher, came to see me every day and inquire if there was anything he could do for me. I think he was glad of this opportunity to talk with one of his kind. The other, who spoke English after a fashion, was a Japanese, Mr. T. Nakashima, official interpreter for the Beppu Municipal Offices. Mr. Nakashima appeared at my bedroom door the morning after my arrival. With much bowing and sibilant sucking in of breath, he announced that he had come to pay his respects and to say that his services and those of the Municipal Offices, including the police, were proffered me free of charge.

He told me that he had spent fourteen years in California and on the strength of that I invited him to dine with me, which he did. During the evening he told me that he had a wife and three children and that he confidently expected to have more, "as all our Japanese ladies are great breeders." Apparently I came through the Japanese test for politeness with honors, or it may have been my white hair, greatly revered in that country, for the next day he sent me a huge bunch of flowers.

My first sand bath was a memorable occasion. With the receding tide I went down to the beach, accompanied by the bow-legged porter, who trotted along by my side, carrying my towels and acting as commander of the expedition. Those baths were not to be undertaken lightly nor in a spirit of levity! It was the most serious, indeed the only, event of the day.

When we reached the public pavilion my own kimono was

243

gently but firmly removed and I was presented with a kimono which covered exactly half of my body—my back. Much thoughtful discussion followed; in response to my entreaties the porter brought me another diminutive garment which I wore in front, desperately hoping the twain would meet somewhere, somehow.

Thus fantastically arrayed, I was led out of the pavilion to face a double row of about fifty faces, all turned expectantly in my direction. Evidently the porter had spread the fame of the foreign lady who was of such noble proportions as to require two kimonos for her bath.

With great ceremony I was escorted to the beach where my grave had been prepared, almost full of hot water. A sturdy-legged gravedigger proceeded to cover me with black, boiling sand. Then he seated himself at the head of my grave, patiently waiting for the moment when I might be allowed to arise, shake myself free of the encumbering sand and ascend to the bathhouse.

At the bathhouse, seated at the head of the steps leading down to the tank, he acted as master of ceremonies during the cleansing bath.

"Drop your kimonos here at the foot of the steps. Then step into the tank," were the instructions he managed to convey with much hissing and gesticulation.

"Can't," I said, "the tank is full."

"Just wait, in a minute two will come out," he replied, recognizing that my requirements for tank space would be in proportion to my demand for kimonos.

I was struggling with an inhibiting sense of embarrassment. How *could* I calmly drop those two kimonos, inadequate though they were? The bathhhouse was open on all sides to the public. To be sure a desk, at which was seated a man fully clothed, divided it into a section each for men and women, but that line of demarcation did not necessarily mean a separation

244

of the sexes, for men, naked as nature made them, wandered unconcernedly around the *zenana*, while women, innocent of even the conventional fig leaf, made themselves equally at home on either side of the desk.

I soon discovered, however, that I was conspicuous only because of my manifestations of modesty. With an effort of which I am still proud, I, a white-haired old lady, old enough to be a grandmother, cast aside the habits of a lifetime, together with the two kimonos, and immersed myself in the tank. But I will confess that my descent into the water was rapid and that I never did acquire the complete freedom *au naturel* enjoyed by my Japanese companions of the bath.

The porter introduced me to my fellow-bathers as a friend of Mr. Heacock, and in their minds I immediately became his wife. I was called Heacock Oku San; my position was unassailable. As long as the genuine Heacock Oku San stays away from Beppu all is well. But if she ever accompanies her husband there, I am very much afraid she will find herself in an equivocal position. I was there first.

I meekly followed the routine of Heacock San with one exception—massage. He always took massage after his baths, but after two treatments I decided it was not necessary for me to subject myself to this torture. I loathe massage; it makes me frantic; and I discovered that I loathed Japanese massage more than any other variety. When I declared my independence the entire hotel staff, headed by the porter, stood before me aghast.

"But, Heacock," he said, and then all the *nesans* echoed his words, "But Heacock. . . ."

"I don't give a damn what Heacock did," I cried, "I will not have massage."

They left me, clattering pigeon-toedly away, wide-eyed in sorrowful amazement. Heacock always had massage. Surely there was something wrong with Heacock's Oku San!

But the next day they were even more amazed. I stopped all

245

treatments. My heart gave out and at the end of the third baking I was dug out of my grave, unconscious, by all the little gravediggers. When I came to, I decided then and there not to tempt the fates by stepping into a grave until the time of my permanent interment.

I no sooner returned to Shanghai than I turned right around again for Japan. My family, for the first time since I'd gone out to China thirty years before, were coming to visit me—all of them: my sister, Irene, her sons, Oscar and Lee, and my younger sisters, Pearl and Lillian. Irene's daughter, Fredonia, and her small son, David, were to come a little later.

The boys had grown into great strapping fellows and we four sisters had grown perceptibly older, but no less anxious to do everything and see everything than when we were young. The boys were thrilled with the novelty of "the little country," but I felt that they had not really been in Japan unless they climbed Fuji.

It was late, only two days before the official closing of the mountain, but we decided to make the ascent anyway. There were eight of us, the two boys, two young ladies from Shanghai, and the four white-haired sisters.

We had just left the Fujiya Hotel in Myanoshita when a storm burst on us in wild fury. Forked lightning cut across the black sky; thunder and a torrential downpour drove us back as fast as we could go to the shelter of the hotel. Two hours later we again started out; it was seven o'clock when we reached Shibashir, the beginning of the ascent. The full moon was hidden by clouds. Word had come down from the mountain that "She" was not safe, all parties were grounded.

While we rested and ate, the moon gave fleeting glimpses of her face. Messages kept coming that "She" was clearing. At nine o'clock Tanaka San, our guide, appeared at the door and told us we could start.

The place suddenly came to life; our eight horses, eight horse boys and several luggage coolies were at the door. Coolies and guides, by the light of gaily colored lanterns, arranged our saddles and puttees. We were to ride astride those enormous mountain horses, each with a man's saddle. The others all mounted with ease, but I struck a snag in the high back of that old saddle. In a white silk uniform, and with legs inadequate as to length, I had started to mount when to my discomfiture the front of my absurdly tight skirt caught on the high back of the saddle. There I lay flat on the horse's back as helpless as if I were in a vise, while my hilarious family and the delighted assembly of horse boys, coolies, and onlookers shrieked instructions at me.

After five hours of steady riding we came to an open space. All about us were dead and petrified trees; while behind us, down on the plain, like a silver sickle in the light of the full moon, lay Crescent Lake. Soon afterward we came out on the bare, rocky slope of the mountain. The sun rose as we reached the sixth station. There is no more glorious sight in the world than a sunrise from Fuji's summit in the clear atmosphere of a morning after a storm.

Those last hours, after we left the horses at the eighth station, were like a nightmare. Breathless, panting, tripping, falling, pushed and dragged up and on we finally reached what might be called the neck of the mountain. There remained perhaps two hundred feet of ascent, though it might as well have been two hundred miles as far as we four sisters were concerned. We stopped and groaned, "No more for us."

But the boys placed their hands in the small of our backs and rushed us up the last stiff climb. We were up. I had shown my family Japan.

Tanaka San went about patting us consolingly, covering us with rugs. He had accomplished a miracle in getting four white-haired women to the mouth of the crater.

The descent was just as difficult. I, being in the lead, took the wrong path over the maze of scoris beds; Irene sprained her hip; and we spent all that day and night at the sixth station. After hours of waiting we found a mountain chair for the invalid and the rest of us journeyed by foot, milk cart and motor to our destination.

Two years later I visited the Fujiya Hotel and inquired about our guide, Tanaka San. Ours, I was told, was the last party he had guided. He accepted the feat of getting four decrepit ladies to the very summit as the crowning glory of his career, and had retired to a life of peace and quiet. I don't blame him.

I have never been one to let well enough alone so after a few weeks in Shanghai I insisted that my sisters and nephews see Tai-shan, China's Holy Mountain. We were carried up the steep slope of the mountain in sedan chairs, each one slung over the shoulders of four nimble-footed bearers. I noticed that for some time the coolies had been looking at me and at each rest place they would gather in little groups, grinning in my direction and exclaiming over and over, *"Sien-nyung, Sien-nyung!"* (The wizard, the wizard!)

My sisters wanted to know what was the matter but I hadn't the slightest idea until suddenly the whole thing dawned on me. Nine years before Dr. Yates, her niece, and my husband and I had made this same trip. On that occasion I had observed that the coolies stopped to rest more often than was usually necessary, and always with great groaning and a general confusion. My curiosity could stand it no longer and finally I hopped out to investigate. The high altitude coupled with the swift uphill running had caused several of the bearers to have nosebleeds of almost hemorrhagic proportions.

I told them I could cure that easily and urged one of the sufferers to take some of the heavy Chinese paper that they always carry with them, and chew it into a wet wad, then pack this between the gum and the fleshy part of the cheek and hold it there. The bleeding stopped almost immediately.

Rheumatics and Reunions

After all these years (a decade is practically a lifetime to a chair bearer) someone in that group had remembered not only the incident but me. Needless to say, when I explained that they were calling me "the wise one" and that they'd remembered me for nine long years, I gained much face in the eyes of my sisters and my nephews.

Our reunion, which had begun so gaily in Japan and continued with such giddiness in China, very nearly ended in tragedy. In the next few weeks I went through one of the hardest experiences of my life.

Just as my nephews left Shanghai their sister, Fredonia, arrived with her little son David. "Fee" for short and for love, and my own little girl, Elizabeth, would have been exactly the same age, and in many ways Fee has always seemed to me to be the realization of my dreams of my own child, while David might well have been my own grandson. Fee, whose first husband had died, had come out to China for her wedding to Malcolm Moss. They went to Japan for their honeymoon and that terrible earthquake of 1923.

My sisters and I were in Peking when the news reached us that Yokohama and most of Tokyo had been destroyed. In that delayed batch of mail there was also a letter from Fee, written August 29, three days before the earthquake. She and Malcolm had been in Myanoshita on their way to Nikko, and had stopped for a two-day visit with David who was in Kamakura with his English nurse. She had written to me,

"Knowing your love for David, I must tell you of the dream he had last night. He told me that in his dream the earth suddenly shook, a terrible shake, and the hotel fell down bang, and a great fire came, and the trees in the forest were on fire and hundreds and hundreds of Japanese came running from the forest into the sea and a great wind was blowing."

It was not until September 20 that I knew they were all alive and well and the next day David and his nurse arrived in

My Days of Strength

Shanghai. They told me that at noon on the day of the earthquake David was playing on the sand. Miss Hazeman had just risen from her chair to say, "It's time for tiffin, David," when she was thrown violently several feet away. David was thrown down three times just as "the hotel fell down bang." That night they slept under the stars while the earth shook and fires raged and the wind blew and the tidal wave broke and washed hundreds of Japanese out to sea.

In the meantime Fee was at Nikko, where nothing was heard of the disaster until noon Sunday when an airplane flew over the Kanaya Hotel to drop a packet containing news of the catastrophe for the Emperor, who was occupying his summer palace nearby. There were no railways and few roads left intact but Malcolm finally found a car and went in search of David. By nightfall he reached Tokyo which was no longer a city but a devil's cauldron boiling over with unspeakable tragedies.

He started at dawn to walk the forty miles through devastated areas to Kamakura. He found David and his nurse safe, crowded in a tent with all the other Europeans who had escaped.

A week later one of our battleships, cruising along the coast to pick up desolate groups which had sought refuge in coves along the shore, reached Kamakura and took them on board.

"And, Aunt Doc," David told me later, "a sailor came and carried me on his shoulder to a big sampan!" (One of Uncle Sam's battleships.)

But as much as I would have liked to I couldn't spend all of the time listening to David for Shanghai was filling with the foreign refugees who had fled Japan and who needed to be fed and clothed.

CHAPTER XXIII

"Plenty Bobbery"

UNFORTUNATELY, AMONG THE RUSSIANS FOR WHOM WE HAD SO much sympathy, there were some who came to stir up discontent. They spread a subtle poison of distrust and rancor in the hearts of certain classes of Chinese and there was a strong suspicion that the frequent strikes were the result of Bolshevist influence. There were Red adherents in every school and college whose duty it was to influence and inflame the youth of China. The same agency was at work in the labor unions. Young, hot-headed Chinese boys were sent to Moscow to imbibe the revolutionary methods of the Soviet, and returned to their own country to put those methods into practice.

At one of the Japanese-owned mills in Shanghai, serious trouble broke out in the spring of 1925. The mill was surrounded by unruly mobs and a Japanese fired into a crowd, killing a workman. The agitation over the death of this "martyr" was particularly violent, fed as it was by two streams of hatred, the old enmity against the Japanese and the Bolshevist propaganda.

On May thirtieth a body of students paraded through the Settlement to fire sentiment against the Japanese. The assembling of crowds at any point in the Settlement is strictly prohibited by law and all speech-making is forbidden, with special emphasis on speeches likely to incite the populace. In defiance of this law, groups of students appeared simultaneously in different parts of the Settlement and, at a given signal, began to harangue the people.

The rapidity with which a crowd collects in Shanghai is

almost unbelievable. The least little thing out of the ordinary brings a mob, peaceable enough if not aroused, but potential powder none the less. In this particular instance the result was a foregone conclusion, for the people had been subjected to inflammatory propaganda for days.

Police appeared immediately; students were asked to disperse quietly, and every possible pacific measure was taken, but it was no use. The students were out to make trouble, and trouble they would make or die in the attempt. The police arrested the ring-leaders, which so enraged their fellow-students that, shouting and yelling, they followed to the very gates of the Louza Police Station, gathering numbers on the way.

All the arms and ammunition were kept in the police station, and with an ugly crowd of several thousand people storming the gates, the affair assumed serious proportions. The police ordered them to disperse at once. The only answer was a more determined attack on the gates; in desperation the police fired, after giving warning of their intention. Several people were killed and many more wounded.

Mrs. Edwin S. Cunningham, the wife of the American Consul-general, happened to come in on the end of this tragic business. After lunching with me, she and Miss Mabel Garrison, the singer, had started out on a shopping expedition, unaware that the trouble brewing for the last week had boiled over. On Nanking Road they were caught in a crowd so dense that the car could hardly move, and as she said, "to walk would have meant walking on the heads of the people."

A policeman suggested that they had better turn into a side street, but they wanted to see what was going on. With the policeman walking by the side of the car, they moved slowly down the street, bumping over hillocks of what later proved to be huge bundles of propagandist literature. As they approached the Louza Police Station they saw five or six dead bodies lying in the gutters and on the sidewalk. The policeman decided that this was not a safe spot for them and escorted them firmly into a side street out of the way of the howling, yelling mob.

Mrs. Cunningham rushed to the consulate to tell her husband the news but he had already been informed by the police.

"Yes, I know what's happened," he assured her. "Hell's broke loose."

The action of the police roused a storm of protest all over the country, and as the men who gave the order to fire were British, it added tremendously to the growing anti-foreign feeling. The Reds, of course, did not let the opportunity slip past them but used it like a flaming torch in the furtherance of their propaganda. Mass meetings were held in many cities, denouncing the Shanghai authorities and particularly the police, and the Chinese newspapers were filled with scathing diatribes against the foreigner.

Opinion among the foreigners as to the justice of the shooting was sharply divided, especially as to whether the police had taken all possible precautions to prevent the development of the situation to a point where the shooting was necessary. During this period the life of the Shanghai foreign community was, to say the least, a hectic one.

The labor unions ordered strikes at all the mills. Trouble was engineered to make the hated foreigner suffer. Again servants were intimidated, their lives threatened if they did not immediately leave the employ of the foreigner.

Mrs. Cunningham had arranged a large dinner party the night of the thirtieth. Just as the first guests were arriving the Boy appeared and told her that all the servants had been threatened with death if they continued to serve the foreigner. The dinner party moved to the Astor House Hotel, where they found the same situation. The servants had departed en bloc, but fortunately there were several French chefs on the staff who managed the cooking while the guests served themselves cafeteria style as best they could. In Shanghai, dinners are seldom canceled for such minor matters as riots, wars or plagues.

Why the American consulate servants and those of the United States Court officials were so peremptorily handled, and those of the British and other consulates left comparatively undisturbed, was never explained.

In China one grows so accustomed to great numbers of efficient servants that doing one's own cooking, bed-making and cleaning seems impossible, especially as establishments there are usually on a scale suited only to a large corps of servants.

Unfortunately for me, my husband was away on furlough at this time. During his absence I occupied a room in the nurses' cottages adjoining the sanatorium. As I turned out my light one morning about two o'clock I realized I had neglected to connect the cottage phone with the hospital switchboard. At that very moment I heard hoarse shouts, and the running feet of many people, apparently coming up the drive which my window faced.

I did not dare turn on the light but seized the first thing which came to my hand, a negligee luckily, and tore down the stairs, hoping to cross the drive and reach the sanatorium before the mob.

When I got outside I discovered, to my intense relief, that the disturbance was not on my property but in the parallel street. Morning brought the news that the police had made a raid on an opium joint, and the wild excitement incident to the capture of the offending law-breakers was the cause of my *mauvais quart d'heure*.

This little episode, anti-climax though it was, forced me to recognize the isolation and helplessness of our situation. I was more than ever appreciative of the attentions of Major Chauncey Holcomb and Captain W. I. Eisler who frequently dropped in at all hours of the night to assure themselves of our safety. In the event of any trouble, they gave me strict orders to phone immediately to the Race Course where they were stationed.

"You may be in the French Concession," they said, "but you belong to us and by God, we'll see you through."

One morning about six o'clock my old amah, looking pinched and worn, came creeping into my room and coming close to the bed whispered,

"Oh Mississee, too muchee trouble. This morning fourteen piecee men have come this side, have talkee every man wantchee go largee walla-walla this afternoon native city. Just now they go. We too muchee fear. No wantchee go that side. This fashion belong velly bad. What thing can do, Mississee?"

As soon as the nurses had had their breakfast, I called all the domestic staff into the music room. They came, a phalanx of forty-eight, all silent and subdued.

"Cook," I said, "this morning my amah have talkee me too much trouble. Have talkee me fourteen men have come this side."

Here my old cook stepped forward and held up his hand as a signal for me to stop.

"Me savee, Mississee," he said. "You no wantchee trouble. I have talkee any man, suppose wantchee go native city can go, but suppose go, I no pay any man come back. Just now belong plenty bobbery, plenty bad peoples, more better evelly man stop this side."

Facing the servants sternly he continued, "Suppose you wantchee go and too much bobbery pay Dr. Fearn, you can go. But no come back. Finish."

"Thank you, Cook," I said, meekly, as they all quietly filed out of the room. Standing at the door, I shook hands with each as he or she passed me. The faithful soul had taken the entire matter out of my hands. None of them went to that mass meeting and not one of them left me.

During this period the volunteer corps was called out, naval forces landed, a state of emergency declared, and Shanghai once more was under martial law. There was a great deal of relief work to be done as the volunteers were mobilized in all for about eighty-six days; days of incessant duty.

It was a terrific strain on the men, and a motor canteen service was organized in co-operation with the British Women's Association and the American Women's Club, to help them keep going.

During the whole of June two motor vans, each driven by four or five young women and loaded with sandwiches, cakes, coffee and chocolate, made two rounds nightly of all the camps, outposts, and such streets as were under military or police patrol, dispensing food and drink. Volunteers, regular soldiers, sailors and marines of every nationality, specials, and Chinese and Sikh policemen; all were fed.

The landing of the marines and soldiers gave us all a greater feeling of security. There is something stabilizing about the sight of blue jackets mounting and countermarching, with their look of impersonal efficiency and disciplined calm.

One Sunday morning the American Women's Club heard that the marines from the American warships were being eaten alive with mosquitoes, and that they could get no sleep because of these pests. The club members decided that nets must be made immediately and telephones began ringing like mad. Every member was asked to come at once to the club, bringing her sewing kit, machine, house tailors, and everything necessary. We determined to make those nets in less than forty-eight hours. The main problem was the netting; for it was Sunday and the foreign shops, the only ones that carried such a thing, were closed tight.

I was delegated to get the netting, Sunday or no Sunday. I jumped into my car and drove downtown, determined to break a store window if there was no other way, but on Tai Ching's corner I saw one of Lane and Crawford's nice young clerks all decked out in golfing togs, waiting for a bus to take him to the recreation grounds. I told him my troubles and he gave up his exercise to open the store. It was good business for I bought out their entire stock of mosquito netting.

There were two full regiments of marines and hundreds and hundreds of yards of netting were used, with nearly every American woman in Shanghai working on them. To finish the job in the time allotted seemed impossible but somehow or other it was done.

I had gone to the officers' headquarters to find out how many nets were needed, silently cursing the stuffed-shirts of the council who had interfered with our mosquito campaign several years before. As I was sitting there chatting a few moments before rushing back to my task, I remembered an old story about one of our southern colonels. I told it to the marines who were standing near by.

"A man came from the North to visit the Colonel. After an evening of great conviviality, the guest retired only to find that sleep was made impossible by swarms of mosquitoes, from which he had no protection whatever. The old Negro who came in with his morning coffee inquired most solicitously as to how he had rested during the night.

" 'Not at all,' said the northerner crossly. 'Those damn mosquitoes never left me alone for a minute. How in the world does the Colonel stand it?'

" 'Well Suh,' the old Negro said, 'it's dis way. De fust part of de night de Colonel, he so drunk dat he don't feel 'em, and in de last part of de night, de mosquitoes is so drunk dat dey can't bite.' "

The boys hooted when I ended by saying that it seemed a pity that Shanghai's tortured protectors weren't even allowed the consolation of getting drunk.

257

My Days of Strength

Life quieted down eventually and ran again in the old grooves, more or less smoothly, but though the wound had begun to heal, one felt that this was not by any means a surface sore. Undercover forces were at work that would cause trouble for years to come.

CHAPTER XXIV

The Light Ladies

For some time the prospect of a country hospital had been brewing. On departing from Shanghai, Mr. Charles Rayner, an old resident, had left an endowment fund for this purpose, and the Municipal Council had expressed a willingness to complete the financing of the project. When it finally opened, the last word in magnificence and comfort, I realized that there was only one thing for me to do—close my hospital. The two hospitals were too much alike in their plan of operation and in too close proximity, both being situated in the country, to permit my carrying on when patronage was derived entirely from the same clientele; also I lacked outside financial support.

The decision was made easier by two circumstances; one a happy instance, and the other the very serious illness of my husband.

At the beginning of his sickness, he had been asked to take over the medical superintendency and management of the new Country Hospital, a great tribute to him and to his work. The members of the Hospital Committee said he was the only man in all Shanghai who could fill the bill, produce order out of the existing chaos, and splice the loose strands in time for the great opening. Before putting this proposition to my husband, the Committee had obtained permission from the Shanghai Municipal Council for him to take over the work and still oversee the General Hospital, which by this time was so well organized that it no longer required his constant supervision.

I was deeply thankful and happy that this honor was his,

glad that this high compliment had been paid him while he was able to appreciate it. This evidence of the confidence of his confreres made those last weeks happier for us both.

As I look back over those seven weeks, it seems impossible that in his state of health he managed to carry out the work entrusted to him. He seemed obsessed with the idea that he must carry it through at no matter what cost to him, and I am convinced that nothing but his indomitable will and high sense of duty kept him up almost until the very end.

Though the machinery of the big organization had been completed, it still had to be shaped into a working whole, the details checked and co-ordinated, and the hospital routine set clicking in smooth running order by the time the doors opened. Even the knowledge of the inevitable result of his illness, Bright's Disease, did not deter my husband. He was driven to the new hospital every day in a car; a bed was fixed for his use in the office from which he directed, advised, organized, and saw that the plans were carried out. The effort expended was almost superhuman; the results accomplished were astounding. His one thought was that he must not fail.

I cannot speak of the last days of his illness. From the beginning we had known that his case was hopeless, but everything that kindness and friendship and medical knowledge could do was done. The last weeks of his life were spent in the work he loved and for which he had such great talent.

He possessed a rare administrative and executive ability, but because he had come to China as a missionary he had refused many attractive opportunities that would have taken him into business. My brother-in-law, Oscar Johnson, was continually offering to set him up in the shoe business; but he always refused, as he always had criticized the practice of entering foreign trade through the missions, as not a few missionaries had done.

To him, smoking and drinking were abominations in the

sight of the Lord. And yet, when he returned to France after bringing back to China several thousand mentally afflicted coolies, he took with him ten thousand cartons of cigarettes for the men in the trenches, and several dozen boxes of the best cigars for the officers. He never overcame his prejudice against drinking, although he did grow more tolerant. As for me, he condemned my lack of interest in the religious life, and felt that my independence was unbecoming to a woman.

For him, everything was made to serve a solemnly religious view of life. Yet there was a constant pull between the narrowness and intolerance of small town Southern Methodism, which tended to restrict and confine him to a groove, and the outward circumstances of his life, which constantly tended to liberate him. China and Yazoo City were in conflict. From a remote town of the mid-South he went first to medical school in Chicago and then to life in China. He could and did condemn Confucianism, but the broadly based culture of Confucianists left him bewildered. He railed against the worldly life of Shanghai, yet he was impressed by the numbers of entirely admirable people who did not count it a sin to take a drink. After years of inveighing against Catholicism he practically died in the midst of his little band of nuns, the nurses of the General Hospital. He was a character of amazing contrasts.

As for me, during the ten years that my sanatorium was in existence, there were frequent periods of utter discouragement, times when I seemed headed straight for financial ruin, when, but for friends and a native stubbornness which forced me to hang on, I would have given up the whole thing. Often now I wonder how I did it. But to whatever it was that upheld me I am grateful, for during those last sad weeks my husband often said to me,

"I didn't approve of your opening this hospital, Annie, but as

I lie here I keep thinking how thankful I am for the care and comfort that surround me, and that it's all due to you."

He died on June 7, 1926.

And then, with almost the same swiftness that marked its purchase, the sale of my sanatorium was accomplished.

The property of the Belgian Consulate on Bubbling Well Road was of great value and much too large for the diplomatic requirements. A corporation sought it as an investment for building purposes, and, as the folly of keeping the property with its expensive and beautiful grounds was patent, the consulate agreed to sell. One of the conditions of the sale, however, was that another site should be provided for the consulate in part payment, an exchange of property with so much cash down.

My lovely place, with its roomy buildings and park-like surroundings, appealed to Mr. Van Haute, the Belgian Consul-general, especially as it was in the best residential section of the French Concession. The transaction was quickly closed, and the actual transfer took place on December 1, 1926, exactly ten years from the day that I had moved in.

Those ten years had witnessed amazing changes in the neighborhood. When I bought the property from Mr. Gerecke, it was in the real country. Only an occasional house within a radius of many blocks saved it from complete isolation. When I left, it was in the very center of a new residential quarter that had sprung up like magic all around us. Buildings seemed to have broken out in the vicinity like an eczematous rash. Roads had been constructed; from my window I could see the belfry of the new American School; while close by was the Community Church. With the numerous residences connected with these institutions, the district had become a small American colony.

Officially my husband was my last patient, but actually it was Singapore Kate, a lady he would whole-heartedly have disapproved of, who wrote finis to this exciting chapter of my life. Her story I shall tell presently. It took time to empty the house and begin the work of demolition. We worked slowly at this task through the hot summer months; and if, ten years before, I had been ignorant of the amount of work and the number of things required to open a hospital, I had realized even less how much physical toil and mental strain was incident to dismantling one. Bleak, discouraging work it was too, for there was none of the hopefulness for the future that had buoyed me in the beginning.

The Country Hospital had taken over my entire staff of nurses, nurse-boys, amahs and other domestics, including my cooks. Miss Beane, who had served as my head nurse for years, had been appointed head matron. I was glad that they were comfortably settled, but I was terrified of the objectless future that stretched before me.

Those last days in Shanghai I remember as one remembers a horrible nightmare. The terrific rush of getting everything out of the house so that I could turn it over to Mr. Van Haute on the first of December; the mad turmoil of packing in the all-too-short intervals between farewell tiffins, teas, and dinners; saying good-by to friends; the empty rooms, the desolation, the awful, awful, anchorless feeling——

It was the last day of a decade spent in that beloved hospital-home. I remember the queer feeling that came over me as, sitting at my desk, the only piece of furniture left in the room, I realized that all my work was done, work that had meant so much to me; there was nothing more to do.

Had it, I wondered, meant so much after all? Had it meant anything to anybody else?

Old friends and patients kept coming to see me all through that long day, and as they strolled around looking at familiar sights, recalling old associations, exclaiming sadly over the emptiness and cheerlessness, my spirits sank lower and lower. I think I had about hit bottom when another basket of flowers was brought in. It was a mass of orchids and with it was a card that I still treasure. It read:

"Dear Dr. Fearn, we are sending you these flowers because we love you. We needed a friend and you were all that to us and more. We hope that you will come back soon."

It was sent by women who had wandered from the straight and narrow path, and for whom I had done the little that I could.

It is hard to explain why that particular basket of flowers and the little note did more than anything else to drag me up out of despondency, but I remember that in the deepening shadows of the twilight I sat there and counted over my friends of the half-world, the light ladies of Shanghai. I had known many of these women, some of them splendid, loyal creatures, all of them generous to a fault. Some had been driven by necessity into a life they would never have chosen voluntarily, and others, of course, had drifted into it through accident or inertia.

Before the influx of White Russians the residents of Shanghai's bordellos were, for the most part, American and British women. I knew them all. I don't believe there was ever a time when there wasn't at least one unmarried mother registered in my hospital under an alias and with the assumed prefix of Mrs. or Mme. I delivered their babies, applied the stomach pump when, desperately discouraged, they took an over-dose of some drug. I closed their eyes in death, officiated at their weddings, and for almost a quarter of a century listened to their heart-breaking stories.

Some of the girls died by their own hand, from drink or dope. Many are leading lonely lives, sick and unwanted, in one of the Rescue Homes in Shanghai. Others really reformed, and I know several who made good marriages and are now society leaders in Shanghai, London and New York. Once, not so long ago, I played bridge at one of Shanghai's most exclusive clubs with a charming gray-haired matron; and only she and I, of all that company, knew that at the turn of the century she had been a member of Shanghai's demi-monde.

Then there is the story of Billy and Barbara, an example of a devotion that one seldom finds. Billy held a high position with a British firm until drink brought him to the verge of delirium tremens. For eighteen years, although he was never any too faithful, he had as his devoted mistress a really charming American woman, Barbara, who never failed to go to him when he needed her either as a nurse or sweetheart.

I had known Billy since my first days in Soochow for he was stationed there then. He had been a friend and a patient, first of mine, and later of my husband. There were many intervening years when we passed out of each other's lives. But one day in 1916, shortly after I had opened my hospital, Barbara and Billy appeared at my door. In response to a note from his Boy, she had gone to him and brought him to my sanatorium in the hope that I might cure him. She showed me the note. It read:

"Dear Missie: Last night master have take one bottle brandy in his room. I think more better you come, Boy."

After a temporary cure he went his way. Eight years later she again brought him to my sanatorium. For many months now Billy had been incapacitated with what had been diagnosed as softening of the brain. He was in a Chinese hospital when Barbara found him this time. The doctors had pronounced him incurable; his family has disinherited him; his firm had asked for his resignation. He had been deserted by everyone but Barbara.

She had stayed by his side in that Chinese hospital until he had recovered his mind sufficiently to be brought to me. After she had seen him settled to her satisfaction she came to my alcove office.

"Dr. Fearn," she said, "now that Billy is under obligations to no one, I think when he leaves this place he should come back to my home as my husband."

I thought so, too, and I said, "All right, Barbara, I'll see that he does."

With the passing of time Billy improved until at last his physician pronounced him well enough to leave. I went to his room to talk to him, carying in my hand the photograph of my small grandnephew, David. He seemed so delighted with this, so genuinely fond of children, that I said,

"See here, Billy, why don't you marry and have children of your own? You'd better be doing it right away. You aren't so young as you once were and you have no time to lose."

"Who!" he exclaimed. "You mean I marry! Who in the world would marry me?"

"Billy," I said, "there is just one woman in all the world who would marry you. Just one woman in all the world you should marry, the woman who has stood by you through everything; the woman who many times has saved your life and who many times has done far more for you than just saving your life; one woman who would be patient with you, who would make you comfortable, who would endure all things as she has endured them for eighteen years at your hands, and for you; and that woman is Barbara."

"Why, she would never marry me," he said.

"Just try her," I said, and threw him a telephone book. "Here, look through this and make out a list of wedding guests."

The wedding took place in my music room in early spring when the daffodils and lilies of the valley were making the world beautiful. The months rolled by and Christmas came. We were busily engaged in preparing Elizabeth's tree when a car drove up and Barbara and her husband entered, carrying between them a huge net stocking.

266

The Light Ladies

"Your Christmas stocking, Doctor," cried Barbara as they laid it the full length of the table.

Everything that the most fastidious woman could desire was in that stocking: a veritable trousseau of embroidered lingerie of the finest handkerchief linen, silk stockings, everything.

As soon as I could catch my breath I turned to her. "My dear, why have you done this lovely thing for me?"

She put her hands on my shoulders and looked in my eyes. Her own were full of tears as she said, "You know I never forget a pal."

Her life for the following six years was not one of unalloyed happiness. A fixed habit cannot be easily broken, but until Billy's death from drink, and even to this day, she has remained a faithful friend.

I understand that now all the prostitutes in Shanghai are not restricted to flats along certain streets, that it is difficult sometimes to segregate the "girls" from the debutantes; but not so long ago it was a simple matter to pick the women outside Shanghai's social pale. One I remember was Emily, who had become a prostitute deliberately to keep her mother and sister from starving. Fortunate in annexing a rich protector, she had given her young sister educational advantages which she herself lacked, and saved the child from any possibility of following the path she had trod. As the young girl grew up, still in ignorance of her sister's profession, she and the "friend" met—things like this sometimes do happen—fell in love, and married. Some kind friend eventually told her all about Emily's past, and from that time on Little Sister refused to speak to her. All went well until the deflation of the rubber boom, when the husband lost everything, and dying suddenly, left his wife and children penniless. The older sister again came to the rescue; although to her dying day the younger sister never spoke to her, it was Emily's money that paid for the food and education of the second generation.

My Days of Strength

Then there was Singapore Kate, one of the most exquisitely beautiful girls I have ever seen, and one of the most notorious of the harlots who traveled up and down the China Coast. Hers is a pitiful story, and I entered it at just about the end. She was married in my hospital and I gave her away.

Singapore Kate, or Kitty as she was then known, lived in Hongkong with an aunt and uncle who, by the time she was sixteen years old, had grown tired of supporting her. They wanted to retire and return to America to spend their remaining days; and to rid themselves of the additional expense of Kitty, they forced her to marry a much older man, a man who professed to love her dearly, but whom she hated. And with just cause, for he was a sadist.

When she could stand his cruelties no longer she ran away and boarded a ship for Europe. She was pregnant, and by the time she reached Singapore she was too ill to continue the journey; she left the ship. She lost her baby, and after an expensive illness she stayed on in Singapore to earn her living and pay her debts, following the only trade she knew.

The name Singapore Kate became a byword up and down the China Coast; she was known from Shanghai to Singapore not only for her profession but for her child-like beauty which, miraculously, did not seem to fade. After working the Orient for five years, she decided to seek greener fields in Europe, and boarded a ship for France. Going up the gangplank she came face to face with the man she feared and hated—her husband. He took possession of her, and that night she rushed screaming from her cabin, brutally bruised and beaten. A young man in the stateroom opposite came to her rescue and took her to the captain, who put her in his custody for the duration of the trip. On reaching England, the young man took her to his mother's home, obtained a divorce for her, and asked her to marry him. She refused, but returned to China with him; and he was devotion itself.

268

One day the doctors informed her that her heart had given out; she had just two months to live and that only if she rested. Then she consented to marry the young man, who brought her to my hospital, begging me to keep her there where she might have rest and care until their marriage. I promised, although officially my hospital had been closed after my husband's death two months before. I assured the young man I would protect Kitty until the wedding day.

"This is a splendid thing you're doing," I told him, "but the marriage won't work. Singapore Kate is too well known a figure on the China Coast for this marriage to bring either of you any happiness."

He was silent for a moment, and then he replied, "Doctor, I'd rather lose my right arm than let that girl down."

They were married in my drawing room. I received with her at the wedding breakfast at the Astor House Hotel afterward. I introduced her to my friends. But it did no good. She definitely was not knowable.

Strangely, her heart ailment disappeared with her marriage.

Then I went away. They went away. Two years later when I was returning to China, I met one of her former protectors on the boat. One afternoon when his wife wasn't around I asked that gentleman if he knew what had become of Singapore Kate.

"I don't know," he answered. "I'm a staid married man now." He suggested that I look her up, and I decided that I would.

We arrived in Shanghai late that night. When I unfolded my paper the next morning, in my room at the Cathay Hotel, the first thing that caught my eye was a notice of the death of Singapore Kate. Pneumonia was given as the cause, but I knew better. I knew it was a combination of too many men, too much champagne, too much cocaine. She just couldn't forget her old profession. Later I learned my diagnosis was right.

But to get back to my hospital on that last, lonely day ——

My Days of Strength

It was quite dark when I finally rose from my desk that night, but I felt less tired, less depressed and discouraged than I had for months. My great adventure had been worth while, if only for that little note. Not only had I spent ten years in work that meant everything to me, but I had found something which left me much richer than when I started. I had found friendship, and I had found a marvelous unstinted gratitude.

That evening I faced the past and the future, and I knew that even with a purposeless old age ahead I was better equipped for whatever might happen than I had been before I ventured to make the dream of a hospital of my own come true.

Chapter XXV

Journey to Regeneration

AFTER THE PAST STRENUOUS MONTHS, A LEISURELY TRAVEL WAS the most perfect change and rest I could imagine, so I invited my grandniece, Frances Edgar, to come from America and join me. I looked forward to revisiting all the familiar sights of the various countries through which we planned to wander, and knew it would be an additional pleasure to see everything through her young eyes.

But before we left China I insisted that Frances must see Peking, certainly not foreseeing that we would have any trouble getting there. To begin with, our boat, presumably an express steamer, lingered lovingly in the vicinity of Shanghai while all the other boats, sailing later, passed us at sea. When finally we crossed Taku Bar there was more delay. The captain advised us to sleep on the ship. He would awaken us at four o'clock in the morning, he said, and we could take rickshaws to the Tangku railway station in plenty of time to catch the Mukden Express.

All that sleepless night sleet and snow fell in a regular blizzard. At three the boy came to our cabin, begging us not to land because of the "too big wind." But we were tired of the boat, and announced that if the rickshaws came we would go. They came and we went.

There was no gangway, but a fifteen foot, open bamboo ladder extended from the deck railing to the wharf over two or three yards of open and rapidly freezing seas. Huge flakes of the sleet and snow cut our faces and hands like whips.

Frances went down the ladder first, shrieking as she descended, "Don't come, Aunt Annie, don't come."

For the first time in my life I felt like taking advice, but I went on. If it had not been pitch black I never could have made it. When I swung from the top of the railing to the ladder I thought my time had certainly come. I clutched the top rail and felt about in the inky dark for the frozen, slippery rung below. I was in my white uniform, and the sealskin coat I wore over it began sliding up around my neck, packing tighter with every downward step; all that I had on beneath was an icy and very wet, silk gauze garment. I got down by a miracle and there was no going back, although the wharf was little more attractive than the ladder.

The coolies yelled, and the few lights only accentuated the surrounding darkness. We headed right into the teeth of a biting wind as we set off in rickshaws to the station. Frances' rickshaw turned over; she lost her hot-water bottle; and we were wet to the skin and stiff with cold as we reached the station just as the train pulled in. Thrusting my purse into Frances' hand, I told her to buy the tickets while I ran ahead to hold the train.

"There are more coming," I cried to every guard I passed, "You must wait, you must hold the train!"

Certain that Frances was just behind me I boarded the train. To my horror, as I turned to look for her I found that we were moving slowly out of the station. I sank down on what I thought was a roll of bedding, and it was not until the bedding rose up and walked that I realized that all those rolls of bedding were sleeping soldiers who were occupying the corridor of the coach.

There stood Frances, with a party from the ship, in a raging blizzard with all the luggage, my purse and the tickets, and here I sat on a troop train with no tickets, no heat, and a frozen hot-water bag. I had several hundred dollars pinned on me in the usual inaccessible places, but under the circumstances, to attempt to extract the bills from their hiding places would have been in bad taste from all points of view.

Somehow I reached Peking, an absolute wreck, sooty black, face and hands smeared with grime, clutching carefully my one possession, an umbrella I'd exchanged for my hot water bag somewhere along the way. Much later that night Frances and the others joined me at the Grand Hotel de Peking, hungry but otherwise none the worse for their experiences.

We had a busy time in Peking, where I visited the Peking Union Medical College of the Rockefeller Foundation. It is a wonderful place, and has done a great deal to spread medical learning in China. However, I think it was a mistake to put this medical center in such an out-of-the-way place. I fear the investigators who came out to select a site were captivated by that ancient capital, as almost everyone is. Peking is one of the world's most interesting spots, but it is off the beaten track so far as the rest of China is concerned. In my opinion Shanghai would have been a far better location.

I knew that my friends in Shanghai would be arranging to give me a final whirl before I left, so Frances and I practiced a little innocent deception and announced our sailing for January twelfth, although we actually booked passage for December the twenty-second. On the day of our sailing the newspapers carried notice of our departure, and it seemed as if all Shanghai came either to the Majestic Hotel where we were stopping, or to the steamer to see us off.

A printed testimonial was to have been presented to me under the auspices of the various American organizations in Shanghai, but it was not completed in time because of my juggling of dates. When the book finally reached me, with the signatures of many hundreds of Shanghai's leading business men, I felt that probably my hospital had served some purpose to others beside myself, and I found inexpressible comfort in the tribute.

My Days of Strength

After lingering in Hongkong and Manila, it was necessary, in order to keep to our schedule, to take the antiquated French boat, the "Angers," to Angkor. Here, while wandering tirelessly among the ruins, Frances, along with much information, acquired a germ. Dengue anywhere in the world is a fever which justifies its name, "breakbone fever," but dengue in the heart of the jungle is a fever of portentous import. However, she recovered quickly; and I was reassured when we reached Colombo and picked up a new set of passengers, for among them were twelve doctors, including Dr. Adelaide Brown of San Francisco, who had been my desk-mate in those far-off years at the Cooper Medical College. It was like going back to medical school again after thirty-three years, but I found talking with the doctors filled me with a longing for my hospital. Dr. Henry Dwight Chapin, the great authority on children's diseases, was among the group, and the day after leaving Colombo we celebrated his seventy-fifth birthday with a dinner; I was the toastmistress. I also enjoyed talking with Dr. Edward C. Otis, the tuberculosis specialist, but I must confess that the shipboard discourses of Dr. Brugler, who called himself the Bureau of Religious Research and who always referred to himself as the Bureau, left me cold.

I was following the same route my husband and I had taken on our first momentous globe-circling trip two decades earlier, and at times the memories flooded me with an exhausting sadness. We arrived in Damascus just at dusk as the Muezzin was calling the hour of prayer from the tall minaret outside our window. Twenty years before my husband and I had stopped at this same hotel, and had been given the same room. It was here that I had brought his righteous wrath down upon my head.

We called that first world trip of ours a bombardment of nouns. I had been delegated the duties of interpreter, and before starting out I had set about learning all the nouns of the languages of the various countries we were to visit. It was my theory that, as a noun is the name of a person, place or thing, all one has to do to obtain any desired place or thing, is to produce the noun. It was a good theory. In practice, it often produced unlooked for and sometimes surprising events and articles. In Damascus my husband, without giving me warning, had asked me to call a carriage. His request was so sudden that the only words in any language that came to my tongue were *plus je vous vois plus je vous aime*.

"What does that mean?" my husband had asked.

When he learned that I had said to a strange cab driver, "The more I see of you, the more I love you," he had walked away in absolute disgust; if it hadn't been for the indissoluble ties which bound us I might never have returned to China.

But I found that Damascus was the same dirty, expensive city. It was almost as expensive as Cairo, but without the latter's luxury. I had reserved a room at Shepheard's for twenty-five dollars gold per day exclusive of everything, even heat; but such swank, such gorgeousness, such jewels among the guests. My unobtrusive white silk uniform must have looked like thirty cents in that assembly of gowns from Worth and Paquin.

One morning I asked the hall boy to call a carriage to take me to the museum. He did nothing about it, and finally I asked him why he had ignored my request.

"But you are not ready, Madame," he answered.

When I replied that I most certainly was he said, "But your hat, lady, and your coat? You have, perhaps, forgotten them?"

"I haven't any," I replied. For seven years I hadn't even owned a hat. It was well for me that my grandniece sustained our reputation for respectability by always appearing properly hatted, gloved and coated.

Frances and I parted in Constantinople. Her illness and my general debility had proved too much for my already weak heart. I retired to my stateroom to continue with the ship to Naples; Frances, chaperoned by Dr. Brown, went on to Paris.

Mr. Cunningham, the Consul-general in Shanghai, had left explicit instructions before departing on his own furlough that everything possible was to be done to aid me in my preparations. One of the vice-consuls had come to my hotel, obtained my signature, the list of the twelve countries I was to visit, and my money. He would take care of my passport, my visas; I had nothing to worry about.

Up to Naples all had been plain sailing. It was Saturday noon and a saint's day to boot when we arrived in Naples and the passport officers came on board. Never dreaming of any irregularity in mine, I handed it to the passport official who glanced at it and put it aside. Other passengers left the ship. I waited. The officers picked up their portfolios and started to leave.

I touched one on the arm. "My passport?" I questioned.

But Madame it appeared had no visa; the American Consulate was closed tighter than a drum, and until the chief of police arrived Madame was not to leave the ship.

All afternoon two policemen walked the deck with me. Time passed and the passengers returned; the hour of sailing approached. I begged to continue with the ship to Marseilles, as I had a French visa, obtain an Italian visa there, and proceed to Genoa. But no. The last attempt on the life of Mussolini had been made by a white-haired woman, and I must be investigated.

The two policemen escorted me ashore to police headquarters where I was placed in a small stone-floored room with iron bars at the window and a policeman at the door. It was cold and I had no coat, as all our warm clothing, useless in the tropics, had been sent ahead to Venice. At last, in desperation, I asked, "What are you going to do with me? I am tired and I want to go to bed."

Finally my policeman companion drove me to what I at first thought was a hotel. It wasn't; it was the steamship company's office, and I sat there while the people congregated to gaze with great curiosity on the white-haired, plump little woman whose intentions toward Mussolini might be questionable.

After unintelligible spaghetti-ing over the telephone I was sent to a hotel with the policeman. At the door of my room I stopped, and asked haughtily if the policeman were supposed to share it with me. He was not. I was not allowed to leave Naples, but, still escorted by my policeman friend, I was permitted to attend services in the cathedral and performances at the opera house.

A few days later, when the consulate re-opened and my passport was put in order, I was allowed to leave. I couldn't get away fast enough; ignoring my bad heart I flew, via Rome and Venice, to Vienna. After my enforced sojourn in Italy and the expensive air trip, I arrived in Vienna with exactly seventy-five cents in my purse and not even a blank check on my bank, the First National Bank in St. Louis, Missouri, which I had often found helpful.

I was considering the Danube as I made my way to the Wiener Bank Verein where in the Anglo-Austrian Department I found a Mr. Edward Edlitsberger to whom I explained my predicament. I had no money, my niece had my letter of credit, and my account was in a bank across the seas in the very middle of America. He evidently believed me when I said I had a bank account, for in the midst of my story he broke in to ask how many thousand shillings I would require to carry me until I could get my money transferred.

Such faith! I closed my eyes and named an enormous sum.

I had arrived in Vienna depleted of strength as well as of cash, and I was discouraged and despondent. I found no joy in the beauty and the music of that city. At my lowest moment I ran across Miss Ruth Benedict, a newspaper woman I had known in Shanghai, who was then writing the life of Dr. Eugen Steinach, one of the pioneers of endocrinology.

"Why don't you," she asked, "try him? He is supposed to be a marvel when it comes to regeneration."

I had been meeting and trying to listen to lectures by a number of famed medical men, such as von Pirquet, noted for his work in the renowned Kinder Klinik, Alfred Adler, the psychoanalyst, Robert Stein, the dermatologist, Professor Singer of diabetic fame, and many others. I talked to them about Steinach. I met his attractive and brainy young associate, Dr. Erwin Last.

They all answered my question with the question, "Why don't you try?"

After all I had nothing to lose. I couldn't possibly feel any worse, and it would be nice to be young again. At that time I had regeneration and rejuvenation mixed in my mind. I had read Gertrude Atherton's story, *Black Oxen,* and I pictured myself as a glamorous, rejuvenated creature. Here I was sixty, but I might as well have been a hundred. I couldn't have felt any older if I'd already passed the century mark.

The treatment I discovered would take thirty days. I've forgotten the exact cost but I do know there was no professional reduction.

I went to Steinach.

"I've heard all about your rejuvenation," I began, "in a book, *Black* ——"

With that he hit the ceiling. It was like waving a red flag before a bull. When at last he calmed down sufficiently to talk coherently, he explained that he and his associates *never* used the word "rejuvenation" for these treatments; that he had never claimed to restore lost youth to his patients, only to bring back the vitality and energy to normal age.

It is unfortunate that unauthorized sources, especially in this country, created this misleading and unscientific word that has done enormous harm to Steinach and his work. Sensational and false announcements and promises of treatments, allegedly originated and performed by Steinach in Vienna, caused a definite and justified opposition among the ethical doctors of America. It will be up to the medical historian to describe how Steinach's ingenious and serious scientific work has been menaced and almost ruined by these accusations.

Steinach's therapeutical aims were to improve the impaired circulation of ageing people, to restore the hormonal equilibrium disturbed by the change of life.

I visited his famous laboratory in the Biologische Versuchsanstalt im Prater where he and his biologist, Dr. H. Kun made many of their animal experiments. They told me that the therapeutic part, animal experiments and treatment, were made in the Department of Physical Therapy of the Mariahilfer Hospital, where Dr. Last had been director for many years. I was satisfied.

Prior to the treatment, I remember, I underwent a very thorough physical examination, which included fluoroscopy, an electrocardiogram, and all the laboratory tests—blood and its chemistry, urine, and status of the hormonal glands—to determine my exact condition. Every locus of minor resistance, which might have been established by a former disease, was checked with minute care. These examinations were performed by a permanent staff under supervision of Dr. Steinach's consultant physician, Dr. Last; other examinations were conducted by such outstanding Viennese specialists as Drs. Stein, Hirsh, Horner, Finsterer, Zweig, Singer, and others whose names I have forgotten.

But not until Steinach had discussed the final result of all these examinations with his personal staff was I ready for my specialized treatment; my chart of diet, exercise, injections and electrical treatment had been determined by my individual report. There is no doubt in my mind that the successful clinical results achieved by Steinach were due to these carefully performed examinations and the therapeutic conclusions drawn therefrom.

These examinations were exceedingly wearing, and how I hated Steinach for a time because he made me walk from where I lived, in a little hotel in the shadow of the University, to his office several blocks away. I hated him because he insisted that I walk back again when I was so tired I could barely drag one foot after the other.

At last I was ready for the treatment. To take it I stripped absolutely naked, then slipped into a kimono, hind side foremost. I was stretched out on a hard bed with my bare back on a lead plate. Lead wristlets and anklets were attached to a static electrical machine; the current was turned on for five minutes the first day, and then increased gradually to a twenty- or thirty-minute period. The electrical treatments were given to improve the circulation of the body as a whole as well as to influence the glands of internal secretion. Glandular extracts of single glands, and combinations of several glands or drugs were then injected; occasionally an X-ray treatment was given.

The first few days I felt that I couldn't stand it. Sometimes I couldn't move. By the end of the first week I was praying to die. On the eighth day I lacked even the strength to dress myself, and I had to send for a maid to help me on with my clothes and accompany me to Steinach's office. I was sent home near to collapse; then, strangely, overnight I grew better. I awoke on the ninth or tenth day feeling refreshed and actually anxious to hop out of bed. By the end of the thirtieth day and the thirtieth treatment I was a new person. I took stock of myself.

My hair was still as white as ever. I obviously was sixty and not sixteen, but my vitality and energy had increased, my blood-pressure had dropped considerably, and certainly my entire circulation had improved. I learned from other women that all the complaints of the menopause—flushes, heart palpitations, and backache—have subsided after this treatment which I would not now hesitate to call a true regeneration.

The effects of the treatment, in my case, lasted more than two years; then I returned to Steinach for another treatment which helped me for a similar length of time. It is with thankfulness that I remember my days in Vienna, although it is with sadness that I contemplate the changes that have occurred since. Many of my old Viennese friends left, or were forced to flee from their homeland and the hospitals and laboratories where they worked so many years. I was glad to learn lately that a number of these doctors, among them Last and Horner and others of Steinach's staff, have settled in New York and other cities of America.

Buoyed by Steinach, I continued my travels until East became West and I arrived in America. There I found friends, more than I could count; I found beauty; I found my family, but I found no peace.

CHAPTER XXVI

Shanghai, My Delight

THE THOUGHT OF SHANGHAI PULLED AT ME INSISTENTLY, COM-
pellingly. I was restless and uprooted in the West; I had
lost my place among my own people. It was beginning to come
home to me that the East does not loosen her hold easily.

One morning at breakfast I announced, "I'm going home."
My family stared at me aghast. My sister, Irene, put down
her cup, much as she might have put down her foot. "This is
home," she exclaimed. "We want you here."

Almost shamefacedly I explained that I must finish out my
cycle of Cathay. So back I sailed wondering with every knot
that brought me nearer Shanghai whether I was being wise in
attempting a return to a life that I had so definitely ended. It
was with mixed feelings that I stood on the deck and watched
the skyline come in view; Shanghai once again.

As I stood by the rail, waiting to land and calling myself
a silly old woman for wanting something that I could never
have—the past—a hand fell on my shoulder. I looked up; it
was Dr. Keiser Nance, one of my babies. He was the vanguard.
Behind him were the Cunninghams from the Consulate; the
Purdys from the United States Court; Julean Arnold, the
American Trade Commissioner, and his wife; scores of
Italians, Chinese, British, business men and diplomats and their
wives; all old friends and all there to welcome me.

I almost cried. No, it wasn't a mistake, my coming back.
This was the same Shanghai I had pictured so often during
my absence, the same bustling, thrilling city, busier than ever.
Here were the hurrying pedestrians, charging from one side

of the street to the other, oblivious of traffic; the same jostling mobs on the pavements and in the gutters; the same shops, the same sounds, the same smells! I had come home.

I settled myself in the Cathay Hotel, right in the midst of the city's confusion. From my windows I could gaze at the ever shifting scene of busy river life, a scene that has never failed to fascinate me, especially on misty nights when the searchlights from the harbor play upon the water and the world seems to be a sea of shimmering gold, and the city spreads out at my feet with its myriad lights on river, ship and shore.

I paused to catch my breath, and then I looked around and found many changes. These changes had not, like mushrooms, sprung up overnight. They had been in progress all the forty-odd years I had lived in China, but now I saw them with new eyes.

I was struck forcibly by the extraordinary emancipation of the Chinese woman of the upper classes. In Soochow, as long ago as 1900, I had seen evidence of what the future might hold for them, but they've come a long way in the three decades since that history-making afternoon when the Governor's wife shattered all traditions by inviting a few foreign ladies to tea.

One night a year or two ago, while dining with friends at a smart night club, I noticed in a mixed official party of foreigners and Chinese a flower-like girl, lovely in the becoming new style feminine costume of sheath dress, slit on either side to the knee. The soft pink satin of the frock was set off by bracelets and a pendant of priceless jade. She was streamlined and beautiful as only a Chinese woman can be.

"Who is she?" I asked, fully expecting the answer to be, "Oh, so-and-so's debutante daughter." I wasn't at all prepared for the reply.

"She is Lee Ya-ching, the aviatrix."

"That fragile hot-house flower actually flies a plane? Impossible!" Later I talked with her and heard her story. Because it revealed her as typical of the modern girl of the new China, I am going to tell it here:

Ya-ching—the free translation of her name is "Red Sky After Sunset"—was lonesome. Never before in her twenty years had she felt so alone and neglected. The cold, gray waters of San Francisco Bay lapped gently around her. Would help never come?

As far as eye could see there were only water, sky and clouds. Not a boat, not a plane in sight. She gave thanks to the gods of her ancestors that her father, Lee Ying-sing, the revolutionist, had insisted she take swimming lessons along with her lessons in shadow-boxing, fencing, English and poetry. She wondered if she had been spared death only to meet it in this icy water. She thought a little about her son, Pax, and her daughter, Molean, safe in China. But mostly she thought about all she had hoped to do for her country. Evidently the fates had decreed that she was not to fly in China; not to teach other young women to zoom into the sky and pilot their planes and deposit teachers of hygiene and a common language in the remote villages. If they had, most certainly they would have prevented her fall from the airplane into these cold California waters. They at least would have seen to it that the instructor-pilot noticed her instead of flying blithely on without a sign.

She swam furiously for a few moments to keep warm, and then lay on her back, paddling lazily. She stopped thinking and watched a bird, circling in the sky; a hawk most likely to peck at her water-logged flesh. The hawk dipped and wheeled with an unbirdlike noise. She waved and hallooed, and the waters closed over her head. When she came up and the wind had blown the salt from her eyes, the plane was disappearing into the clouds. But at her hand floated a life belt. She strapped it on swiftly, and then with calm, Oriental philosophy relaxed to wait—for what she did not know.

Help came soon after; an army amphibian with tall, strong

284

men to lift her on board, fly her to the airport, and speed her to the emergency hospital. Lee Ya-ching was saved after all. From the time she fell, when the flying instructor had made a sudden loop, until her rescue, she was in the water only twenty minutes. But to Miss Lee this twenty minutes of the afternoon of May 15, 1935, seemed a lifetime.

When I first saw her she had just returned to China after completing her air education at the Boeing School in Alameda, California. She was busy trying to convince hard-hearted government officials that women would be just as capable in aviation as they had proved themselves to be in the fields of medicine, law, finance and education. She flew in air exhibitions designed to make all China air-minded; and she proudly showed me her licenses—the first non-commercial pilot's license issued to a Chinese woman flier in China by the American Department of Commerce, a Swiss license, and the first and only private pilot's license to fly over Shanghai.

Ya-ching has crowded a number of things into her short and somewhat tragic life. She was born in Hongkong in 1913 during the political exile of her father, one of Sun Yat-sen's aides. At the age of fifteen she stopped her studies at the McTyiere School in Shanghai to recoup the family fortunes by marrying an elderly statesman who took her to Geneva with him. It was there, restless and lonely, that she learned to fly. Her husband forbade it, but she took lessons secretly. When he discovered her deception the storm broke. She was kept at home a prisoner. She was unhappy and he was unhappy. This May and December marriage was not working out so successfully as similar unions had in the good old days. There was a financial settlement; the children were sent home to his family; and Ya-ching, resuming her maiden name in true Western fashion, hastened across the Atlantic to learn more about aviation in America.

She is typical of the modern Chinese woman, determined, dynamic, youthful and dainty in appearance, but adaptable and practical. When war broke out in 1937 she gave up her flying; donning white cap and apron, she turned to the imperative and immediate task of caring for the wounded soldiers and civilian refugees in the cold, bleak hospital barracks.

There are hundreds just like her; women who see what their country lacks, who, on their return from travel and study abroad, set about at once trying to improve existing conditions. They have brains; they open schools; they teach athletics and hygiene. No longer is it necessary for foreign physicians, men or women, to go out to China, for some of the best doctors in pediatrics, obstetrics, urology, dermatology and other medical divisions are Chinese—and many of them Chinese *women* at that.

When Ling Tsu and Foh-me were struggling to study medicine in that first co-educational medical school in Soochow, no one dreamed that the door they were pushing against so desperately would open to such freedom and opportunity.

Education has had an immense influence in loosening the chains that shackled Chinese women. Before the period of reform which followed the Boxer uprising, rare indeed was the woman who had the most elementary schooling. The new system introduced in 1902 ignored the girls; but mothers of the upper classes snatched at the opportunity to start schools of their own for their daughters and the daughters of their friends. The two pioneer schools for Chinese women, the McTyiere School of the Southern Methodist Church, and St. Mary's Girls' School of the Protestant Episcopal Church, deserve much credit for giving thousands of these young women a knowledge of the ways of the modern world.

When the McTyiere School, with which I was always more or less closely associated, opened nearly fifty years ago, an incident occurred which was significant of the Chinese attitude toward women. Officials of the neighboring provinces, even representatives from Peking, had assembled to do honor to the occasion. The guests were received by the Bishop and the most prominent men of the Mission. There was not a woman to be seen.

Finished with inspecting the building and drinking the inevitable tea, the guests gathered in whispering groups. At last one Chinese plucked up courage to ask the Bishop if it would be possible to see this wonderful woman whose idea it had been to start the school, the Honorable Presence into whose keeping they were asked to intrust their daughters.

After some discussion it was arranged. Miss Laura Haygood, a woman of fifty or thereabouts, of fine bearing and great dignity, took her stand with hands folded across her stomach, Buddha fashion, and eyes downcast, in the very center of the dining room, facing the doors leading into the drawing room. Then the doors were thrown open and the assembled guests, for one brief instant, gazed upon her in the complete silence of extreme respect.

Not all the Chinese were so respectful toward Miss Haygood, however, and the school had a discouraging time of it in the early days. Many fathers forbade their daughters to attend. They were convinced that the school was a new-fangled foreign brothel, and they employed watchers to stand outside and count the men who entered the building. They were sure the girls were used for immoral purposes.

To quiet their fears Miss Haygood made a rule that no men could enter the grounds, except on very special occasions and then only under the most rigid chaperonage. But one day, unaware of all the red tape that must be unwound before entrance might be gained, a dignified old Methodist Bishop came to pay a call. He was stopped by the gatekeeper who, arms outstretched, barred the way.

"Stop!" commanded the gatekeeper. "You can't come in."

"But," sputtered the old gentleman, "I am the Bishop."

287

My Days of Strength

"You may be the Lord Jesus Christ," answered the gateman, "but unless Miss Haygood says so you can't come in."

For many years an old leper in the last horrible stages of the disease stood outside this same gate. He would not move an inch until in desperation Miss Haygood pensioned him, paying him so much a month to keep out of sight. "Miss Haygood's Leper" he was called, and after her death he was looked upon as mission property, a legacy from that great woman whose life was full of good works. Death, the solver of so many problems, at last released him and, incidentally, all of us who contributed to his support.

Many years ago I used to watch a serious, pig-tailed little girl poring over her books at McTyiere's. Her pig-tails have since been discarded for a boyish bob, and for ten years now she has been hard at work ridding China of many of its old customs and superstitions, and teaching the women of all classes the rudiments of hygiene and sanitation. She is Mei-ling, the youngest of the three famous Soong sisters, Mme. Sun Yat-sen, Mme. H. H. Kung, and Mme. Chiang Kai-shek, and the acknowledged leader of the new women of China.

It was during the turbulent years from 1925 to 1927 that the name Chiang Kai-shek began to rise like a hopeful star from the seemingly hopeless morass of Chinese politics. Coupled with his name at first was the dread name of Borodin, the Communist who started the push from Canton, driving all the foreigners before him. But before the army reached Shanghai, Chiang had broken with Borodin, and turned officially against the Communists.

The next year China was electrified by the courtship and marriage of Chiang Kai-shek and Soong Mei-ling. It was not long before this Buddhist war lord was as good a Methodist as his American educated wife. I was in the United States when Mei-ling was married, and I felt flattered indeed when the Soong family cabled me an invitation to the wedding on De-

"The Cushion"—Rice Christian Boy— carrying one of the silver trays.

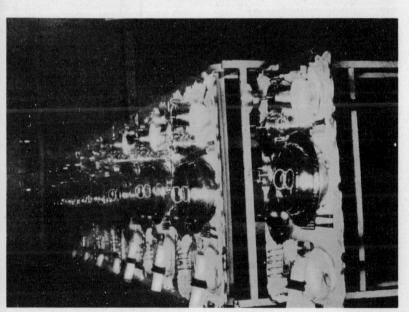

The famous silver trays, ready to go up.

My diplomatic dinner for Mrs. Theodore Roosevelt, Sr. at the Cathay Hotel in Shanghai, 1934. I am standing just behind Mrs. Roosevelt, who is seated between Countess Ciano (Edda Mussolini) left, and Mme. Becerra of Chile, right; next is Lady Calder-Marshall and standing behind them is Count Ciano. Sun Fo, president of the Legislative Yuan and the son of the illustrious Sun Yat-sen, is standing at my left. Behind me is the late Judge Milton D. Purdy of the U.S. Court for China. Behind him is Lord Li Ching-Mei, the cember 1, 1927. I had known Mei-ling and her family almost since my first days in China. Her father was an outstanding Methodist minister and her mother one of the finest women I have known anywhere.

Along with the rest of the world, I have been interested in following the development of that family which has come to be called "The Soong Dynasty," with special reference to the three sisters, the brother, T. V. Soong, China's financial wizard, and Ai Ling Soong's husband, Dr. H. H. Kung, whom in late years I have come to know well.

After taking notice of China's new life, the next step was to make a new life for myself. I had never been idle, and I couldn't begin at this late date; I disliked even the thought of being an onlooker. There was no reason why I should sit back, for in looking around I had discovered that there was plenty for me to do. Although there were continually changes all around me there was no apparent change in one thing—the suffering of China's children.

Friends advised me against getting involved in charitable undertakings. The more outspoken called me "crazy" but I'd been called crazy many times, especially when, nearly fifty years old and with no money, I had started a hospital and run it on an extravagant scale. But age, I've always contended, is of no moment; life should be measured by experiences and accomplishments, and not by birthdays. I didn't start to study medicine until I was twenty-two, a ripe old age for a girl in 1889. I was twenty-six before I graduated and went out to China, and it was not until I was over forty that I began to practice medicine seriously in Shanghai. Horticulturally, I suppose, I might be considered a late bloomer. Now, at sixty plus, a new life was unfolding for me. I turned my attention to the needs of children, Chinese and American.

Back in 1912 I had helped start a school in a small rented building. The parents of most American children of school age were patients of mine, and as I treated their ills I listened to their troubles. Their greatest worry was the lack of proper educational facilities. Many of the children were my babies, so the problem was very close to my heart. I decided that something must be done; got together a few people, missionaries and business men, who were of the same opinion; and in this way the Shanghai-American school was established.

From the original small enrollment of twenty, by 1930 the school had grown to almost one thousand students. From the very beginning the school had been on its own; unlike the British, French and Japanese schools, it did not receive a government subsidy. By this time there was urgent need of money; there was talk of closing the school, and in any case, unless sufficient funds were available to employ capable teachers, the school would be demoted to class B rank—its graduates would not be assured unconditional entrance into colleges and universities—while schools of other foreign nationalities in Shanghai would remain in class A.

The Standard Oil and the Dollar Steamship Companies were among the first to recognize the need for a good American school; they realized that their men in the Far East would not work well if they were discontented, and that they could not be happy unless their children were assured a decent education. John D. Rockefeller, Jr., personally underwrote the campaign expenses of $60,000. When Mr. Howard Cole of the Standard Oil cabled me to come to America and work with Dr. E. J. Anderson, the school principal, in conducting a financial campaign, and when officials of the National City bank seconded that invitation, I was more than willing to undertake the task and contribute my time and services.

If the devil himself had chosen it the time could not have been worse. I arrived in America in the very middle of the depression period of 1930-1931, but in spite of bad times we succeeded in raising enough money to build the boys' dormitory and auditorium, and to guarantee the school $25,000 per year for five years. At the close of the campaign, worn and weary, I returned to China to devote most of my time to the Chinese children. My chief interest now, along with the American school, became the National Child Welfare Association of China, of which Dr. Kung is president.

In 1932, after the Chinese agreed to the Japanese demands and were assured that there would be no fighting, I sailed for Manila to visit my friends, Judge and Mrs. Milton Purdy, who already were vacationing there. Two hours after the agreement was signed and after I had sailed, "the 1932 Incident" occurred. I remained in Manila until after hostilities ceased, and in my absence Mrs. Cunningham took over my work as assistant chairman of the Association. She rescued children, saw that they were fed, clothed and their bodies repaired, exposing herself to shot and shell time and time again. Even after I returned to Shanghai there was still much to be done for the war orphans, the maimed, the refugee babies, their widowed and starving mothers. I went through the Revolution of 1913 all over again.

Our work continued after the war was long forgotten. We started out improperly financed, and my job, it developed, was raising money to care for the six hundred children in our orphanages and to maintain the schools, clinics and crèches. The Chinese children were so eager to be clean, so eager to learn, so loyal and industrious; they even made their own clothes and shoes.

Twice a week we had bath parties when all the children of the neighborhood clamored to get scrubbed. No economy was practiced with soap and water; heads were shaved clean, finger- and toe-nails cut, and the rags covering the children taken off, bundled up, and sent away for sterilization.

The children of China are pathetic in their ills. In America or Europe an ailing child informs the world of its aches and pains, but the Chinese child just lies quietly and waits until the doctor tells him that he is cured.

I spent a great deal of time at the orphanages and the clinics, bringing visitors and hoping they would be moved by what they saw and give liberally to the cause. There were always horrid sights to see: children covered with abscesses and boils from malnutrition; boys and girls lying almost lifeless with perforated cheeks through which the teeth and gums could be seen—all victims of tuberculosis.

The Chinese men and women, themselves, are doing great things to improve the general standard of health, but they have many serious handicaps. One is the lack of a common language; every hundred miles in China there is a different dialect. However, Dr. James Yen's mass education movement is now overcoming this by leaps and bounds. Heading the handicaps are the Japanese and their too, too frequent visitations. General Wu Te-chen, when Mayor of Greater Shanghai, did much to sanitate the native Chinese area by building model tenement villages and a marvelous civic center, all completely demolished by the Japanese.

Chinese doctors, after receiving the best medical training obtainable in the Occident, have returned to their country to give generously of their knowledge. One of the most generous was the late Dr. W. S. New. Then there are the innumerable doctors of the Lester Chinese Hospital, St. Luke's and other hospitals for the Chinese, who are doing their best to rid Shanghai of dirt and disease.

Government officials, too, are being liberal in the furtherance of public welfare. This in itself is a big step, for when I first went out to China the Chinese were loath to help anyone outside the members of their particular families.

In recent years I worked in close association with Dr. Kung. He is noted as an astute financier and a clever politician, but I knew him as a large-hearted philanthropist. I remember once approaching him about a raise in salary for one of the clerks of the National China Child Welfare Association, supposing of course that the man's salary was paid from the Association's funds. To my surprise, it developed that his salary came from Dr. Kung's own pocket; we sat down right then and there for a heart to heart talk on the subject of philanthropy. His favorite course, he told me, was to educate young people and set them up in some kind of work.

Even with considerable help from the Chinese there was much for the foreigner to do, and I found I was working harder running money-making affairs for the American School and the Child Welfare than I had ever dreamed of doing at the Soochow Woman's Hospital, the Margaret Williamson Clinic or the Fearn Sanatorium.

I liked the work and I liked the people. Everyone turned out to help me, European nobility in diplomatic circles, high officials and a gangster!

If it hadn't been for Tu Yueh-sung, the man of mystery generally conceded to be Shanghai's Number One Gangster, many is the time one of my entertainments for charity might have failed.

I remember one occasion when I had organized a program for the China Child Welfare, but couldn't find a star performer any place. I was sick with discouragement, when I thought suddenly of the powerful Mr. Tu. I hurried to him and poured out my story. He listened with the greatest sympathy, and immediately dispatched a message to Peking for one of China's most famous singers, who, needless to say, came speedily. Mr. Tu took a box at the recital and contributed a generous sum, besides sending the singer thirty-four baskets of flowers.

I never quite got up the courage to ask Mr. Tu to dinner but I wanted to. My family say it is a disease, like alcoholism or opium-smoking; but when I meet people I enjoy I usually invite them to come and have dinner with me; and they usually come. When I arrived in Soochow and met the Governor of the Province I invited him to dinner, an unheard-of thing and quite a shock to the missionaries, but he accepted.

Those early day dinners were pretty funny but also fun. I remember one night an old Chinese mandarin dined at my home in Soochow. At that time dairy products were used only to a very limited extent by the Chinese; cheese and butter were scarcely known. The mandarin helped himself to a dainty little butterball by slipping his long fingernail under it. Holding it to his nose, he took a whiff of its fragrance, and then with a shiver he slapped it back on the dish again, remarking, "*Chi mien*—smells like cow."

But those days have long since passed; now the Chinese dine with foreigners and eat Western food with perfect table manners, and the foreigners dine with Oriental hosts and eat "Chinese chow" and have great difficulty manipulating the chopsticks.

The last dinner I attended at the Union Club, members of which include representatives of all nations, and of which my old friend, Sir Robert Calder-Marshall, is president, I sat next an impeccably groomed Chinese who spoke English with an Oxford accent. Pidgin English, the literal translation of the idiom, was used exclusively by the English-speaking Chinese thirty or forty years ago. Now one hears it only from one's servants, and even they, likely as not, speak straight though limited English. The passing of pidgin English means progress, but it also means the loss of another charm of the old China.

People have always told me that I had a flair for bringing people together, and that if ever I have any claim to fame it will be not for my ability as a doctor but as a hostess. I only know that I like people and parties and that I've never been so busy that I couldn't take time out to entertain.

I know well the three classes of foreigners in Shanghai—the

missionaries, the diplomats, and the businessmen—and I usually invited a few from each group to my parties, another social error.

But one party I gave was as completely official as it was international. Mrs. Theodore Roosevelt, Sr., was on her way to Manila to visit her son, T. R., Jr., who was then Governor-general of the Philippines. When word came that she was to arrive in Shanghai Mr. Cunningham, the Consul-general, was away, but he telephoned asking me to be official hostess with Judge Purdy the official host. The consulate cabled Mrs. Roosevelt in mid-ocean, asking her to accept my hospitality and be my guest at dinner. Her answer came at ten o'clock on Saturday night. She would come. By midnight everyone had accepted my dinner invitation except the French Minister, who was away in Peking, and a high Chinese official.

My telephone rang at two o'clock Sunday morning. At the other end was the sleepy voice of Mr. Yui Ming, head of the Shanghai Bureau of the Waichaipu (Foreign Office). He had just been awakened by a messenger who had come by plane from Nanking on behalf of the National government. The messenger had been sent to accept the dinner invitation in the name of the several officials and to ask that Mrs. Roosevelt might be the guest of the Chinese government.

I thanked him but said, "No, she is my guest, but do come to the party."

They came, I remember. Everyone came to honor the widow of T. R. Not one country missed sending a representative. Italy was represented by Mussolini's daughter, Edda, and her husband, Count Ciano; China by Sun Fo, the son of Sun Yat-sen, by Lord Li Ching Mai, the son of the great Li Hung-chang and Lady Li, and by Mme. Tang Shao Yi (the wife of the man who had loaned me the money to build my hospital); Great Britain by Sir Robert and Lady Calder-Marshall, Sir Frederick and Lady Maze, Lady Pearce, and so on down the list.

My Days of Strength

It was the high spot of my career as a Shanghai hostess, and I think too it spoke well for my prowess as a physician and hospital director; for as I looked down that long table I recognized at least a dozen ex-patients, Chinese and foreign. Indeed it is one of the joys of my life to know that my warmest friendships had their beginnings in a physician-patient relationship, many of them starting in my hospital.

One of my dearest friends is a charming woman whose appendix I removed on the top of a mountain just at dawn after one of the worst storms I have ever experienced. This emergency operation occurred away back in 1903 when I was vacationing at Mokanshan, a mountain resort near Hangchow. I was called shortly after midnight, and never will I forget how I struggled up that mountainside with the rain beating against my face, and the wind whipping me from side to side on a narrow shelf-like path which could be seen only in the occasional frightening flashes of lightning.

The woman was in excruciating pain when I arrived. She showed every sign of appendicitis and at first I thought it was a ruptured appendix. I had brought along my emergency kit, all I had with me in Mokanshan, but fortunately it contained a few ligatures, needles and dressings. I made the incision with a silver pocket knife which I sterilized as well as possible. Luckily the appendix was not ruptured, but it did burst just as I removed it. As soon as the storm abated and the patient could be moved, I had her brought to my cottage where I combined the duties of doctor and nurse.

When I attend a diplomatic dinner, visit a Chinese orphanage, sit on the platform at the Chinese American School, head a drive for funds or just walk up Nanking Road—everywhere I see faces of those with whom I have sorrowed or with whom I have rejoiced. Is it any wonder then that I say "My Shanghai"?

So with one thing telescoping into another, what started out as a grand lark for one year extended into an adventure of forty-four, and I am fulfilling my cycle of Cathay. It was just at the beginning of the last "Trouble" that I started out on my fifteenth trip around the world, a trip that will eventually take me back to Shanghai; for even after four decades my feeling for this city is still best described in the one word I cabled to my mother when first I saw it—"Delight!"

Date Due